# THE SYSTEM OF LIBERTY

"Classical liberalism" refers to a political philosophy in which liberty plays the central role. This book demonstrates a conceptual unity within the manifestations of classical liberalism by tracing the history of several interrelated and reinforcing themes. Concepts such as order, justice, rights, and freedom have imparted unity to this diverse political ideology by integrating context and meaning. However, they have also sparked conflict, as classical liberals split on a number of issues, such as legitimate exceptions to the "presumption of liberty," the meaning of "the public good," natural rights versus utilitarianism, the role of the state in education, and the rights of resistance and revolution. This book explores these conflicts and their implications for contemporary liberal and libertarian thought.

George H. Smith is an independent scholar and writes a weekly column for the Cato Institute's Libertarianism.org titled "Excursions Into the History of Libertarian Thought." He is the author of *Atheism: The Case Against God* (1974); *Atheism, Ayn Rand, and Other Heresies* (1991); and audio series on "Great Political Thinkers," "The Meaning of the U.S. Constitution," and "The Ideas of Liberty." His articles and book reviews have appeared in such publications as *The New York Times*, *Newsday*, *Reason*, *Liberty*, the *Journal of Libertarian Studies*, *Free Inquiry*, and *The Humanist*.

# The System of Liberty

## THEMES IN THE HISTORY OF
## CLASSICAL LIBERALISM

### GEORGE H. SMITH

CATO
INSTITUTE

CAMBRIDGE
UNIVERSITY PRESS

CAMBRIDGE UNIVERSITY PRESS
Cambridge, New York, Melbourne, Madrid, Cape Town,
Singapore, São Paulo, Delhi, Mexico City

Cambridge University Press
32 Avenue of the Americas, New York, NY 10013-2473, USA

www.cambridge.org
Information on this title: www.cambridge.org/9780521182096

First published 2013

Printed in the United States of America

*A catalog record for this publication is available from the British Library.*

*Library of Congress Cataloging in Publication Data*

Smith, George H., 1949–
The system of liberty : themes in the history of classical liberalism / George H. Smith.
  pages cm
Includes bibliographical references and index.
ISBN 978-1-107-00507-5 – ISBN 978-0-521-18209-6 (pbk.)
1. Liberalism.  2. Liberty.  3. Individualism.  I. Title.
JC574.S54  2013
320.51′2–dc23      2012039029

ISBN 978-1-107-00507-5 Hardback
ISBN 978-0-521-18209-6 Paperback

To

*Walter E. Grinder, to whom I owe more intellectual debts than*

*I can ever repay*

*and*

*Treg Loyden, who believed in this book*

# Contents

# Acknowledgments

This book was made possible by the generous financial assistance of the Cato Institute. I especially wish to thank two people at Cato.

Tom G. Palmer, a colleague of mine for many years, was involved with this project from the beginning. Dr. Palmer's contributions over a period of years, which included suggested revisions in two drafts, were invaluable.

David Boaz, executive vice president of the Cato Institute, shepherded this book through its final stages. His patience and encouragement in the face of repeated delays were worthy of a saint.

# Introduction

Liberal individualism – or "classical liberalism," as it is often called – has a long and rich ancestry, but it did not begin to take shape as a coherent and integrated political theory until the seventeenth century. It was in that century that challenges to the theory of political absolutism came to fruition in the writing of the Levellers, Algernon Sidney, John Locke, and other individualists. Against the theory of state sovereignty, which had gained traction with the rise of the modern nation-state, liberals countered with a theory of self-sovereignty, according to which all moral rights and duties ultimately reside in individuals and can be delegated to governments only with the consent of the governed.

This book is not a history of classical liberalism per se; rather, it covers some basic themes and controversies that run throughout the history of liberalism, especially those that divided liberals into different camps, such as natural-rights versus utilitarian liberalism. Such internecine conflicts seem to go with the territory of political movements that enjoy some measure of success. After a common foe has been vanquished – as was largely the case with political absolutism by the mid-eighteenth century – the victors tend to turn their gaze inward, toward the fundamental premises of their own philosophy, in an effort to develop that philosophy in a systematic fashion. And with sustained reflection on how liberal principles can best deal with the problems of political philosophy came differences of opinion about the foundation and proper application of those principles.

Despite these differences, liberals shared common ground on a number of key issues that imparted unity to an otherwise variegated tradition. One such issue was the importance of ideas in effecting social and political change. Although liberals understood that self-interest is a powerful motive in human affairs, they also understood that self-interest is not a primary. Rather, how people view their own interests will ultimately depend on their beliefs about human nature, social interaction, the proper roles of coercion and persuasion,

1

and a host of other abstract issues. As David Hume put it, "though men be much governed by interest; yet even interest itself, and all human affairs, are entirely governed by *opinion*."[1]

This accounts for the stress that liberals placed on rational, or *enlightened*, self-interest – or what Bishop Butler felicitously described as "cool self-love." Most liberals agreed that a society that permits a maximum amount of individual freedom will serve the long-range interests of everyone in that society, and this belief caused them to stress the role of education as a means of teaching people the value of freedom.

The value of individual freedom was another point of agreement among liberals; indeed, this may be called the defining characteristic of classical liberalism. In the words of the liberal historian Lord Acton, a liberal is a person "whose polar star is liberty – who deems those things right in politics which, taken all round, promote, increase, perpetuate freedom, and those things wrong which impede it." The true liberal views liberty as an end, not merely as a means; it is a value that is not "exchangeable for any amount, however large, of national greatness and glory, of prosperity and wealth, of enlightenment or morality."[2]

In moral terms, this focus on individual freedom, wherein freedom functions as a "polar star" to guide political decisions and institutions, was formulated during different historical stages of liberalism as self-proprietorship, self-sovereignty, self-ownership, and so forth. Such terms, which emphasized the moral priority of the individual over any social collective or political agency, expressed the natural right of individuals to use their bodies, freedom, labor, and justly acquired property as they see fit, so long as they respect the equal freedom of others.

At the core of this stress on external freedom was an internal power that liberals called "liberty of conscience." This was the moral foundation of the struggle for religious freedom, which was the first great liberal crusade and the arena where liberals scored their earliest victories. As liberty of conscience came to be regarded as the principal inalienable right of human beings, this emphasis was applied over time to other spheres of human activity, as we see in the Declaration of Independence where Thomas Jefferson highlighted the "unalienable" rights to life, liberty, and the pursuit of happiness.

---

[1] David Hume, "Whether the British Government Inclines More to Absolute Monarchy, or to a Republic," in *Essays: Moral, Political, and Literary*, rev. ed., ed. Eugene F. Miller (Indianapolis: Liberty Classics, 1987), 51.

[2] Lord Acton, "Selections from the Acton Legacy," in *Selected Writings of Lord Acton*, vol. 3, *Essays in Religion, Politics, and Morality*, ed. J. Rufus Fears (Indianapolis: Liberty Classics, 1988), 543.

Of course, the trajectory of liberal ideas was more complex than the preceding summary might indicate. One factor that contributed to this complexity was the very notion of freedom that so fascinated liberal philosophers and social theorists. According to this conception, which is often called "negative freedom," social and political freedom consists of the absence of external compulsion and constraint by other human beings. In thus viewing freedom as the absence of coercion, liberals confronted the difficult problem of tracking the effects of this elusive concept in social relationships. Because voluntary relationships encompass a wide range of human actions, from those that are wise and virtuous to those that are foolish and immoral, it can be extraordinarily difficult to determine the long-range consequences of freedom on society at large.

What is the relationship between freedom and virtue? Or between freedom and social order? Or between freedom and economic prosperity? Or between freedom and personal happiness? Since freedom, conceived as the absence of coercion, is an invisible element in human relationships, liberals needed to develop theories in economics, sociology, psychology, and other fields to answer these and similar questions. This ambitious undertaking – whose most systematic pioneers were David Hume, Adam Smith, and other luminaries of the Scottish Enlightenment – resulted in more than a liberal *political* theory. It resulted in something far more complex, namely an *interdisciplinary* approach, or ideology, in which freedom was analyzed from many different perspectives.

Freedom was a major theme in seventeenth-century political philosophy, and it became a major theme in the social sciences that began to emerge as distinctive disciplines in the eighteenth century. In framing their conceptions of a good society, liberals engaged in two kinds of investigation, one normative (or prescriptive) and the other positive (or descriptive). The normative part of what they frequently called "moral science" – which included all aspects of human behavior in which moral agency is involved – addressed the nature of justice, whereas the positive part addressed the problem of social order. *What is justice? What is social order?* For classical liberals, these were essential questions not only for those fields of inquiry that we now call moral and political philosophy but for the social sciences as well.

Something remarkable happened in the seventeenth century, as John Locke and other philosophers began to think the unthinkable and imagine the unimaginable. They suggested, if only indirectly, that government is not absolutely necessary for the existence of society, that social order and even justice can be maintained to some degree without political institutions. Just as the authority of religious institutions had previously been undermined by Protestant Reformers, so the authority of political institutions now faced a serious challenge from liberal individualists. At the hands of John Locke and later individualists, such as Thomas Paine, government became a convenience, not an absolute necessity, and with this view came the argument that it would be better to have no government at all rather than suffer the oppressions of a tyrannical government.

This was a radical position indeed, one that undercut the widespread belief (one held even by philosophers who rejected absolutism) that government is a divinely mandated institution. The venerable Augustinian doctrine that government is a punishment and remedy for sin faced a serious challenge, and this caused many opponents of liberalism to charge that liberal individualists were in fact latent anarchists. According to these critics, liberal principles, if consistently applied, are unable to justify *any* kind of government and so must logically leave us in an anarchistic "state of nature" instead.

Although this "specter of anarchy" argument was the most common refrain of liberalism's critics for over two centuries, it has received scant attention from modern historians of classical liberalism. I have therefore devoted considerable space to this controversy, especially in Chapter 5 ("The Anarchy Game").

Another factor that contributed to the fear that liberal principles promoted anarchy was the radical edge of Lockean theory, specifically, its appeal to natural rights to justify resistance to unjust laws and revolution against despotic governments. These fears came to a head after the atrocities of the French Revolution convinced many observers – including Edmund Burke, Jeremy Bentham, and others who were otherwise sympathetic to the liberal political agenda – that the doctrine of natural and inalienable rights was a dangerous chimera that needed to be expunged from the domain of political philosophy.

Thus did the French Revolution become a watershed not only in the history of Europe but in the history of liberalism as well, for it was after this epochal event that Lockean natural-rights liberalism lost much of its influence to other forms of liberalism (e.g., the utilitarianism of Jeremy Bentham) that sought to avoid the radical implications of the earlier approach. As with other themes, this one is interwoven throughout the book, but the main discussion appears in Chapter 6 ("The Radical Edge of Liberalism").

If these excursions into anarchy and revolution are the most dramatic features of the history of liberalism, they are not the most fundamental. Liberals dealt with the same problems that have vexed political philosophers for centuries, and, like their colleagues, liberals were sometimes unclear in their formulation of basic principles and ambivalent about how those principles should be applied to practical problems. Hence, after discussing some differences between "old" and "new" liberalism in Chapter 1, I continue with an analysis of the role played by the presumption of liberty in classical liberalism, and (in Chapter 2) with how liberals viewed that ambiguous concept known variously as the "public good," "common good," and "social utility."

In Chapter 3, I examine how liberals viewed political philosophy and how the perennial problems of that discipline informed their thinking about freedom and government. This discussion is continued in Chapter 4, which discusses the liberal distinction between state sovereignty and self-sovereignty.

Skipping over the next two chapters, which I mentioned previously, we come to Chapter 7, which is an overview of the negative conception of freedom embraced by classical liberals and its broader implications for social and political theory. Chapter 8 illustrates two important debates that emerged in nineteenth-century liberalism. The first, that between Benthamite utilitarianism and an older school of natural-rights liberalism, had profound implications for the future of liberalism. A case can be made that the triumph of Benthamism, having reduced the value of freedom to calculations of social utility, ripped the moral heart from liberalism and thereby ensured its demise within a matter of decades.

The second part of Chapter 8 deals with another internecine conflict, namely the debate between those liberals who advocated a role for the state in education and those liberal "voluntaryists" who called for a complete separation of school and state. Only rarely has the voluntaryist wing of liberalism received attention from historians, despite the fact that it was for decades a vibrant movement whose proponents called upon an older form of Lockean liberalism to support their arguments.

Chapter 9 seeks to correct a few of the common misconceptions about liberalism, especially the charge that it involved a shallow "social atomism" and that its more radical advocates, such as Herbert Spencer and William Graham Sumner, were guilty of advocating an ill-defined but presumably horrendous evil called "Social Darwinism." Chapter 10 is an overview of "methodological individualism" – an approach that was fundamental to the liberal treatment of the social sciences and a controversy that still commands the attention of social and political philosophers.

A short digression on the use of an important term in this book should help to clarify its purpose. At various points in this book I use the label "Lockean paradigm." By this I mean a constellation of key concepts that has historically been used to address the fundamental and recurring problems of political philosophy. The concepts include natural rights, social contract, consent, property, and the rights of resistance and revolution.

Although Locke did not originate these concepts or how they functioned in political controversies, they have been more closely linked to his name than any other philosopher. Indeed, when considering a person who defended similar ideas before Locke was even born, we are apt to describe those ideas, if integrated in a certain manner, as "Lockean."

We do this partly from habit and partly because we assume that the label "Lockean" will convey information to reasonably well-educated people. For example, Richard Overton and John Lilburne were prominent Levellers who defended self-proprietorship, private property, and government by consent before John Locke was a teenager. However, if we were pressed to give some- one a highly condensed description of what Overton and Lilburne believed, we would probably convey more information by dubbing their ideas "Lockean" rather than "Leveller-like."

I will thus use the adjective "Lockean" in a generic sense, much as some people use the word "Kleenex" to signify a type of tissue rather than a specific brand. To the various objections that might be raised against this procedure, I can only plead that no grand historical thesis is implied by my use of "Lockean paradigm." This is a purely heuristic device, a matter of convenience, nothing more.

Although much of this book deals with the internal problems of classical liberalism, and although I believe that liberals failed to resolve some of these problems, my sympathies with this school of thought will quickly become apparent to readers. In their search for answers to difficult questions, the classical liberals may not have been successful in every respect. But they did have many successes, both theoretical and practical, in their effort to justify and explain individual freedom, and we owe them an incalculable debt for many of the freedoms we enjoy today.

# 1

# Liberalism, Old and New

## I

In the late nineteenth century, liberals in Europe and America discovered that they were victims of a linguistic coup. They found that they were no longer regarded as liberals per se but as *old* liberals – a qualification that had been foisted upon them by self-proclaimed *new* liberals.

Old liberals had defended individual freedom in a variety of spheres, including commerce, religion, speech, and press. Many were known for their opposition to slavery, military conscription, victimless crime laws, imperialism, and wars fought for reasons other than self-defense. They were among the first to speak out for the equal rights of women and the right of children to be free from physical abuse.

Freedom, for these liberals, signified the absence of physical coercion and threats of coercion – a conception that is commonly known as "negative freedom," because it imposes on others only the negative obligation to restrain from interfering with the equal freedom of others. One is truly free when one can act on one's own judgment in pursuit of one's own goals, enter into voluntary relationships with other people, and dispose of one's person and property as one sees fit, so long as one respects the equal freedom of other people to do the same. This moral and practical commitment to freedom naturally led liberals to view government with cautious, skeptical eyes. If governments have a crucial role to play in protecting the lives and property of their citizens, governments also pose the greatest threat to the freedoms of those citizens they should protect. It was from their conviction that coercion should play a minimal role in social relationships that liberals derived the principle of *limited* government, that is, a government whose powers are restricted to the protection and enforcement of individual rights.

Old liberalism, according to its critics, was old in more ways than one. Not only was it an outmoded ideology but its defenders were a dying breed. In 1900, a writer for the *Nation* explained it this way:

> Liberalism is a declining almost a defunct force. Only a remnant, old men for the most part, still uphold the Liberal doctrine, and when they are gone, it will have no champions.[3]

This was an accurate observation: When Herbert Spencer, the dean of old liberalism, died in 1903, there was no one to take his place. By 1905, when A.V. Dicey published his classic account of nineteenth-century English liberalism, the victory of new liberalism was complete. As Dicey put it,

> Liberalism itself has at last learned to place no small confidence in the beneficent effects of State control; but this trust, whether well founded or not, is utterly foreign to the liberalism of 1832.[4]

Old liberalism remained effectively dormant for decades. When it experienced a rebirth after World War II, it was usually called "classical liberalism" (or "libertarianism" in its more radical manifestations) to distinguish it from the welfare-state liberalism that had established a virtual monopoly on the label in the English-speaking world.

The old liberals did not go down without a fight. "[I]t seems needful," wrote Herbert Spencer in 1888, "to remind everyone what Liberalism was in the past, that they may perceive its unlikeness to the so-called Liberalism of the present."[5]

> They do not remember that, in one or other way, all . . . truly Liberal changes diminished compulsory cooperation throughout social life and increased voluntary cooperation. They have forgotten that, in one direction or other, they diminished the range of governmental authority, and increased the area within which each citizen may act unchecked. They have lost sight of the truth that in past times Liberalism habitually stood for individual freedom *versus* State-coercion.[6]

Old liberals – or what Spencer preferred to call "true" liberals – disliked the implication of the modifier "new," which suggested something progressive, as

---

[3] Quoted in L.T. Hobhouse, *Liberalism* (New York: Oxford University Press, 1964), 5.

[4] Albert Venn Dicey, *Lectures on the Relation Between Law and Public Opinion in England During the Nineteenth Century*, 2nd ed. (London: Macmillan, 1914), 39.

[5] Herbert Spencer, "The New Toryism," in *The Man Versus the State*, ed. Eric Mack (Indianapolis: Liberty Classics, 1981), 10.

[6] Ibid., 10.

if new liberals had improved on the theory of old liberalism while retaining what was worthwhile and discarding what had become obsolete. The term "liberal" carried favorable connotations; in addition to its association with "liberty" ("liberal" derives from *liber*, the Latin word for "free"), the adjectival form had long been used to mean magnanimous, open-minded, and tolerant. The label therefore suggested something more than a political doctrine; it suggested a humanistic outlook, a moral and social ideology in which the happiness of the individual is a key concern.

Given these implications, it is understandable why many social reformers who disliked the *laissez-faire* tendencies of traditional liberalism did not wish to jettison the label. They claimed that the new liberalism was based on a more sophisticated notion of freedom and therefore represented intellectual progress. As Spencer viewed the matter, though, the new liberalism was essentially old wine in a new bottle. The old wine in this case was paternalism, a doctrine that called for state intervention in voluntary relationships on the grounds that the state has the parental-like duty to protect individuals from the potentially harmful effects of their own uncoerced decisions and actions.

Spencer, using the conventional terminology of English politics, characterized the new liberals as "Tories of a new type."[7] Tories had traditionally sought to expand the range of governmental activity; similarly, the new liberalism "has to an increasing extent adopted the policy of dictating the actions of citizens, and, by consequence, diminishing the range throughout which their actions remain free."[8]

Spencer did not impugn the motives of the new liberals; in calling for greater governmental inference in the lives of individuals, they were actuated by a sincere desire to further the public good. This is one reason why Spencer characterized the new liberalism as a "new type," or "new species," of Toryism, rather than a reversion to Toryism in its traditional form. The old Tories called on government to promote the interests of the landed aristocracy, whereas the new Tories saw themselves as champions of the working class and looked to government to mitigate what they regarded as social injustices. Moreover, whereas Tories had traditionally defended monarchical power and opposed democratic reforms, the new Tories justified their policies by claiming they reflected the will of the people, as manifested in a parliament that had become increasingly democratic through the Reform Acts of 1832, 1867, and 1884.

Although old liberals also supported democratic reforms, Spencer pointed out that they fought for limits on government power, however that power

---

[7] Ibid., 5.
[8] Ibid., 10.

might manifest itself. Liberals opposed the *principle* of absolute sovereignty, regardless of whether this sovereignty is said to reside in the king, the parliament, or the people: "The real issue is whether the lives of citizens are more interfered with than they were; not the nature of the agency which interferes with them."[9] An unlimited power placed in the people (or, more precisely, a majority of the people) is just as dangerous as an unlimited power placed in a king.

> If men use their liberty in such a way as to surrender their liberty, are they thereafter any the less slaves? If people by a *plebiscite* elect a man despot over them do they remain free because the despotism was of their own making? Are the coercive edicts issued by him to be regarded as legitimate because they are the ultimate outcome of their own votes?[10]

Restrictions on the equal freedom of individuals are no more defensible if they "proceed from a popularly-chosen body" than if they originate with the decrees of an absolute monarch. Just as "true Liberalism in the past disputed the assumption of a monarch's unlimited authority, so true Liberalism in the present will dispute the assumption of unlimited parliamentary authority."[11]

According to Spencer, the new liberals substituted a theory of unlimited popular sovereignty for the older Tory theory of unlimited monarchical sovereignty, and in so doing they abandoned the true liberal principle of limited government. This is a major reason why Spencer did not regard the "new" liberalism as a species of liberalism at all; it was not an improvement or revision of true liberal principles but an abandonment of those selfsame principles. The new liberalism was indeed a variant of an older political tradition, but that tradition was paternalistic Toryism, not liberalism.

Of course, the new liberals rejected Spencer's analysis, especially his argument that they had forsaken a concern for individual freedom. Instead, they claimed to have unmasked the deficiencies in the anemic conception of negative freedom defended by old liberals, replacing it with a richer, more authentic conception of *positive* freedom. In the process, they had deconstructed the theory of natural rights used by old liberals (especially those in the Lockean tradition) to place arbitrary limits on the activities of government, exposing it as a chimera that ignored the social nature of human beings.

New liberals, while conceding that old liberals had served a useful purpose in their day by working for the repeal of many onerous and unnecessary

9   Ibid., 24.
10   Ibid., 25.
11   Ibid., 26.

laws, castigated free-market policies as an inadequate remedy for the injustices of nineteenth-century industrial capitalism. They alleged that old liberalism sanctioned economic exploitation by forbidding the state to interfere in the supposedly voluntary contractual arrangements between workers and employers.

In 1911, in what is perhaps the best explanation and defense of new liberalism, L.T. Hobhouse presented this summary of the "restricted view of the function of government" defended by the Manchester school of old liberalism[12]:

> Government had to maintain order, to restrain men from violence and fraud, to hold them secure in person and property against foreign and domestic enemies, to give them redress against injury, that so they may rely on reaping where they had sown, may enjoy the fruits of their industry, may enter unimpeded into what arrangements they will with one another for their mutual benefit.[13]

Although Richard Cobden (the most prominent representative of the Manchester school) opposed factory acts that authorized governmental interference in voluntary contracts between workers and employers, he supported legal restrictions on child labor. Hobhouse asked why this exception to the sanctity of "free contract" in the case of "helpless children" should not logically be extended to adults who, owing to circumstances over which they have no control, are relatively helpless vis-à-vis their employers:

> If the child was helpless, was the grown-up person, man or woman, in a much better position? Here was the owner of a mill employing five-hundred hands. Here was an operative possessed of no alternative means of subsistence seeking employment. Suppose them to bargain as to terms. If the bargain failed, the employer lost one man and had four hundred and ninety-nine to keep his mill going. At worst he might for a day or two, until another operative appeared,

---

[12] The Manchester school was associated with Richard Cobden and John Bright, who, as leaders of the Anti-Corn Law League, played key roles in the popular agitation that resulted in the repeal (in 1846) of duties on grain imported into Britain. As we shall see, some old liberals were more consistent than others in upholding an economic policy of *laissez-faire*. Hobhouse refers to the Manchester school specifically because its members were among the most consistent advocates of voluntary contracts and other free-market policies. Since even these avid defenders of the free market admitted that a government should intervene in some social arrangements that are nominally free (e.g., to prevent the exploitation of children), Hobhouse argued that there is no reason, in principle, why these exceptions should not be expanded to include a broader range of circumstances. This method of argument was intended to show that, contrary to Spencer's argument discussed earlier, the new liberalism was not a radical theoretical departure from the old liberalism; instead it represented a different *application* of the same basic principles.

[13] Hobhouse, *Liberalism*, 46.

have a little difficulty in working a single machine. During the same days the operative might have nothing to eat, and might see his children going hungry. Where was the effective liberty in such an arrangement?[14]

Thus Hobhouse rejected the negative freedom of old liberalism as a nominal freedom without substance:

> In the matter of contract true freedom postulates substantial equality between the parties. In proportion as one party is in a position of vantage, he is able to dictate his terms. In proportion as the other party is in a weak position, he must accept unfavourable terms. [L]iberty without equality is a name of noble sound and squalid result.[15]

This style of argument was by no means original to Hobhouse; he relied heavily on the arguments of the philosopher T.H. Green (1836–1882), whose influence on subsequent liberal thought was immense, especially in Britain.[16] Indeed, in the realm of theory it would not be an exaggeration to describe Green as the founding father of new liberalism.

In a lecture delivered in 1881, Green pointed out that parliament had recently passed a number of acts pertaining to labor, education, and public health that "limit a man's power of doing what he will with what he considers his own," and that therefore violate the principle defended by many old liberals, namely "the supposed inherent right of every man to do what he will with his own."[17] Unlike earlier reforms supported by old liberals, which had "complete freedom of contract" as their underlying principle and whose purpose was "to set men at liberty to dispose of what they had made their own," later reforms supported by new liberals took "a seemingly different direction" insofar as they "put restraints on the individual in doing what he will with his own."[18]

This account of the essential difference between old and new liberalism closely resembles the account given by Herbert Spencer seven years later

[14]  Ibid., 46–47.

[15]  Ibid., 47–48.

[16]  "The roster of public figures acknowledging [Green's] influence included two Prime Ministers (Herbert Asquith, Henry Campbell-Bannerman) and Members of Parliament (Richard Haldane, Arthur Acland), prominent civil servants (Robert Morant, William Beveridge), and a host of government officials, administrators, philanthropists, reformers and social workers." Gertrude Himmelfarb, *Poverty and Compassion: The Moral Imagination of the Late Victorians* (New York: Alfred A. Knopf 1991), 247.

[17]  T.H. Green, "Liberal Legislation and Freedom of Contract," in *The Political Theory of T.H. Green: Selected Writings*, ed. John R. Rodman (New York: Meredith Publishing Co., 1964), 44–45.

[18]  Ibid., 48.

(which we examined previously). Green, in noting that old liberals will resist the new liberal legislation "in the name of individual liberty," anticipated the reaction of Spencer. But whereas Spencer would later contend that the new liberalism was a violation of true liberal principles, Green took the opposite viewpoint. In a manner that Hobhouse would later echo, Green maintained that liberals, old and new, "probably all agree that freedom, rightly understood, is the greatest of all blessings; that its attainment is the true end of all our effort as citizens."[19]

The devil here lies in the detail "rightly understood." As Green explains:

> But when we thus speak of freedom, we should carefully consider what we mean by it. We do not mean merely freedom to do as we like irrespectively of what it is that we like. We do not mean a freedom that can be enjoyed by one man or one set of men at the cost of a loss of freedom to others. When we speak of freedom as something to be so highly prized, we mean a positive power or capacity of doing or enjoying something worth doing or enjoying and that, too, something that we do or enjoy in common with others. We mean by it a power which each man exercises through the help or security given him by his fellow-men, and which he in turn helps to secure for them. When we measure the progress of a society by its growth in freedom, we measure it by the increasing development and exercise on the whole of those powers of contributing to social good with which we believe the members of the society to be endowed; in short, by the greater power on the part of the citizens as a body to make the most and best of themselves. Thus, though of course there can be no freedom among men who act not willingly but under compulsion, yet on the other hand *the mere removal of compulsion, the mere enabling a man to do as he likes, is in itself no contribution to true freedom.*[20]

This is the classic statement, rich with Hegelian overtones, of what Green calls "freedom in the positive sense: in other words, the liberation of the powers of all men equally for contributions to a common good."[21] To what extent did this conception of liberty render the new liberalism incompatible with the old? A closer examination of some key concepts in classical liberalism, including how the "public good" was viewed by old liberals, will better enable us to answer this question.

---

[19] Ibid., 51.

[20] Ibid., 51–52; emphasis added.

[21] Ibid., 53. For a critical analysis of positive freedom, see the classic essay by Isaiah Berlin, "Two Concepts of Liberty," in *Liberty*, ed. Henry Hardy (Oxford: Oxford University Press, 2002), 166–217.

II

The term "liberalism" appears to have originated in France in the early 1800s, when it was used to describe the individualistic ideology of Benjamin Constant, Madame de Staël and other critics of Napoleon.[22] Both Constant and de Staël were vigorous advocates of private property and free-market economics. According to Constant, there is an "inherent right" to dispose of one's property with "unlimited freedom" – a theme that was echoed by de Staël when she wrote that "governments must protect property instead of rivaling it."[23] Moreover, both Constant and de Staël defended freedom of speech, press, religion, and other personal and civil rights that characterized classical liberalism.

Although "liberalism" was apparently not used by eighteenth-century writers, they did use the adjective "liberal" to qualify nouns such as "policies," "measures," and "sentiments" to mean "pro-freedom" and "tolerant." For example, in the *Wealth of Nations* (1776), Adam Smith referred repeatedly to the "liberal and generous system" of free trade and to the "liberal plan of equality, liberty, and justice" wherein every person, "as long as he does not violate the laws of justice, is left perfectly free to pursue his own interest his own way."[24]

There is an interesting parallel here to "mercantilism," which denotes the system of commercial regulations and trade restrictions that typified the policies of European governments well into the eighteenth century. Although the word "mercantilism" is sometimes attributed to Adam Smith, he did not actually use it but spoke instead of the "mercantile system." We don't know who first shortened "mercantile system" into the single word "mercantilism," but educated guesswork would suggest that Smith's French disciples similarly transformed his "liberal system" into "liberalism" – meaning thereby a system of liberal, or pro-liberty, ideas.

"Liberal," when used to signify a political party or movement, is probably of Spanish origin. When a Cortes, or legislative assembly, was formed in 1810, it was dominated by self-proclaimed *Liberales* who wished to transform

---

[22] On the origins of the terms "liberal" and "liberalism," see A. Nefftzer's article, "Liberalism," in *Cyclopedia of Political Science*, ed. John J. Lalor (New York: Maynard Merrill, and Co., 1899). (This three-volume work is a valuable source of articles by classical liberals, especially the French followers of J.B. Say.) Lord Acton claimed that the term "liberalism" was first used around 1807 by Chateaubriand; see *Selected Writings*, III: 543.

[23] Quoted in Anthony Arblaster, *The Rise and Decline of Western Liberalism* (Oxford: Basil Blackwell, 1984), 233.

[24] Adam Smith, *An Inquiry into the Nature and Causes of the Wealth of Nations*, ed. R.H. Campbell, A.S. Skinner, and W.B. Todd (Indianapolis: Liberty Classics, 1981), 2: 671, 687. (This is a reprint of the 1979 edition by Oxford University Press.)

Spain into a constitutional monarchy. These *Liberales*, inspired by the French Constitution of 1791, drafted the Spanish Constitution of 1812, which abolished a number of feudal institutions, sold off common lands, and enshrined the rights of private property.

It was shortly after the end of the Napoleonic Wars in 1815 that "liberal" made its appearance in English political debates. Like the traditional labels "Whig" and "Tory," "liberal" was originally a term of opprobrium – a smear aimed at those English radicals who were sympathetic to natural rights, especially the rights of resistance and revolution and other "Jacobinal" principles associated with the French Revolution. Not until 1822, when Leigh Hunt launched his periodical *The Liberal*, did the word begin to take on more positive connotations.[25]

To sharpen our conception of liberalism, we need to discuss the history of another term, namely *laissez-faire*. According to the standard historical account, a variation of this term dates from around 1680, when Colbert, chief economic adviser to Louis XIV, asked a group of merchants what the government could do to help them. To this one merchant shot back, *"Laissez-nous faire"* – "leave us alone."[26]

The expression *"Laissez-faire, laissez passer"* ("Let it be, let it pass") and the abbreviated *laissez-faire* were used by French economic writers during the first half of the eighteenth century, and *laissez-faire* became something of a catchword among the French school of economists known as "Physiocrats." (The word "physiocracy" is itself significant, for it means "the rule of nature" – which suggests an economic order that is governed by natural laws, that is, causal forces that cannot be abrogated by human will or decree.)

Although *laissez-faire* generally refers to the economic doctrine of free trade, classical liberals often used it in a broader sense to signify a hands-off governmental policy in various spheres. "We advocate *laissez-faire* in education, as in trade," wrote Thomas Hodgskin in *The Economist* in 1847, and we find the

---

[25] Élie Halévy, *The Liberal Awakening, 1815–1830*, trans. E.I. Watkin (New York: Barnes and Noble, 1961), 81–82. Although *The Liberal*, which featured "liberalities in the shape of Poetry, Essays, Tales, Translations, and other amenities" by Lord Byron's circle, was more literary than political, its radical perspective provoked "a universal outcry," according to the publisher John Murray – who was fined 100 pounds for publishing a "gross, impious and slanderous" libel on George III. Only four issues of *The Liberal* were published. For an earlier periodical, the *Examiner* (which championed abolition of the slave trade, Catholic emancipation, parliamentary reform, and other liberal causes), Leigh Hunt and his brother were fined 500 pounds and served two years in prison, specifically for one of their attacks on the Prince of Wales. See Ian Jack, *English Literature, 1815–1832* (Oxford: Clarendon Press, 1963), 319–22.

[26] See Scott Gordon, *The History and Philosophy of Social Science* (London: Routledge, 1991), 223.

same expression applied by liberals to indicate religious liberty, freedom of the press, and the like. Thus, although it is appropriate that classical liberalism is sometimes called *laissez-faire* liberalism, this should not lead us to suppose that liberals were concerned exclusively with economic issues.

Some historians warn against linking *laissez-faire* and liberalism, because the classical economists were not consistent defenders of unregulated markets. Moreover, liberals sometimes disagreed among themselves, such as, on whether the government should intervene in education and, if so, to what extent.[27]

This brings us to a basic issue that must be addressed by every historian of ideas: How can we define an ideological tradition – that is, a value-based belief system that develops over time – in the face of inconsistencies and disagreements among its advocates? One way to answer this question is to see what liberals themselves had to say about this matter.

Although many liberals deviated from the principle of *laissez-faire*, it is significant that these exceptions were recognized *as exceptions*; and an exception has meaning only in contrast to a general rule. *Laissez-faire* in all spheres, personal, social, and economic, was the fundamental presumption of liberalism – its default setting, so to speak – and all deviations from this norm stood in need of justification.[28]

Among liberals the burden of proof rested with the person who advocated any governmental policy that appeared to violate the presumption of liberty. As Scott Gordon has noted, some classical liberals used the term *laissez-faire* "to mean that in considering the exercise of governmental power the burden of proof should be on those who propose to constrain private actions rather than on those who contend that they should be let alone."[29] Similarly, A.V. Dicey refers to "a presumption" that was prevalent in England between 1830 and 1860 "in favor of individual liberty – that is, of *laissez faire*."[30]

John Stuart Mill – a liberal who knew a lot about exceptions to *laissez-faire*, having advocated many of them himself – put the matter well: "Even in those portions of conduct which do affect the interests of others, the onus of making out a case always lies on the defenders of legal prohibitions."[31] After arguing

---

[27]  For an account of liberal opposition to state education, see George H. Smith, "Nineteenth-Century Opponents of State Education: Prophets of Modern Revisionism," in *The Public School Monopoly*, ed. Robert B. Everhart (Cambridge, Mass.: Ballinger, 1982), 109–44.

[28]  The same point is made by Arblaster, *The Rise and Decline of Western Liberalism*, 252.

[29]  Gordon, *The History and Philosophy of Social Science*, 221.

[30]  Dicey, *Lectures on the Relation Between Law and Public Opinion*, 258.

[31]  John Stuart Mill, *Principles of Political Economy* (New York: The Colonial Press, 1899), 2: 444.

that people should normally be left free to pursue their own interests as they deem fit, Mill goes on to say this:

> The preceding are the principal reasons, of a general character, in favor of restricting to the narrowest compass the intervention of a public authority in the business of the community; and few will dispute the more than sufficiency of these reasons, to throw, in every instance, the burden of making out a strong case, not on those who resist, but on those who recommend, government interference. Letting alone, in short, should be the general practice; every departure from it, unless required by some great good, is a certain evil.[32]

This onus-of-proof principle, which takes the presumption of liberty as its starting point, is evident at various places in the *Wealth of Nations*. When Adam Smith defended government measures that run counter to *laissez-faire*, he typically identified such measures as exceptions to the general rule and tried to justify them. Consider Smith's discussion of the paper money (or promissory notes) issued by British banks. Smith called for prohibiting notes under five pounds, believing this would reduce the likelihood of fraud committed on poor people by unscrupulous, fly-by-night bankers. Further,

> To restrain private people, it may be said, from receiving in payment the promissory notes of a banker, for any sum whether great or small, when they themselves are willing to receive them; or, to restrain a banker from issuing such notes, when all his neighbors are willing to accept of them, is a manifest violation of that natural liberty which it is the proper business of law, not to infringe, but to support. Such regulations may, no doubt, be considered as in some respects a violation of natural liberty.[33]

Another remark about the need to justify exceptions to *laissez-faire* appears in Smith's discussion of when it may be advisable to restrict the exportation of grain. To hinder the farmer from selling his produce to foreign markets "is evidently to sacrifice the ordinary laws of justice to an idea of public utility, to a sort of reasons of state." This violation of natural liberty, according to Smith, can be "pardoned only in cases of the most urgent necessity."[34]

The presumption of liberty was explicitly endorsed by James Madison, who stated that he approved of some exceptions to "the rule of laissez-faire" but opposed "converting the exceptions into the rule." As Madison saw the matter,

[32] Ibid., 2: 451.
[33] Smith, *Wealth of Nations*, 1: 324.
[34] Ibid., 1: 539.

this defeasible presumption provided a reasonable alternative to "the extremes of doing nothing and providing everything."[35]

In 1893, J. Shield Nicholson (professor of political economy at the University of Edinburgh) explained how the presumption of liberty informed the thinking of those classical economists who generally favored a policy of *laissez-faire*:

> [The classical economists] considered the presumption against State interference to be established. The rule, it is true, was never absolute and unqualified. Adam Smith himself indicated some of the most important of these exceptions, and the list has been extended by his successors. But these exceptions were all based on reasoned principles, [and] in spite of all these exceptions... the presumption remained undisturbed.[36]

When a liberal posited an exception to the presumption of liberty, there always seemed to be another liberal around who was willing to criticize that exception as unjustified. We see this in a criticism of Adam Smith written in 1787 by Jeremy Bentham, who took Smith to task for advocating a legal limit on interest rates. Smith, according to Bentham, had succumbed to the popular prejudice against usurers (or loan sharks, as we might call them today). For centuries the word "usury" had been saddled with unfavorable connotations, and those who called for laws against moneylenders were simply cashing in on this popular prejudice. Bentham put it this way:

> Usury is a bad thing, and as such ought to be prevented; usurers are a bad sort of men, a very bad sort of men, and as such ought to be punished and suppressed. These are among the string of propositions which every man finds handed down to him from his progenitors – which most men are disposed to accede to without examination.[37]

Moneylenders are an innocent and even meritorious class of men who deserve praise rather than censure for performing an important public service. Adam Smith had defended engrossers, forestallers, wholesalers in grain,

---

35  Letter to Frederick List (Feb. 3, 1829), in *The Complete Madison: His Basic Writings*, ed. Saul K. Padover (New York: Harper and Brothers, 1953), 275.

36  J. Shield Nicholson, "The Reaction in Favor of the Classical Political Economy," in *Essays in Economic Method*, ed. R.L. Smyth (New York: McGraw-Hill, 1963), 120.

37  Jeremy Bentham, *Defence of Usury*, quoted in Élie Halévy, *The Growth of Philosophic Radicalism*, trans. Mary Morris (New York: Macmillan, 1928), 112. Bentham's tract attracted a good deal of public attention and was probably the single most important factor in converting English opinion to free-market interest rates. Adam Smith (quoted in ibid., 113) called it the work of a "superior man" and said that Bentham "has given me some hard knocks, but in so handsome a manner that I cannot complain."

and other social pariahs. Hence Bentham, in defending equal freedom for usurers, claimed that he was merely following in the footsteps of his master by upholding the presumption of liberty for this unpopular minority.

III

The presumption of liberty generated a complex dynamic in the liberal community. Insofar as liberals joined hands and followed Acton's "polar star" of liberty when pursuing political objectives, we can trace the external history of a movement that sought to liberate individuals from the coercive hand of government in a variety of spheres. However, insofar as liberals disagreed among themselves about legitimate exceptions to the presumption of liberty, we can trace the internal history of a movement that, riddled with serious conflicts, inevitably gave birth to ideological factions.

The basic problem that attends the presumption of liberty may be stated as follows: If, speaking as classical liberals, we agree that a government may override the presumption of liberty in some situations, this requires that we be able to *identify* those situations and set them apart from situations in which exceptions to the presumption of liberty cannot be justified. In other words, we need *defeasibility criteria*; we need standards that enable us to ascertain when the presumption of liberty should be defeated, or overridden, and when it should not.

Lurking within this problem is another problem of even greater significance. We must wonder how individual freedom can function as the supreme political value if that value may be trumped by another political value. Implicit in the search for a criterion of defeasibility that can annul, invalidate, suspend, or otherwise override the presumption of liberty is the suggestion that freedom is an instrumental value that should be defended only when it serves as a means to a greater good – and this approach seems to undermine the assertion that liberals upheld freedom as the supreme political value.

Many liberals appealed to the "public good" (or some variant of this idea[38]) as the primary criterion of defeasibility. They held that governments are

---

[38] Throughout the history of classical liberalism – indeed, throughout the history of political philosophy in general – we find a number of expressions that served the same function in political discourse as the "public good," such as "common good," "social good," "general welfare," and "social utility." Although some philosophers (especially those who were influenced by economic reasoning) believed that social utility can be measured and is therefore more precise than appeals to the public (or social) good, this claim falls beyond the scope of the present discussion. All that is relevant here is the fact that such terms frequently served as criteria of defeasibility.

authorized to override the presumption of liberty when this action would promote the public good. Since (as noted previously) this approach implies that freedom is an instrumental value – a means to the end of the public good – we would expect it to be defended by utilitarian liberals. Nevertheless, it was also defended by some prominent natural-rights liberals, such as John Locke: "The public good is the rule and measure of all law-making."[39]

This remark highlights the pivotal role played by the public good in liberal theory. Unless liberals were able to fill that empty vessel called the "public good" with a definite meaning, one that severely restricts the number of occasions when a government can legitimately override the presumption of liberty in the name of the public good, they ran the risk of reducing that presumption to an empty ideological gesture. After all, even Robert Filmer, Thomas Hobbes, and other absolutists agreed with the principle that governments should respect the freedom of individuals unless such freedom conflicts with the public good. But this truism leaves two key questions unanswered: First, *what* does it mean to speak of the public good? Second, *who* should decide whether a particular law is consistent with the public good?

In some respects the latter question is more crucial than the former. Even if we tighten up our notion of the "public good" by giving it a definite meaning and formulating it as a general rule, this rule cannot possibly anticipate and specify the many variables that we will encounter in particular cases. General rules do not apply themselves; such application requires a mental act known as "judgment."[40]

Suppose we agree that the presumption of liberty should apply except when it is incompatible with the public good, and suppose (like Bentham) we define the public good as "the greatest happiness for the greatest number." Our agreement at this highly abstract level is no assurance that we will also agree about particular cases. For example, censorship of pornography may increase the greatest happiness for the greatest number of people, according to my calculations, whereas your calculations may cause you to reach the opposite conclusion.

---

[39] John Locke, *A Letter Concerning Toleration*, trans. William Popple, in *The Second Treatise of Government and A Letter Concerning Toleration*, ed. J.W. Gough (Oxford: Basil Blackwell, 1946), 142.

[40] Aristotle called attention to this problem in his defense of the principle that rightly constituted laws rather than personal rule should be the "final sovereign." Even those who uphold the rule of law must take into account "those matters on which law is unable, owing to the difficulty of framing general rules for all contingencies, to make an exact pronouncement." *The Politics of Aristotle*, trans. Ernest Barker (Oxford: Oxford University Press, 1952), *Politics*, 1282b.

This problem (which attends every utilitarian calculation, regardless of the standard of measurement) is so obvious and has been discussed by so many philosophers that it scarcely seems worth mentioning. However, this problem was not viewed by Thomas Hodgskin, Herbert Spencer and other natural-rights liberals as the most troubling implication of utilitarianism. What especially alarmed them was the fact that, regardless of how liberal philosophers may resolve their differences of opinion about whether a given law serves the "public good" (however this term may be defined), this matter will ultimately be determined by the *government*. Since a major purpose of the presumption of liberty is to limit the power of government, to concede that this selfsame government should decide when that presumption does and does not apply is akin to having the fox guard the henhouse.

I shall discuss this problem in more detail in the next chapter. For the remainder of this chapter I explore a different conception of the public good, one that refers not to any particular value (or constellation of values) but to the *intentions* of a ruler.

In the course of explaining why a concern for the public good is a prerequisite of every legitimate government, John Locke quotes his ideological enemy and champion of absolute monarchy, James I, to buttress his case. King James correctly argued that a legitimate king makes the "Good of the Publick" the purpose of his government, whereas a tyrant uses his power to promote his personal interests at the expense of the public good.[41]

This point was almost as old as political philosophy itself, as we see in Aristotle's remark that tyranny is said to exist whenever a king governs "with a view to his own advantage rather than that of his subjects."[42] Further, according to Thomas Aquinas, "what renders government unjust is the fact that the private good of the ruler is sought at the expense of the good of the community. The further it departs from the common good, therefore, the more unjust will the government be." When a ruler "seeks gain for himself and not the good of the community" he is a tyrant rather than a legitimate king.[43]

This conception of tyranny permitted some latitude when the actions of a sovereign were judged. Liberals conceded that kings and other rulers are fallible and so may make mistakes from time to time, even with the best of intentions. However, they also pointed out that we cannot peer into the minds of rulers, so we must judge their intentions by their actions. Although isolated

---

[41] John Locke, *Two Treatises of Government*, rev. ed., ed. Peter Laslett (New York: New American Library, 1963), II: §200.

[42] *The Politics of Aristotle*, 1295a.

[43] Thomas Aquinas, *On the Government of Princes*, in *St. Thomas Aquinas, Political Writings*, ed. and trans. R.W. Dyson (Cambridge: Cambridge University Press, 2002), 12, 8.

acts of injustice are not evidence of tyrannical intent, this is not true when such acts occur on a regular basis and exhibit a pattern. When this occurs we may reasonably conclude that the injustices were the result of a design – a deliberate plan to sacrifice the liberties of the people for the benefit of the rulers themselves, their family members and cronies, or their political and financial supporters.

This was the substance of the charge of "corruption" – a popular and important word in the liberal lexicon, especially during the seventeenth and eighteenth centuries. A government was said to be corrupt when it used its powers and financial resources to further private interests at the expense of the public good. This is what Thomas Jefferson, James Madison, and other critics of Alexander Hamilton had in mind when they accused him of attempting to replicate the British system of corruption in the newly formed American government. As they saw the matter, Hamilton's plan for a national bank and governmental support of private industries (in the form of tariffs, bounties, etc.) was a throwback to mercantilism – a system of economic regulations in which merchants, manufacturers, and other private parties profited through an alliance with the state at the expense of other private parties (mainly agricultural interests) and the public in general. This is why Jefferson and others in his tradition viewed free trade as something more than a beneficial commercial policy; it was also a "natural right,"[44] that is, an aspect of equal treatment under the law that is indispensable to the public good.

Of course, Hamilton and others who supported an alliance between business and government denied that their policies were contrary to the public good. While conceding that their policies would benefit private interests (a point too obvious to be denied), they also trotted out arguments to show how their interventionist policies would strengthen the national economy and thereby serve the public good overall.

The conflict between Hamilton and Jefferson is a good illustration of the basic theme of this chapter. Although Hamilton had some favorable things to say about free trade, Jefferson was committed to commercial freedom in a way that Hamilton was not. Jefferson's belief that free trade is a natural right generated a *moral* commitment to this policy that Hamilton did not share; nevertheless, like many of his fellow liberals Jefferson viewed this as a presumption, not as an inflexible rule. As to what was necessary to defeat this presumption, Jefferson provided an answer during his second term as president, when he supported a drastic trade embargo in the hope that it would prevent

---

[44] Thomas Jefferson, A *Summary View of the Rights of British America*, in *Thomas Jefferson: Writings*, ed. Merrill Peterson (New York: The Library of America, 1984), 108.

the United States from becoming embroiled in the war between Britain and France – a conflict that Jefferson characterized as "the present paroxysm of the insanity of Europe."[45]

It has often been said that Jefferson's support of the Embargo Act (December 22, 1807) was "inconsistent with his basic philosophy of government."[46] That this is a plausible charge can be seen in the remarks of a sympathetic biographer, Dumas Malone, who wrote this about Jeffersonian support for the Embargo Act: "By this act avowed champions of individual liberties had imposed on their fellow citizens the gravest economic restrictions that Americans had known since adoption of the Constitution."[47]

This fact is ironic, to say the least, but an obvious problem with the charge of inconsistency is that it fails to take into account the role of the presumption of liberty in Jefferson's brand of liberalism. We have already discussed this doctrine in detail, so there is no need to belabor the point – but I don't wish to leave the impression that Jeffersonian liberals regarded all types of rights and freedom as nothing more than defeasible presumptions. This was not the case.

Those liberals who, like Jefferson, distinguished between alienable and inalienable rights typically maintained that only alienable rights should be regarded as defeasible presumptions. Under no circumstances could a government legitimately violate *inalienable* rights, so rights in this category were viewed as absolute.[48]

Eighteenth-century liberals ranked liberty of conscience as the most fundamental inalienable right: It is a right that cannot be transferred, abandoned, forfeited, or waived under any circumstances. In contrast, rights that apply to external property (along with those commercial activities that deal with such property) were viewed as alienable. This meant that free trade, though a natural right, was a presumptive right that could be overridden in some

---

[45] Quoted in Noble E. Cunningham, Jr., *In Pursuit of Reason: The Life of Thomas Jefferson* (Baton Rouge: Louisiana State University Press, 1987), 315.

[46] Ibid.

[47] Dumas Malone, *Jefferson the President: Second Term, 1805–1809* (Boston: Little, Brown, and Co., 1974), 640.

[48] Inalienable rights were linked to our ability to judge between right and wrong (commonly known as the "faculty of conscience"), so the violation of an inalienable right was regarded as an assault on our moral agency, which is an essential aspect of our individuality as human beings. Lord Acton (*Selected Writings*, III: 544) – who argued that "Liberalism is ultimately founded on idea of conscience" – had this in mind when he wrote that the "public good is not to be considered if it is to be purchased at the expense of the individual." Inalienable rights established a bright line that no government should be permitted to cross, regardless of what the "public good" may seem to require.

circumstances, if this was deemed necessary for the public good. But what were these circumstances? Although Jefferson never discussed this problem in detail from a philosophical point of view, he obviously regarded the prospect of war as a sufficient reason to override the presumption of liberty in regard to trade.

From the standpoint of our present discussion, Jefferson's support of the Embargo Act constitutes one of the most fascinating and instructive chapters in the history of American liberalism. For one thing, given the ideological hand wringing that this crisis provoked, it shows that the Jeffersonians took their principles very seriously indeed. For example, although Secretary of the Treasury Albert Gallatin reluctantly supported the embargo, he also cautioned that violating the presumption of liberty might bring about harmful effects that had not been anticipated. Just days before the Embargo Act became law, Gallatin wrote this to Jefferson:

> Government prohibitions do always more mischief than had been calculated; and it is not without much hesitation that a statesman should hazard to regulate the concerns of individuals as if he could do it better than themselves.[49]

Gallatin proved a capable prophet, for Jefferson's desire to avoid war by prohibiting trade with France and Britain (both had violated the rights of American merchants and sailors) produced unintended consequences galore. For instance, the plan itself would prove unworkable if only France and Britain were targets of the embargo, since there was no realistic way to control the destination of American ships after they had set sail. It was therefore necessary to ban virtually *all* exports from American ports, regardless of their intended destination, and this is exactly what the Embargo Act did:

> *Be it enacted*, That an embargo be, and hereby is laid on all ships and vessels in the ports and places within the limits or jurisdiction of the United States, cleared or not cleared, bound to any foreign port or place; and that no clearance be furnished to any ship or vessel bound to such foreign port or place, except vessels under the immediate direction of the President of the United States. . . . [50]

The Embargo Act precipitated economic crises throughout the nation, and it met with widespread opposition and resistance, especially among New England merchants. In response, Jefferson branded dissidents and smugglers as traitors, implemented draconian methods of enforcement (some of which

---

[49] Quoted in Dumas Malone, *Jefferson the President: Second Term*, 482.

[50] See *Documents of American History*, ed. Henry Steele Commager (New York: Appleton-Century-Crofts, 1949), I: 202.

were so severe that his closest political friends took him to task), and expanded presidential powers to a degree that offended even the most ardent Federalists. In short, those free-trade liberals who supported the embargo as an exception to the presumption of liberty found themselves fulfilling their own warnings about the dangers of political power.[51]

Our discussion of the potentially broad range of exceptions permitted by the presumption of liberty has brought us, full circle, back to the new liberalism discussed earlier in this chapter. New liberals were no more of a homogenous group than old liberals had been, and though many of them embraced the "positive liberty" of T.H. Green (which reflected a Hegelian influence), many did not. The latter group did not need to renovate the basic concepts of classical liberalism to justify a more expansive role for government; they merely had to climb aboard the Benthamite train and ride it to its logical destination.

A.V. Dicey, referring to "the unlimited scorn entertained by every Benthamite for the social contract and for natural rights," put it this way: "This contempt...deprived individual liberty of one of its safeguards." Without this safeguard, "the principle of utility became an argument in favour, not of individual freedom, but of the absolutism of the State."[52]

---

[51] For details, see Dumas Malone, *Jefferson the President: Second Term*, 636–40. For an explanation of why the embargo was not the only alternative to war, see Dumas Malone, *Empire for Liberty: The Genesis and Growth of the United States* (New York: Appleton-Century-Crofts, 1960), I: 366–69.

[52] Dicey, *Lectures on the Relation Between Law and Public Opinion, in England*, 309–10.

**2**

# Liberalism and the Public Good

I

We have seen that public good (or some variant thereof) was the most frequently cited liberal rationale for overriding the presumption of liberty in favor
of state intervention. Adam Smith's contention (quoted earlier) that violations
of liberty can be "pardoned only in cases of the most urgent necessity" typifies
this approach. We find a similar approach in David Hume, who grounded
property rights and other principles of justice in social utility:

> Does any one scruple, in extraordinary cases, to violate all regard to the
> private property of individuals, and sacrifice to public interest a distinction,
> which had been established for the sake of that interest? The safety of the
> people is the supreme law: All other particular laws are subordinate to it, and
> dependent on it: And if, in the *common* course of things, they be followed and
> regarded; it is only because the public safety and interest *commonly* demand
> so equal and impartial an administration.[53]

Catholic philosophers had long maintained that the ordinary rules of justice do not apply in emergency situations, and the same position was upheld
by two major Protestant exponents of natural law in the seventeenth century,
Hugo Grotius and Samuel Pufendorf. As Grotius pointed out, "Even amongst
Divines it is a received Opinion, that whoever shall take from another what is
absolutely necessary for the Preservation of his own Life, is not from thence
to be accounted guilty of Theft."[54] This is justifiable because in cases of

---

53 David Hume, *Enquiries Concerning Human Understanding and Concerning the Principles of
   Morals*, 3rd ed., ed. P.H. Nidditch (Oxford: Clarendon Press, 1975), 196.
54 Hugo Grotius, *The Rights of War and Peace*, trans. Jean Barbeyrac (1738), ed. Richard Tuck
   (Indianapolis: Liberty Fund, 2005), II: 434. Grotius (ibid., 436) adds that when necessity
   compels me to take the property of another person, "I certainly ought to make that Man
   Restitution as soon as I am able to do it." This latter claim was criticized by Samuel Pufendorf,

"absolute necessity" private property reverts to its primitive condition of common ownership and so may be used by anyone in need without violating property rights.

Although Grotius and Pufendorf are not properly classified as liberals (their political conclusions were closer to the absolutism that liberals opposed), their method of justifying the principles of justice is similar to that of David Hume and other utilitarians with liberal sympathies.[55] Even defenders of natural rights agreed with Hume that the rules of justice are "absolutely requisite to the well-being of mankind and existence of society," and that this "utility" is indispensable to our conception of justice.[56] (Where they took issue is with Hume's assertion that social utility is the "sole foundation" of justice.[57])

Most early liberals considered social utility and natural rights to be perfectly compatible. Natural-rights liberals in particular agreed with John Locke that "the rightness of an action does not depend on its utility; on the contrary, its utility is a result of its rightness."[58] A similar idea had been expressed over fifty years earlier by Grotius, who characterized natural law as the "mother" of utility while noting that the law of nature "has the reinforcement of expediency."[59] Thus, as a leading historian of this tradition has cautioned, "To draw a stark contrast between natural law and all those theories which make an appeal to utility is simplistic."[60]

The belief in the compatibility of natural rights and the public good is what led early liberals to insist that the presumption of liberty should be overridden only in exceptional cases (which is why this subject often appears in discussions of war). But in calling attention to this permissive function, whereby the public good permitted exceptions to the presumption of liberty, we should not suppose that this was its only role in liberal theory. On the

---

who pointed out that one cannot legitimately demand restitution from a person who is merely exercising his or her right to act as he does. See *On the Law of Nature and Nations*, trans. C.H. and W.A. Oldfather (Oxford: Clarendon Press, 1934), 304.

[55] Although Hume is often portrayed as a critic of the natural-law tradition, his criticisms are directed primarily at the *rationalist* wing of that tradition, as exemplified by Samuel Clarke, William Wollaston, and others. For a discussion that places Hume in the natural-law tradition and shows his similarities to Grotius and Pufendorf, see Stephen Buckle, *Natural Law and the Theory of Property: Grotius to Hume* (Oxford: Clarendon Press, 1991), 234–98.

[56] Hume, *Enquiries*, 199.

[57] Ibid., 203.

[58] John Locke, "Essays on the Law of Nature," in *Locke: Political Essays*, ed. Mark Goldie (Cambridge: Cambridge University Press, 1997), 133.

[59] Hugo Grotius, *Prolegomena to the Law of War and Peace*, trans. Francis W. Kelsey (Indianapolis: Bobbs-Merrill, 1957), 13.

[60] Stephen Buckle, *Natural Law and the Theory of Property: Grotius to Hume* (Oxford: Clarendon Press, 1991), 22.

contrary, the principal function of the public good in natural-rights liberalism was to *restrict* the activities of government to the enforcement of rights. For these liberals, to say that a government ought to further the public good *means* that a government ought to protect the natural rights of its citizens in normal circumstances. Natural rights were conceived as the primary constituents of the public good.

Fully to appreciate this view of the relationship between rights and the public good, the common good, social utility, and so forth requires that we understand the liberal conception of "society." Antoine Destutt de Tracy – whose works were greatly admired by Jefferson and other American liberals – gave this succinct account:

> Society is purely and solely a continual series of exchanges. It is never any thing else, in any epoch of its duration, from its commencement the most unformed, to its greatest perfection. And this is the greatest eulogy we can give to it, for exchange is an admirable transaction, in which the two contracting parties always both gain; consequently society is an uninterrupted succession of advantages, unceasingly renewed for all its members.[61]

Although this conception of society, which stresses mutually advantageous exchanges, reflects the influence of Adam Smith, J.B. Say, and other free-market economists, Destutt was not thinking solely of economic transactions. When people interact voluntarily with other people, they do so because they expect to gain something of value – a value that will contribute to their personal conception of a good life. But this "pursuit of happiness" (as liberals often called it) requires the freedom to act on one's own judgment, without coercive interference by others, and this freedom is defined and delimited by the notion of natural rights. Rights are conceptual formulations of the conditions that make possible the pursuit of happiness in a social context.

In the technical language of modern philosophy, rights make the pursuit of happiness *compossible*; in other words, they enable individuals – many of whom entertain different ideas about happiness – to pursue happiness simultaneously without conflict.[62] Since happiness is a fundamental good

---

[61] Count Destutt de Tracy, *A Treatise on Political Economy*, trans. Thomas Jefferson (George-town: Joseph Milligan, 1817), First Part, 6. A facsimile reprint of the *Treatise* is included in John M. Dorsey, *Psychology of Political Science: With Special Consideration for the Political Acumen of Destutt de Tracy* (Detroit: Center for Health Education, 1973). Despite the highly eccentric nature of Dorsey's book, it contains a useful "selection of writings culled from historical and contemporary references to Tracy family background, personal development and works."

[62] The concept of compossibility is fleshed out in Hillel Steiner, "The Structure of a Theory of Compossible Rights," *Journal of Philosophy* 74 (1977): 767–75 and in Steiner, *An Essay on Rights* (Oxford: Blackwell, 1994).

sought by every human being, a government promotes this common good when it protects individual rights.

Lockean liberals had an individualistic conception of society. They held that all rights are ultimately the rights of individuals and that society – or, more specifically, a government that is authorized to act on behalf of society – cannot claim special rights over and above the rights of individuals. Thus when liberals spoke, as they frequently did, of measures that promote the "public happiness," they meant not that "society" is an entity capable of experiencing happiness but that the measure in question establishes conditions that empower individuals to pursue happiness equally under the law, each in his or her own way.

The identification of the public good with natural rights is found as early as the fourteenth century in the writings of William of Ockham, a pioneer in rights theory. Regarding Ockham's agreement with a maxim of canon law, according to which laws should be instituted "for the common utility of its citizens," Brian Tierney notes:

> In using such language Ockham was not propounding a utilitarian theory of government in opposition to a rights-based theory in the manner of some later utilitarians. Rather he maintained that their common utility normally required rulers to respect the natural rights of their subjects.... It seems that, for Ockham, common utility prevailed over private rights [only] in the last resort.[63]

James Madison expressly identified the public good (or that which is for "the benefit of the people") with natural rights. In 1789, while attempting to persuade an indifferent Congress of the need for constitutional amendments that would protect individual rights (a proposal that eventually became the Bill of Rights), Madison recommended that a declaration be affixed to the Constitution that read, in part, "That government is instituted, and ought to be exercised for the benefit of the people; which consists in the enjoyment of life and liberty, with the right of acquiring and using property, and generally of pursuing and obtaining happiness and safety."[64]

In maintaining that the benefit of the people "consists" in protecting their rights to life, liberty, property, and the pursuit of happiness, Madison articulated the natural-rights paradigm of the "public good." This usage illustrates the *restrictive* function of the public good in classical liberalism, in contrast to the *permissive* function that we examined earlier. According to this paradigm

---

[63] Brian Tierney, *The Idea of Natural Rights: Studies on Natural Rights, Natural Law, and Church Law, 1150–1625* (Grand Rapids: William B. Eerdmans Publishing, 1997), 190–91.

[64] *James Madison: Writings*, ed. Jack N. Rakove (New York: The Library of America, 1999), 441.

of the public good, governments must normally *restrict* their activities to the
protection of rights because only in this way can they further the public good.

John Locke (who in many respects deserves to be called the father of natural-
rights liberalism) refers to the "public good" many times in his political writings; though it is not always clear what he means by the term – a problem that
has generated widely different interpretations by modern commentators – a
careful reading leaves little doubt that Locke generally equated the "public
good" with the protection of rights. To quote Jerome Huyler,

> Throughout his writings, Locke professes his commitment to the public
> good and general welfare. But it is not correct to conclude that this consists in
> whatever the public, or a majority, or any interested segment of society decides
> will be good or will conduce to its welfare. From both a moral and practical
> standpoint the public good consists in the protection and preservation of
> property, which includes "life, liberty and estate."[65]

Although Locke defended this liberal paradigm, he invoked the public good
for other reasons as well. Let us now take a brief look at four of the roles that
the public good plays in Locke's political theory.

1. Locke's first significant discussion of the "public good" in his *Two Treatises of Government* occurs in the *First Treatise*, in a discussion of the difference
between property rights and governmental power. The power that a sovereign
exercises over his or her subjects is not a type of property right, according to
Locke, because property rights exist "for the benefit and sole Advantage of the
Proprietor, so that he may even destroy the thing, that he has Property in by his
use of it, where need requires." Rulers do not have this property right over their
subjects; instead, they must act "for the good of the Governed," and this they
do by protecting their subjects from the "Violence or Injury of others." Unlike
a property owner, rulers (in their capacity as sovereign) use legitimate violence
not to protect their property but to compel men "to observe the positive Laws
of the Society, made conformable to the Laws of Nature, for the public good,
i.e., the good of every particular member of that Society, as far as by common
Rules, it can be provided for; the Sword is not given the Magistrate for his own
good alone."[66]

Locke needed to stress the difference between political power and property
rights because, according to the patriarchal theory defended by his dead adversary, Sir Robert Filmer, political power originated in the dominion over the
earth and its creatures that God had supposedly bestowed upon Adam. Even

---

[65] Jerome Huyler, *Locke in America: The Moral Philosophy of the Founding Era* (Lawrence:
University Press of Kansas, 1995), 170–71.

[66] Locke, *Two Treatises*, I: §92.

if one agrees with Filmer's reading of Genesis (which Locke did not), Locke pointed out that property rights are not the same as the rights associated with political sovereignty, since the latter must be exercised for the public good.[67]

As indicated by the preceding remarks, Locke equated the public good with protecting the right of individuals to be free from the "violence and injury" of others. That Locke had an individualistic conception of the public good is evident from his statement that the public good consists of "the good of every particular member" of a society. Moreoever, in noting that measures for the public good must be formulated in terms of "general rules," Locke stated the liberal doctrine that laws passed in the name of the public good must apply universally and equally; they cannot favor one individual or group over others.

Many of Locke's references to the "public good" illustrate its restrictive function in a similar manner. This approach flows from Locke's belief that a government can legitimately claim only those powers that have been delegated to it by individuals. Since no individual can place himself or herself under the arbitrary rule of another person[68] or justifiably claim an arbitrary power over the lives and property of other people, no government can claim such rights. Hence the "utmost bounds" of political power are *"limited to the publick good of the Society. It is a Power, that hath no other end but preservation, and therefore can never have a right to destroy, enslave, or designedly to impoverish the Subjects."*[69]

2. Another reference to the public good appears near the beginning of the *Second Treatise*, where Locke explained what he means by political power:

> *Political Power* then I take to be a *Right* of making Laws with Penalties of Death, and consequently all less Penalties, for the Regulating and Preserving

---

[67] See Ruth Grant, *John Locke's Liberalism* (Chicago: University of Chicago Press, 1987), 58ff. Grant presents a compelling case for the traditional view of Locke as an advocate of limited government liberalism. In addition, she maintains, contrary to many of Locke's critics, that his defense of natural law and natural rights is consistent with the epistemological theories presented in *An Essay Concerning Human Understanding*.

[68] Although later Lockeans would invoke the principle of inalienable rights to argue that certain rights cannot be delegated to governments, even with the consent of the rights-bearer, this was not Locke's position in regard to "arbitrary" power over a person's life. He argued instead that, as God's property, we do not have the right to destroy ourselves. Consequently, since we cannot transfer a *nonexistent* right, no government can claim this right over its subjects (*Two Treatises*, II: §6, §23). On this subject, see A. John Simmons, *On the Edge of Anarchy: Locke, Consent, and the Limits of Society* (Princeton: Princeton University Press, 1993), 101–46. As Simmons (102) puts it, "Indeed, what Locke actually wrote on the subject strongly suggests that he may *not* have had the idea of inalienable rights (in political contexts) clearly in mind at any point in his writings." Contrary to Simmons, however, I think that Locke regarded liberty of conscience (as defended in *A Letter Concerning Toleration*) as an inalienable right, even though he did not use the word "inalienable."

[69] Locke, *Two Treatises*, II: §135.

of Property, and of employing the force of the Community, in the Execution of such Laws, and in the defence of the Common-wealth from Foreign Injury, and all this only for the Publick Good.[70]

Locke here invoked the "public good" to emphasize his belief that governments do not exist to advance the private interests of rulers.

3. A more controversial and problematic discussion of the public good appears in Locke's discussion of the prerogative power that should be vested in the executive branch of a government. For Locke there were two basic branches of government, the legislative and the executive; and since the essence of sovereignty lies in the power to enact laws, the supreme power rests with the legislative branch. But in matters pertaining to the public good for which laws prove inadequate, "those must necessarily be left to the discretion of him, that has the Executive Power in his hands, to be ordered by him, as the publick good and advantage shall require: nay, 'tis fit that the Laws themselves should in some Cases give way to the Executive Power. . . . " Furthermore, "This Power to act according to discretion, for the publick good, without the prescription of the Law, and sometimes even against it, *is* that which is called *Prerogative*."[71]

Locke illustrated the need for a prerogative power that can contravene the ordinary rules of justice as follows: Suppose a house is on fire, and to prevent the fire from spreading throughout a town it is necessary to pull down the adjacent house of an innocent man. A strict observance of property rights, as embodied in a just legal code, would normally prohibit the destruction of private property; however, since the public good clearly requires that the house be destroyed in this case, the prerogative to authorize this action should be vested in the executive.

Another example of prerogative power is the right of the executive to pardon criminals when he or she thinks that punishing them would not advance the public good. Locke distinguished between two aspects of punishment, namely, the personal right of a victim to receive restitution from the person who injured him or her, and the public right to confine or kill a criminal. (The latter serves the dual purpose of restraining the criminal so he or she cannot commit additional crimes and deterring other people from committing similar crimes.) Locke then argued that the power to pardon should extend only to criminal penalties, not to civil reparations; the executive should not be able to absolve a criminal of his or her duty to restitute the victim.[72] This is because

---

[70]  Locke, *Two Treatises*, II: §3.

[71]  Ibid., II: §159, §160.

[72]  See ibid., II: §11.

restitution pertains to the private good of individuals, whereas the restraint of a criminal is for the public good and therefore falls within the discretionary prerogative powers of the executive.

4. Consider Locke's discussion of the public good in the following passage:

> But though Men when they enter into Society, give up the Equality, Liberty, and Executive Power they had in the State of Nature, into the hands of Society, to be so far disposed of by the Legislative, as the good of the Society shall require; yet it being only with an intention in every one the better to preserve himself his Liberty and Property; (For no rational Creature can be supposed to change his condition with an intention to the worse) the power of the Society, or *Legislative* constituted by them, *can never be suppos'd to extend farther than the common good*; but is obliged to secure every ones Property by providing them against those three defects above-mentioned, that made the State of Nature so unsafe and uneasie.[73]

Here as elsewhere, Locke indicated that concern for the public good restricts what a government may do; specifically, a government must provide better protection for those rights that would otherwise be insecure in a society without government (i.e., a state of nature). But there is a good deal of wiggle room in this proviso. To say that a legislature, having been entrusted by the people with certain rights, should act "as the good the Society shall require" in order to protect those rights, leaves considerable discretion in the hands of the legislature.

Locke's rather vague remarks on this subject (such as his claim that "men give up all their Natural Power to the Society, which they enter into"[74]) have prompted some commentators to conclude that Locke wished to vest virtually unlimited powers in government to regulate property, to the point where he would not have objected to the schemes of redistribution found in modern welfare states. This interpretation, however, flatly contradicts Locke's many statements that a government should provide better protection for private property than would be available in a state of nature: "The great and *chief end . . .* of Mens uniting into Commonwealths, and putting themselves under Government, *is the Preservation of their Property.*"[75]

The most reasonable interpretation of this issue is that Locke was thinking of those many areas of civil law that are indeterminate, insofar as they cannot be specifically determined by referring to the principles of natural law. For

---

[73] Ibid., II: §131.

[74] Ibid., II: §136.

[75] Ibid., II: §124. As indicated in §123, Locke is here using "property" in a broad sense to mean rights in general, specifically the rights to life, liberty, and "estates." This latter term signifies external *things* that are owned.

example, although we may believe that the general features of a contract can be deduced from a theory of natural rights, this is not true of its *specific* features, such as those conditions that must be fulfilled before an agreement is regarded as legally binding. There are many legal procedures that are conventional in this sense, but this does not necessarily mean that the fundamental principles on which those conventions are based are conventional as well.[76]

Philosophers of natural law conceded that many details of a legal system are optional, so it is possible for a variety of legal systems, which differ in matters of procedure, to be compatible with justice. This is probably what Locke had in mind when he insisted, on the one hand, that a government should protect property rights and, on the other hand, that a government has considerable discretion in deciding which laws it should enact for the purpose of protecting those rights. (This position is similar to Locke's belief that various forms of government, from a democracy to a constitutional monarchy, are consistent with the demands of justice, provided they are based on the consent of the governed.) Such matters are indifferent from a juridical perspective; they are not specifically demanded or forbidden by the principles of justice. Hence they fall within a discretionary range of options from which a government may choose, and the public good should be the criterion used by a government in making this choice.

In summary, we have seen that Locke appeals to the public good for at least four different reasons: first, to restrict the powers of government (in normal circumstances) to the protection of rights; second, to stress that rulers may not use their power to advance their private interests at the expense of the ruled; third, to authorize a government to override the principles of justice in exceptional cases, when this serves the public good; and fourth, to enable a government to fill the procedural gaps of a legal system that cannot be specified by the principles of natural law alone.

Among these purposes it was the third that caused the most problems for subsequent generations of liberals. Although they agreed that the presumption of liberty may be overridden in exceptional cases, it proved extraordinarily difficult to specify with precision the criteria that should be used to identify an "exceptional" case. In addition (as I noted in the last chapter), liberals were haunted by the problem of *who* should decide when rights should be sacrificed in the name of the public good. For example, later advocates of a republican form of government, however much they admired Locke, were deeply suspicious of the executive branch of government and so were troubled by Locke's defense of prerogative powers. As Madison put it in an ad hominem

---

[76] See Grant, *John Locke's Liberalism*, 32.

pique, Locke's judgment on this issue was "warped" by his allegiance to the English system of monarchy: "The chapter on prerogative [in the *Second Treatise*] shews how much the reason of the philosopher was clouded by the royalism of the Englishman."[77]

II

Because liberals agreed that rights are compatible with – indeed, indispensable to – the public good, it can be difficult to classify a given philosopher as either a natural-rights liberal *or* a utilitarian liberal. The difference consists mainly in this: Utilitarians justified rights *solely* on the grounds of their social utility, whereas proponents of natural rights considered social utility to be a *consequence* of observing moral principles that are ultimately justified in terms of human nature – especially the role of reason in judging which actions will enable a person to live a good life. As Benjamin Constant put it, "Right is a principle; utility is only a result. Right is a cause; utility is only an effect."[78]

Although many natural-rights liberals conceded that freedom is a presumption rather than an inflexible rule, their belief in the status of rights as fundamental moral principles led them to insist on limits to what a government may do in the name of the public good. For example, they would not permit the violation of *inalienable* rights, such as liberty of conscience, under any circumstances. As John Locke put it, "liberty of conscience is every man's natural right," so "nobody ought to be compelled in matters of religion either by law or force." Hence "the magistrate ought not to forbid the preaching or professing of any speculative opinion in any church, because they have no manner of relation to the civil rights of the subjects." If a Catholic believes that what others would call "bread" is really the body of Christ, or if a Jew does not believe that the New Testament is the word of God, these and similar convictions do not "alter anything in men's civil rights," so they are not the proper concern of government: "The business of laws is not to provide for the truth of opinions, but for the safety and security of the commonwealth, and of every particular man's goods and person."[79]

Locke and other natural-rights liberals would not condone the suppression of a peaceful but unpopular religious minority merely because a government might judge this policy to be conducive to the public good. Nor does a

---

[77] "*Helvidius*," No. *I*, in *Madison: Writings*, 540.

[78] Benjamin Constant, *Principles of Politics Applicable to All Governments*, trans. Dennis O'Keeffe (Indianapolis: Liberty Fund, 2003), 41.

[79] Locke, *A Letter Concerning Toleration*, 150–51.

government have a right to violate the property rights of the members of one religion to benefit the members of another religion. "But," Locke asked, "what if the magistrate believe such a law as this to be for the public good?" He replied that the "private judgment" of the magistrate about what will promote the public good, when this judgment violates the fundamental purpose of government (which is to secure those natural rights that would be insecure in a state of nature), does not "give him any new right of imposing laws upon his subjects, which neither was in the constitution of the government granted him, nor ever was in the power of the people to grant...."[80]

These remarks illustrate how natural rights impose limits on the power of government that could not be justified in a strictly utilitarian account that upholds the legitimacy of any law that furthers social utility. According to Lockean liberals, the fundamental purpose of government is to protect rights, not to promote the welfare of individuals per se. They regarded the protection of rights as a necessary, but not sufficient, condition of a good life. As Locke pointed out, a "good life" requires more than the possession and use of external property; it also involves religious beliefs and other values that are a matter of conscience – and there is a "great danger" that one of these "jurisdictions" will entrench upon the other. A government is a "keeper of the public peace," not an overseer of souls, so it is empowered to promote the collective interests of individuals (and thereby serve the public good) *only* insofar as its activities do *not* encroach upon the private sphere of conscience.[81]

The crucial role played by inalienable rights in restricting the power of government can be seen in Locke's discussion of what should happen if "the magistrate should enjoin anything by his authority that appears unlawful to the conscience of a private person." This will rarely occur, according to Locke, if the ruler truly has the public good in mind; but if it should occur and a person cannot obey a law in good conscience, his or her response should depend on the kind of law in question.

If a law falls, in principle, within the proper jurisdiction of government, then a conscientious objector should resort to passive disobedience; in other words, he or she should refuse to obey the law and then submit to the legal penalty for disobedience. This is required because "the private judgment of any person concerning a law enacted in political matters, for the public good, does not take away the obligation of that law, nor deserve a dispensation." If, however, the law falls outside the legitimate jurisdiction of government – if, for example, it compels people "to embrace a strange religion, and join in the

---

[80] Ibid., 154.
[81] Ibid., 151.

worship and ceremonies of another church" – then "men are not in these cases obliged by that law, against their consciences" and are authorized to resist its enforcement.[82] As Locke put it in the *Second Treatise*, tyranny is *"the exercise of Power beyond Right,"* and when a ruler exceeds his or her legitimate power, "he may be opposed, as any other Man, who by force invades the Right of another."[83]

In sum, "force and compulsion" have no legitimate role in the sphere of conscience. "Nobody is obliged in that matter to yield obedience unto the admonitions or injunctions of another, further than he himself is persuaded. Every man in that has the supreme and absolute authority of judging for himself."[84]

We thus see that the doctrine of inalienable rights imposes an a priori restriction on the power of government. Whether a legal incursion into the sphere of conscience really promotes the public good is irrelevant, since matters of conscience are exempt from calculations of this kind. The jurisdiction of government is confined to those external actions that affect rights, so the public good can serve as a standard of legislation only within that delimited sphere.

This a priori restriction on the power of government is what fundamentally distinguishes natural-rights liberalism from utilitarian liberalism. A consistent utilitarian could not impose a priori limits on the power of government in this manner. Although he or she might *conclude* that governmental incursions into the sphere of conscience do not promote the public good and therefore should not be undertaken, he or she could not *preclude* such actions beforehand, as a matter of moral principle, before making the necessary calculations.

Although Locke's principles would appear to demand universal freedom of religion, this was not his position. On the contrary, he expressly denies that Catholics and atheists should be tolerated. Locke avoids the obvious contradiction by claiming that toleration should be denied to Catholics and atheists, not because of their religious convictions per se, but because of the *political* implications of those convictions.[85]

According to Locke, "no opinions contrary to human society, or those moral rules which are necessary to the preservation of civil society, are to be tolerated by the magistrate." Furthermore, since he believed that some

---

[82] Ibid., 153.

[83] Locke, *Two Treatises*, II: §199, §201.

[84] Locke, *A Letter Concerning Toleration*, 152–53.

[85] This had been a standard rationale for religious persecution since the reign of Queen Elizabeth. Those Nonconformists and Catholics who were persecuted under Elizabeth were accused of treason, not heresy, because of political doctrines deemed subversive to the state. See J.W. Allen, *A History of Political Thought in the Sixteenth Century* (New York: Barnes and Noble, 1960), 231ff.

Catholic doctrines – for example, that the excommunication of a king releases his subjects from the duty of obedience, that only Catholics should be tolerated by Catholic sovereigns, and that Catholics owe primary allegiance to the pope – are politically subversive, he concluded that Catholics "have no right to be tolerated by the magistrate." Similarly, "those are not all to be tolerated who deny the being of a God." This is justified because belief in God is the foundation of morality, so those who deny the existence of God have no reason to respect the sanctity of those "promises, covenants, and oaths" that constitute the foundation of civil society.[86]

Whatever one may think of these arguments, they at least illustrate, if in a peculiar way, Locke's commitment to the doctrine that personal matters of conscience should be immune to governmental interference. Before Locke could justify the suppression of Catholics and atheists in the name of the public good, he had to shift their convictions from the private domain of conscience to public domain of beliefs with political implications, for only then could he invoke the public good as a reason for government intervention. The problem, of course, is that this maneuver is so elastic as to potentially nullify the function of inalienable rights by bringing a broad spectrum of beliefs and self-regarding actions within the purview of government coercion.

III

Having discussed the role of natural rights in delimiting the sphere in which appeals to the public good can serve as a guide to legislation, let us now turn to how utilitarian liberals approached this issue. As noted before, since early liberals often blended their discussions of natural rights with appeals to social utility, it can prove difficult to label a given liberal in an either/or manner. Nevertheless, we can frequently identify a dominant tendency, and a utilitarian tendency is evident in the liberal theory of Joseph Priestley (1733–1804), the famous chemist, dissenting minister, and English champion of American liberties.

According to Priestley, "That the happiness of the whole community is the ultimate end of government can never be doubted, and all claims of individuals inconsistent with the public good are absolutely null and void." But if this utilitarian goal is beyond doubt, matters are far less simple when it comes to ascertaining what political measures will achieve this goal most efficiently: "There is a real difficulty in determining what general rules, respecting the

---

[86]  Locke, *A Letter Concerning Toleration*, 154–56.

extent of the power of government, or of governors, are most conducive to the public good."[87]

Priestley began his analysis by drawing a distinction "of the greatest importance," namely the difference between "the *form* and the *extent of power* in a government." Any form of government – be it "a monarchy, an aristocracy, or even a republic" – can be tyrannical if it wields excessive power. The key issue is whether "people enjoy more or fewer of their natural rights." "If the power of government be very extensive, and the subjects of it have, consequently, little power over their own actions, that government is tyrannical, and oppressive," regardless of the form of the government in question. From the perspective of an individual who values freedom, it is a matter of little consequence "whether his life, his liberty, or his property were at the mercy of one, of a few, or of a great number of people. . . . " The justice of a government is ultimately determined by whether or not it leaves "a man the most valuable of his private rights," so the extent of power exercised by a particular government is more fundamental, morally speaking, than the form of that government.[88]

Priestley disagreed with the maxim that collective decisions ("the joint understanding of all the members of a state") are generally preferable to individual decisions: "In truth, the greater part of human actions are of such a nature, that more inconvenience would follow from their being fixed by laws, than from their being left to every man's arbitrary will." Social cooperation is advantageous chiefly because it enables us to enlist the assistance of others in gaining values that would be unattainable by our solitary efforts, such as when we seek restitution from those who have injured us. Laws are defective when, instead of assisting us in this manner, they are "injurious to the natural rights and civil liberties of mankind, when they lay a man under unnecessary restrictions, by controlling his conduct, and preventing him from serving himself, with respect to those things, in which they can yield him no real assistance, and in providing for which he is in no danger of injuring others."[89]

Despite his adherence to these general principles, Priestley warned that "the proper extent of civil government is not easily circumscribed within

---

[87] Joseph Priestley, *An Essay on the First Principles of Government, and on the Nature of Political, Civil, and Religious Freedom*, 2nd ed. (1771), in *Joseph Priestley: Political Writings*, ed. Peter Miller (Cambridge: Cambridge University Press, 1993), 31.

[88] Ibid., 28–29. Priestley's distinction was often expressed as the difference between the *principle* of a government and its *form*. The former pertains to the fundamental purpose for which legitimate governments are instituted, such as the protection of individual rights. Although eighteenth-century liberals generally preferred a republican form of government, they emphasized that this form derives its value from its ability to preserve freedom better than other forms.

[89] Ibid., 30–31.

exact limits," and this is where a consideration of the public good came into play. He identified two schools of thought about the relationship between government and the public good. According to one theory, "the legislature should make express provision for every thing which can even indirectly, remotely, and consequentially, affect the public good." This approach stands in contrast to the liberal theory, according to which government should concern itself only with matters of justice (i.e., the protection of rights) while leaving more tangential matters to the voluntary decisions and actions of individuals. Liberals believe that "it is for the advantage of society, upon the whole" that social matters not directly concerned with justice "be left to take their own natural course, and that the legislature cannot interfere in them, without defeating its own great object, the public good."[90]

This is Priestley's version of the presumption of liberty: As a general rule we should be free to act on our own judgments, without the coercive intervention of government, so long as we do not violate the rights of others. That Priestley believed this to be a *defeasible* presumption is indicated by his observation that we should not rely on a priori arguments when determining the proper extent of government power, but that "experiments only [i.e., experience] can determine how far this power of the legislature ought to extend." Moreover, "till a sufficient number of experiments have been made, it becomes the wisdom of the civil magistracy to take as little upon its hands as possible, and never to interfere, without the greatest caution, in things that do not immediately affect the lives, liberty, or property of the members of the community."[91]

In presenting minimal government (whose functions are basically confined to the protection of individual rights) as a presumption that should operate until and unless experience proves that the public good can be better served by vesting government with more expansive powers, Priestley expressly identified the public good as the principal defeasibility criterion to which we can appeal to override the presumption of liberty. Although Priestley did not personally advocate more extensive powers, he maintained that people who have voluntarily formed or joined a political society "may subject themselves to whatever restrictions they please; and, consequently, that the supreme civil magistrate, on whom the whole power of society is devolved, may make what laws they please." Hence the relevant issue is not whether violations of the presumption of liberty are just; instead, "the question is, what restrictions and laws are wise, and calculated to promote the public good. . . . "[92]

---

[90]  Ibid.
[91]  Ibid., 31–32.
[92]  Ibid., 32.

We could scarcely ask for a more pertinent discussion of the role played by the public good in utilitarian versions of liberalism than that provided by Joseph Priestley. Although there is a palpable tension between his appeal to natural rights, which at times seem to function as an ultimate standard of judgment in political affairs, and his appeal to social utility, he insisted that we are incapable of "arguing *a priori* in matters of government," and that we should rely on experience to tell us which measures further the public good and which do not.

This conclusion was the worst nightmare of natural-rights liberals. Although the liberal critics of utilitarianism agreed with Priestley that the public good is best served when a government restricts its activities to the protection of natural rights, they also knew that people will inevitably disagree not only about what means are best suited to the public good but also about the nature of the "public good" itself. It is therefore no surprise, in view of these fundamental disagreements about the goal to be attained, that "experiments" (by which Priestley meant the sustained and systematic study of events in the political world) will teach different things to different people. If I believe that economic equality is a key element of the public good, even if this goal will result in less wealth overall, then experience may teach me that a free market is detrimental to the public good. If, on the other hand, you believe that equal freedom under the law is a fundamental aspect of the public good, then you may insist that free markets are indispensable to the public good.

It was owing to problems like this that natural-rights liberals insisted that moral limits should be imposed on government *before* calculations of social utility even come into play. They recognized of course that these moral limits may have little or no practical effect, that they may be violated under any form of government, that, as Locke put it, "the magistrate, being the stronger will have his will, and carry the point." Nevertheless, as Locke retorted, "the question is not here concerning the doubtfulness of the event, but the rule of right."[93] And, according to natural-rights liberals, it was precisely this "rule of right" that was put in serious jeopardy by those liberals who based their defense of freedom solely on social utility, and who thereby abandoned even the most fundamental freedoms, such as liberty of conscience, to the fickle and self-serving assessments of rulers.

A similar point was later made by F.A. Hayek. Although Hayek was not a proponent of natural rights – he held, for example, that coercion is bad because it hinders the development of a person's mental powers and thereby prevents him (or her) "from making the greatest contribution that he is capable

---

[93] Locke, *A Letter Concerning Toleration*, 154.

of to the community"[94] – he shared the concern of natural-rights liberals that utilitarian calculations would render the principles of freedom unstable and vulnerable to the shifting sands of public opinion and political expediency. Hayek was therefore highly critical of those classical liberals for whom the principle of *laissez-faire* "was never more than a rule of thumb." To view freedom as a mere presumption that can be readily defeated by appeals to the public good is "not adequate to decide what is and what is not permissible in a free system," because people "will not refrain from those restrictions on individual liberty that appear to them the simplest and most direct remedy of a recognized evil."[95] Hayek continues:

> The preservation of a free system is so difficult precisely because it requires a constant rejection of measures which appear to be required to secure particular results, on no stronger grounds than that they conflict with a general rule, and frequently without knowing what will be the costs of not observing the rule in the particular instance. A successful defence of freedom must therefore be dogmatic and make no concessions to expediency, even where it is not possible to show that, beside the known beneficial effects, some particular harmful result would also follow from its infringement. Freedom will prevail only if it is accepted as a general principle whose application to particular instances requires no justification. It is thus a misunderstanding to blame classical liberalism for having been too doctrinaire. Its defect was not that it adhered too stubbornly to principles, but rather that it lacked principles sufficiently definite to provide clear guidance. . . . [96]

Hayek's solution to this problem lay in his conception of general rules, and since he frequently recommended the approach defended by David Hume, let us take a brief look at how Hume dealt with this issue.[97]

If Hume's belief that "nothing less than the most extreme necessity"[98] can warrant violations of justice seems closer to the position of natural-rights liberals than to their utilitarian cousins, this is because of his conviction that such principles will further social utility only if they are treated as "general inflexible rules" in normal circumstances. The principles of justice "are highly

---

[94]  F.A. Hayek, *The Constitution of Liberty* (Chicago: University of Chicago Press, 1960), 134.

[95]  F.A. Hayek, *Law, Legislation, and Liberty*, vol. 1, *Rules and Order* (Chicago: University of Chicago Press, 1973), 61.

[96]  Ibid.

[97]  See F.A. Hayek, "The Legal and Political Philosophy of David Hume," in *Hume: A Collection of Critical Essays*, ed. V.C. Chappell (New York: Anchor Books, 1966), 335–60. Although I think Hayek underestimates the extent to which Hume believed that the rules of justice are the product of reason, this article contains important insights about Hume's approach to the evolution of moral and juridical norms.

[98]  Hume, *Enquiries*, 206.

useful, or indeed absolutely necessary to the well-being of mankind: but the benefit resulting from them is not the consequence of every individual single act; but arise from the whole scheme or system concurred in by the whole, or the greater part of the society." Although observing the rules of justice will not always result in desirable consequences from a moral point of view, it is essential to the peace and preservation of society that they be applied "without taking into consideration the characters, situations, and connexions of the person concerned, or any particular consequences which may result. . . . "[99]

Hume's approach, which is essentially a philosophical defense of the traditional idea of an impartial "rule of law," leaves little room for exceptions to the rules of justice, since it does not permit each case to be evaluated on its merits so far as its contribution to social utility is concerned. Rather, Hume argued that the social utility of a juridical system is not due merely to the direct effects of each constituent rule, considered separately and in isolation, but rather to the indirect, long-range benefits of the system as a whole, which contributes stability and predictability to a social system. To this a natural-rights liberal might object that the same thing could be said of a despotic legal system, and that a defender of this system could rebut demands for greater freedom with Humean arguments about the utility of the despotic system as a whole.

Classical liberals are sometimes ridiculed (unfairly, in my judgment) for their belief that history is a "lamp of experience" from which the present generation can learn valuable lessons. If there is a lesson to be learned from the aspect of liberalism that we have explored to this point, it is that freedom has been defended from a number of different perspectives, and that the internecine conflicts within liberalism about which defense is the best defense are conflicts that seem to come with the territory. If so, such conflicts will exist so long as there are people who believe that freedom is worth defending.

IV

Liberal concerns over ambiguity in the notion of the public good, and their fears that appeals to the public good would open the door for a wide range of government intervention, were more than a theoretical issue. The practical import of the problem manifested itself during debates over ratification of the U.S. Constitution.

Specifically, the "general welfare" clause (Article 1, Section 8) provoked strenuous objections by opponents of the Constitution ("Antifederalists") that

---

[99] Ibid., 304–05. Modern philosophers have dubbed this approach "rule utilitarianism," in contrast to "act utilitarianism." The former assesses the overall utility of a general principle, or rule, whereas the latter assesses the utility of particular acts.

this gave to Congress a blank check to pass any legislation it deemed conducive to the public good. In response, James Madison and other defenders of the Constitution ("Federalists") maintained that the general welfare clause is not a grant of unlimited power but merely a statement of the general *purpose* for which Congress could levy taxes. The powers of Congress, they insisted, are specified in the list of enumerated power that follows the general welfare clause. Article 1, Section 8 of the U.S. Constitution begins as follows:

> The Congress shall have Power To lay and collect Taxes, Duties, Imposts and Excises, to pay the Debts and provide for the common Defense and general Welfare of the United States; but all Duties Imposts and Excises shall be uniform throughout the United States; . . . .

This clause ends with a semicolon, after which we find a list of the so-called enumerated powers granted to Congress, including "To borrow Money on the credit of the United States; to regulate Commerce with foreign Nations, and among the several States, and with the Indian tribes; To establish an uniform Rule of Naturalization," and so on.

The basic point of contention was whether the grant of power of Congress to provide for the "general welfare of the United States" specifies the *purpose* of the enumerated powers, or whether it is a separate and distinct power apart from the enumerated powers – a power whose range would ultimately be determined by Congress itself.[100]

Antifederalists protested that the general welfare clause would be construed as a separate and distinct power; since "general welfare" has no clear meaning, it would effectively nullify the enumerated powers by granting an undefined and therefore indefinite power to Congress. One Antifederalist, writing under the pseudonym "Brutus," expressed this concern as follows:

> It will . . . be matter of opinion, what tends to the general welfare; and the Congress will be the only judges in the matter. To provide for the general welfare, is an abstract proposition, which mankind differ in the explanation of, as much as they do on any political or moral proposition that can be proposed; the most opposite measures may be pursued by different parties, and both may profess, that they have in view the general welfare; and both sides may be honest in their professions, or both may have sinister views. Those who advocate this new constitution declare, they are influenced by a regard to the general welfare; those who oppose it, declare they are moved

---

[100] It is important to keep in mind that the Constitution did not originally include a Bill of Rights. This was a major complaint of the Antifederalists (along with some of the Constitution's supporters, such as Thomas Jefferson), and it was largely owing to the persistent efforts of the Antifederalists that the first ten amendments were added in 1791.

by the same principle; and I have no doubt but a number of both sides are honest in their professions; and yet nothing is more certain than this, that to adopt this constitution, and not to adopt it, cannot both of them be promotive of the general welfare.[101]

When one is confronted with a vague term such as "general welfare," the key question is this: *Who* shall decide in what the "general welfare" consists? If Congress is vested with the power to decide this matter for itself, "it is a truth confirmed by the unerring experience of ages that every man and every body of men, invested with power, are ever disposed to increase it, and to acquire a superiority over every thing that stands in their way."[102]

In *The Federalist* (#41), James Madison responded to the fears voiced by Antifederalists about the general welfare clause. Articulating the view that would later become a mainstay of strict constructionism, he argued that the power to provide for the general welfare was never intended to be a separate and distinct power granted to Congress, and that the meaning of the "general welfare" is confined to the subsequent list of enumerated powers.

Perhaps the most interesting aspect of Madison's discussion is the contempt he expressed for those Antifederalists who warned that this clause would grant virtually unlimited powers to Congress: "No stronger proof could be given of the distress under which these writers labour for objections, than their stooping to such a misconstruction."[103] Madison claimed that the Antifederalist argument would be plausible only if the Constitution contained "no other enumeration or definition of the powers of the Congress." However, this argument is not plausible, given that the general terms "common defense and general welfare" are immediately followed by a list of enumerated powers and are "not even separated by a longer pause than a semicolon." It is not reasonable to suppose that "one part of the same sentence be excluded altogether from a share in the meaning," and that "the clear and precise expressions" of the enumerated powers be denied any role in defining "the more doubtful and indefinite terms." After all, why would the enumerated powers have been included in the first place – what purpose would they serve? – if they would effectively be nullified by a general, undefined, and indefinite grant of power to promote the "general welfare"?[104]

---

[101] *The Anti-Federalist: Writings by the Opponents of the Constitution*, ed. Herbert J. Storing (Chicago: University of Chicago Press, 1985), 142–43.

[102] Ibid., 112–13.

[103] Alexander Hamilton, James Madison, and John Jay, *The Federalist Papers*, ed. Garry Wills (New York: Bantam Books, 1982), 209.

[104] Ibid., 209–10.

So obvious did this interpretation seem to Madison that he could not take the Antifederalist argument seriously. To claim that the enumerated powers should play no role in explaining or qualifying the meaning of "general welfare" can have no other effect than "to confound and mislead" the American people. Americans must therefore decide whether the framers of the Constitution deliberately set out to deceive them, or whether Antifederalists were deliberately distorting the meaning of the general welfare clause in order to inflame the deep-seated fear of a government with unlimited power. Of course, there was no doubt in Madison's mind about the correct explanation.

Thus did Madison emphatically deny that the general welfare clause "amounts to an unlimited concession to exercise every power which may be alleged to be necessary for the common defence or general welfare."[105] As part of his argument that the term "general welfare" is simply a caption that is explained by the subsequent list of enumerated powers, Madison noted that the relevant terms were copied from the Articles of Confederation (Article III), which says that the American states have entered "into a firm league of friendship with each other, for their common defence, the security of their Liberties, and their mutual and general welfare." And according to Article VIII of the same document, "All charges of war, and all other expences that shall be incurred for the common defence or general welfare" shall be "defrayed out of a common treasury."[106]

How should these references to the "general welfare" in the Articles of Confederation be construed? Madison contended that the "general welfare" specified a *purpose* (along with the common defense) for which specific powers had been delegated to the Confederation Congress to serve as *means*. The general welfare, in other words, was not itself a delegated power, nor was Congress authorized to do anything it deemed appropriate to promote the general welfare. Rather, the Articles authorized Congress to exercise only those powers that had been expressly delegated to it, and the states had given this authorization so that Congress could advance the general welfare.[107] Therefore, since the identical words appear in the Constitution, it is unreasonable to suppose that they mean anything other than what they meant in the Articles of Confederation.

Madison's interpretation was echoed during the Virginia ratifying convention (June, 1788) by Governor Edmund Randolph (who, like Madison, had

---

[105] Ibid., 209.

[106] Commager, *Documents*, 111–13.

[107] This interpretation of the Articles of Confederation was bolstered by Article II, according to which every state retained its "sovereignty, freedom and independence," as well as "every Power, Jurisdiction, and right" that was not "expressly delegated" to the general government.

served as a delegate to the Constitutional Convention). After accusing Antifederalists of using highly colored rhetoric to exaggerate "the dangers of giving the General Government an indefinite power of providing for the general welfare," Randolph insists that "no such power is given." The "general welfare" is not a separate and independent power but merely specifies the purpose for which Congress is empowered to levy taxes. To interpret it as a grant of indefinite power is "absurd" – "treason against common language" – because it would make nonsense out of the subsequent list of enumerated powers.[108]

Despite Madison's condescending attitude toward the objections of Antifederalists, and despite Randolph's charge that their interpretation was "absurd" and "treason against common language," it didn't take long for the prediction of Antifederalists – namely that the general welfare clause would be construed as a grant of indefinite power to Congress – to become true. In late 1791, Alexander Hamilton (then Secretary of the Treasury in the Washington administration) produced his highly influential *Report on Manufactures*. In this detailed defense of governmental intervention to promote various industries in the United States, Hamilton defends bounties as necessary to make certain industries viable in America.

The problem for Hamilton was that the Constitution nowhere authorizes the payment of such bounties; indeed, to the extent to which bounties benefit particular industries at the expense of taxpayers, farmers, and other industries, they would seem to run afoul of the requirement that taxes serve the general welfare rather than special interests.

The first thing Hamilton needed to do was to argue that bounties, however much they may seem to benefit some people at the expense of others, are conducive to the growth of an economy and therefore further the general welfare. Even if we grant this, though, the problem remains that bounties are not included in the list of enumerated powers. Hamilton met this objection by outlining his broad interpretation of the general welfare clause – an interpretation that would later receive the sanction of the U.S. Supreme Court.

Hamilton maintained "the terms 'general welfare' were doubtless intended to signify more than was expressed" by the enumerated powers; "otherwise numerous exigencies incident to the affairs of a Nation would have been left without a provision." Hamilton continues:

> The phrase is as comprehensive as any that could have been used because it was not fit that the constitutional authority of the Union, to appropriate

---

[108] *The Debate on the Constitution: Federalist and Antifederalist Speeches, Articles, and Letters During the Struggle over Ratification*, ed. Bernard Bailyn (New York: The Library of America, 1993), 2: 956.

its revenues should have been restricted within narrower limits than the 'General Welfare' and because this necessarily embraces a vast variety of particulars, which are susceptible neither of specification nor of definition.

It is therefore of necessity left to the discretion of the National Legislature, to pronounce, upon the objects, which concern the general Welfare, and for which under that description, an appropriation of money is requisite and proper. And there seems to be no room for a doubt that whatever concerns the general Interests of *learning* of *Agriculture* of *Manufacturers* and of *Commerce* are within the sphere of the national Councils *as far as regards its application of Money.*[109]

In 1936, the broad interpretation of the general welfare clause that Madison contemptuously dismissed as a bogeyman of the Antifederalists was embraced by the U.S. Supreme Court. After summarizing Madison's argument that the general welfare clause should not be construed as a separate and distinct power granted to Congress but instead "amounted to no more than a reference to the other powers enumerated in the subsequent clauses of the same section," Justice Roberts, writing for the majority, goes on to summarize the broad interpretation defended by Alexander Hamilton (and later embraced by Justice Story in his celebrated *Commentaries*):

> Hamilton . . . maintained the clause confers a power separate and distinct from those later enumerated, is not restricted in meaning by the grant of them, and Congress consequently has a substantive power to tax and to appropriate limited only by the requirement that it shall be exercised for the general welfare.[110]

Roberts accepts this as the correct interpretation, which means that the power of Congress to tax is not limited to the specific powers enumerated in Article 1, Section 8, but is justified so long as it serves the "general welfare" – a term whose meaning is *not* confined to those enumerated powers.

[109] Hamilton, *Writings*, 702.
[110] For an abridged version of the majority decision in *United States v. Butler*, see William B. Lockhart, Yale Kamisar, and Jesse H. Choper, *Constitutional Law: Cases, Comments, Questions*, 4th ed. (St. Paul: West Publishing Co., 1975), 214–18.

# 3

# Liberal Ideology and Political Philosophy

Liberalism is an extremely diverse political tradition, and tracing the history of liberal ideas has long been a cottage industry for intellectual historians. Many debates have emerged from these investigations, some of which revolve around the ideas and influence of John Locke. For example, was Locke's brand of individualism a continuation of, or radical departure from, the classical natural-law tradition? To what extent were America's founding fathers indebted to Locke? Did they owe more to Francis Hutcheson and other luminaries of the Scottish Enlightenment than they did to Locke? Did they draw less from the tradition of Lockean individualism and more from the tradition of "classical republicanism" that was rooted in Aristotelian political theory – or, perhaps, the tradition of "civic humanism" that had ties to Machiavelli?

If such questions are difficult to answer, this is largely because of the problems inherent in defining a political tradition. In tracing the development and influence of a particular tradition, we can easily lose sight of the fact that intellectual traditions are mental constructs created by historians. When we determine that the fundamental ideas of a philosopher are similar to the ideas of earlier philosophers, we are tempted to speak of a "tradition" or "school of thought" to which all of these philosophers belonged. One among many problems in this procedure is how to identify which ideas should serve as the essential, and therefore defining, characteristics of a tradition.

I have used a minimalist approach in my treatment of the "liberal tradition"; specifically, I have followed Acton's lead in viewing liberals as those political philosophers whose "polar star" was liberty. Another way of saying this is that liberals embraced freedom as their highest political value. They tended to evaluate political measures and institutions in terms of their impact on individual freedom, favoring those measures and institutions that advanced the cause of freedom and criticizing those that hindered that cause.

Even this inclusive approach is problematic, since philosophers with many different (and often conflicting) beliefs have professed their commitment to freedom. That this agreement is more verbal than real becomes evident when we examine the widely different meanings that philosophers have ascribed to the word "freedom," so it is necessary to specify that liberals subscribed to what has become known as the negative conception of freedom. Although liberals acknowledged different kinds of freedom – Richard Price, for example, spoke of physical, moral, religious, and civil liberty – they also agreed with Price that "there is one general idea that runs through them all; I mean the idea of self-direction, or self-government." Moreover, "In all these cases there is a force which stands opposed to the agent's own will, and which, as far as it operates, produces servitude."[111]

Another problem with my conception of a liberal is that not every philosopher whom I place in this category expressly endorsed freedom as his or her highest political value. Some never discussed the problems of political philosophy in these terms, while others (as we have seen) supported freedom only to the extent that it contributed to some notion of the public good. Because of these and similar problems, it is better to think of Acton's polar star as an ideal type instead of a formal definition.

Max Weber developed his theory of ideal types to deal with the kind of problems that we encounter in tracing the history of liberalism. An ideal type is a mental construct whose parts are selected, arranged, and combined into a single mental unit for the purpose of analysis. As Weber put it, an ideal type is formed by the "one-sided *accentuation* of one or more points of view" and by the synthesis of a great many singular phenomena, which are arranged "according to those one-sidedly emphasized viewpoints into a unified *analytical* construct."[112]

More simply, ideal types are simplified models, stylized concepts that are neither causal generalizations (as we find in natural science) nor formal definitions (as we find in logic and mathematics). Ideal types are not descriptions of reality per se; rather, they serve as benchmarks that enable us to compare diverse historical phenomena in terms of their similarities and differences to the ideal type.

---

[111] Richard Price, *Observations on the Nature of Civil Liberty* (1776), in *Richard Price: Political Writings*, ed. D.O. Thomas (Cambridge: Cambridge University Press, 1991), 21–22.

[112] Max Weber, "Ideal Types and Theory Construction," in *Readings in the Philosophy of the Social Sciences*, ed. May Brodbeck (New York: Macmillan, 1968), 497.

Hence when I say that Acton's "polar star" is an ideal type of liberalism, I mean that it is serviceable as a basis of comparison; we can use it to determine the similarities and differences among different types of liberalism, as well as the peculiarities of individual liberals. As for whom should be thrown into the pot in the first place so their ideas can be compared in this manner, this is largely a judgment call, one that depends to some degree on conventional labels. As illustrated in the first two chapters, I have used the presumption of liberty as a rough guide. If a political philosopher focuses on individual freedom as a value that deserves special consideration, then I regard this as a good reason to place that philosopher in the liberal tradition.

In the final analysis, it matters not in the least whether there exists a consensus about whether a given philosopher should be dubbed a "liberal." If that philosopher defended individual freedom to a significant degree and had interesting things to say on this topic, then this is all that matters for the purpose of this book.

II

When we are discussing the meaning of liberalism, it is useful to distinguish between (1) liberal sentiments, (2) liberal principles, (3) liberal theories, and (4) liberal ideologies.

1. By liberal sentiments, I mean expressions of the value of freedom that are not formalized as general principles or justified as part of a general theory of liberalism. We often find liberal sentiments in the writings of philosophers and literary figures whose philosophical views on freedom and government would disqualify them as liberals in the strict sense. Montaigne is a good example of such a philosopher. Although it would be problematic at best to classify Montaigne as a liberal, liberal sentiments do recur throughout his *Essays*, as in this example:

> No prison has received me, not even for a visit. Imagination makes the sight of one, even from the outside, unpleasant to me. I am so sick for freedom that if anyone should forbid me access to some corner of the Indies, I should live distinctly less comfortably. And as long as I find earth or air open elsewhere I shall not lurk in any place where I have to hide.[113]

2. By a liberal principle, I mean a general statement of the value of liberty in a particular sphere of human activity for which some justification is

---

[113] *The Complete Essays of Montaigne*, trans. Donald M. Frame (Stanford: Stanford University Press, 1965), 820.

offered. Like liberal sentiments, liberal principles need not signify a broader commitment to a liberal political theory. For example, it is not unusual to find defenders of absolute sovereignty, such as Jean Bodin (1530–1596), who also defended the principle of religious toleration. A policy of religious toleration was sometimes recommended to absolute monarchs for its pragmatic value, as the best way to maintain peace and social order within their kingdoms; in such cases, this liberal (i.e, pro-freedom) principle was consistent with a belief in anti-liberal policies in other spheres.

3. At a higher level of abstraction we find liberal theories. A liberal theory is an interrelated system of principles that defend individual freedom as the highest political value. Such theories typically include a moral defense of freedom and a normative theory of government, according to which the basic purpose of government is to protect individual rights. Hence liberal theories tend to fall within the province of political philosophy.

4. More comprehensive still are liberal ideologies. By a liberal ideology, I mean an integrated system of theories in various intellectual disciplines (ethics, political philosophy, economics, sociology, etc.) that are connected, directly or indirectly, to the primary value of freedom. In short, a liberal ideology is a comprehensive, interdisciplinary belief system that revolves around the idea of freedom.

"Ideology" is a contentious term, one that has been used in a variety of ways for over two centuries. The word was coined around 1800 by the French liberal Destutt de Tracy, who used it to denote the science (or systematic investigation) of ideas. An adherent of the "sensationalist" school of epistemology (whose most notable French proponent was Condillac), Tracy believed that all ideas originate in our sensory experiences and that we can clarify the meanings of the words we use – including terms such as "property," "rights," and other magnets of political controversy – by tracing their roots to our perceptions of the physical world. Hence in *Les éléments de l'idéologie*, Tracy explores the genesis and development of ideas and indicates how the sciences (including the moral sciences that deal with human action) can be constructed on an objective foundation. This was an ambitious agenda indeed; in the words of one historian, ideology "would reconstruct politics, economics and ethics from the ground up, moving from the simplest process of sensation to the loftiest regions of spirit."[114] (Thomas Jefferson admired Tracy's work in this

---

[114] Terry Eagleton, *Ideology: An Introduction* (London: Verso, 1991), 66. My discussion of Tracy and the reaction the ideologists provoked from Napoleon draws heavily from Eagleton. For another historical overview of the term "ideology," see Mostafa Rejai, "Ideology," in *Dictionary*

field, calling it "a production of the first order in the science of our thinking faculty, or of the understanding."[115])

As a liberal who believed that a clarification of ideas would serve the cause of freedom by dissolving the illusions on which authoritarian regimes depend, Tracy soon ran afoul of Napoleon, who coined the word "ideologue" as a pejorative label for subversive "windbags" and "visionaries" who undermine the foundations of political authority. "You ideologues," Napoleon complained, "destroy all illusions, and the age of illusions is for individuals as for peoples the age of happiness."[116]

As Napoleon's military fortunes took a turn for the worse, he became obsessed with denouncing the ideologues, even blaming them for the disasters of his Russian campaign. Tracy and other liberal ideologues were unwilling to sacrifice their principles for the sake of expediency, and their stubborn insistence that political authority requires a rational justification made it difficult to maintain a compliant citizenry that would obey Napoleon instead of criticize him. According to Napoleon, the rationalistic doctrine of the ideologues, which refused to accommodate itself to "a knowledge of the human heart and . . . the lessons of history" was responsible for "all the misfortunes which have befallen our beloved France."[117]

It is thus to Napoleon that we owe the pejorative connotation that the term "ideologue" carries to this day. We often think of an ideologue as an intellectual who is so absorbed in the ethereal world of abstractions that he is unable to deal with the practical requirements of politics. In this view, ideologues range from incompetent but relatively harmless dreamers and visionaries to dangerous fanatics (such as the Jacobins of the French Revolution) who will not hesitate to sacrifice lives in their relentless pursuit of an ideal, utopian society.

---

of the *History of Ideas*, ed. Philip P. Wiener (New York: Charles Scribner's Sons, 1973), 2: 552–59.

[115] Letter to Joseph Milligan (April 6, 1816), in *The Life and Selected Writings of Thomas Jefferson*, ed. Adrienne Koch and William Peden (New York: Modern Library, 1944), 664. Dumas Malone speculates that Jefferson, despite his praise for *The Elements of Ideology*, "probably never got through the whole of it since he did not care much for abstractions"; *Jefferson and His Time*, vol. 6, *The Sage of Monticello* (Boston: Little, Brown, and Co., 1981), 208. Be this as it may, Jefferson played a key role in translating and distributing two other books by Tracy: *A Commentary and Review of Montesquieu's Spirit of Laws* (Philadelphia, 1811) and *A Treatise on Political Economy* (Georgetown, 1817). The latter work (which included a preface by Jefferson) was adopted as a textbook at the College of William and Mary, and it subsequently became a standard text on political economy at many American universities, especially in the South, where Tracy's *laissez-faire* ideas received a sympathetic hearing.

[116] Quoted in Eagleton, *Ideology*, 67.

[117] Quoted in ibid., 67–68.

If "ideologue" conveys roughly the same meaning today that it did when first coined, the same cannot be said of "ideology" – a word that is rarely if ever used with the same meaning that Tracy imparted to it. For one thing, the term now refers to a belief system of some kind, not to a cognitive discipline that investigates the origin of that belief system. According to the *American Heritage Dictionary*, an ideology is "A set of doctrines or beliefs that form the basis of a political, economic, or other system."

If this value-neutral definition of "ideology" does not comport with the negative implications that the word frequently conveys in modern discourse, this is largely because of the work of Marx and Engels, who gave the word a distinctive meaning that would profoundly influence future generations of social theorists. Engels coined the expression "false consciousness" to convey the notion that an ideology is something more than a belief system; it is a belief system that functions as a distorting medium, one that renders us unable to perceive the world (or at least the moral, social, and cultural world of human beings) in an objective fashion.

As indicated previously, I use the term "liberal ideology" to signify an *inter-disciplinary* approach to liberalism, one that attempts to integrate the diverse perspectives of various disciplines into a comprehensive treatment. More specifically, the term "ideology" refers to a value-based belief system; it is an integrated system of ideas that are connected, directly or indirectly, to a primary value commitment. The major components of this definition are as follows.

By "idea," I mean any cognitive phenomenon or phenomena that is or are viewed subjectively as a single mental unit. A concept, definition, theory, belief, paradigm, and so forth – whether simple or complex, whether one or many – is called an idea when regarded as a distinct part (one unit) of an ideology. Furthermore, this ideology itself, considered as a single mental construct, or unit, is also an idea. Simply put, the term "idea," as used here, is to the inner world of abstraction what the term "thing" is to the external world of physical objects.

By "primary value commitment," I mean, first, a valuation that exists in the consciousness of a person, a value to which that person is subjectively committed; second, a value that is primary, that is, fundamental within a given cognitive sphere (religion, ethics, politics, etc.). In a liberal ideology, individual freedom is the primary value commitment in the sphere of political theory.

By "integrated system," I mean an organized structure of diverse ideas, which are shaped into a self-contained unity according to their common relationship to a regulative principle. The system is functional; in other words, the parts contribute to the same overall end. The primary value, in the case of an ideology, is the regulative principle and unifying theme.

An ideology is the interpretative framework that enables us to classify our social experiences and integrate them into consistent patterns. An ideology greatly affects how we perceive and respond to the social world of institutional relationships. An ideology provides a conceptual framework that influences how we see social and political "problems," how we evaluate them, and which "solutions" we will accept as legitimate.

### III

Although we can find liberal sentiments, principles, and even theories in ancient and medieval philosophy, liberal ideology is a distinctively modern phenomenon, one that did not begin to take hold until the early seventeenth century. This development owed a great deal to the turn taken by political philosophy in the sixteenth century, with the rise of modern nation-states. As defenders of these nation-states presented arguments for political absolutism, critics of absolutism were pressed to find a philosophical justification for their opposition, which sometimes manifested itself in resistance and revolution. And, as if guided by the inner logic of ideas, they found an alternative to the principle of state sovereignty in the principle of *self-sovereignty*.

Although the idea of self-sovereignty first arose in arguments for religious toleration, it was soon applied to other spheres of human activity. Political philosophy was essential to this development, for it was by means of this discipline that liberals sought to draw a bright line between the coercive sphere of state activity and the voluntary sphere of social interaction. This was the primary function of the theory of natural rights; such rights specified the circumstances in which force may be used by a government.

Let us now take a closer look at political philosophy and how some fundamental themes in liberalism emerged from this discipline.

Political philosophy is the systematic, reflective investigation of political relationships and institutions from a normative perspective. To call political philosophy "systematic" is simply to identify it as an intellectual *discipline* – in contrast to a casual, ad hoc foray into political subjects. To call it "reflective" means that the political philosopher consciously reflects on his or her *methods* of investigation and strives to base his or her conclusions on a method that will impart consistency, coherence, and some kind of verifiability to these conclusions.[118]

---

[118] Traditionally, any systematic and reflective investigation of a given subject matter was called a "science," especially if it produced authentic knowledge rather than mere "opinion." (The label was applied both to the cognitive activity itself and to the organized body of knowledge that resulted from that activity.) Metaphysics, ethics, and even theology qualified as sciences in this general sense; nonetheless, this neutral usage, according to which "science" referred

A traditional way of defining intellectual disciplines is in terms of their "matter" and "form." The subject matter of a discipline is that which it studies; the form of a discipline is the perspective, or point of view, from which the subject matter is studied.

To call political philosophy a "normative" discipline (its "form," or point of view) means that political philosophy does not merely describe political phenomena but also employs norms, or standards of value, to *evaluate* political concepts, beliefs, arguments, actions, and relations. This prescriptive aspect is commonly said to constitute the essential difference between political *philosophy* and political *science*. The latter (we are told) is purely descriptive in character; the political scientist employs empirical methods to relate facts about political phenomena that can be objectively verified. Even when dealing with subjective beliefs about (say) political legitimacy, political scientists do not impose their own value judgments on their subject matter. They do not attempt to determine whether such beliefs are right or wrong, justified or unjustified, but confine themselves to describing those beliefs impartially.

Whether "political science" always lives up to the rigorous demands of a value-free discipline is open to doubt. (When a political scientist classifies some regimes as "authoritarian," it is difficult to believe that a negative value judgment is not being imported into the analysis, if only implicitly.) Fortunately, we needn't concern ourselves here with this controversy, since our focus is on political *philosophy*, which is clearly a value-laden undertaking.

As for our subject matter, to say that political philosophy studies "political" relationships and institutions won't get us very far until and unless we reach an understanding about the meaning of "political." Here, as we shall see, unanimity is hard to come by. Not only in philosophy but in history and the social sciences as well, substantial disagreements over the subject matter and scope of a discipline are the rule rather than the exception. Such disagreements have spawned acrimonious methodological debates, with the result that practitioners of the same nominal discipline sometimes appear to have little more in common than a label.

Becoming a political philosopher is not like joining an organization in which the conditions of membership and procedural rules have been clearly

to any intellectual discipline, has fallen into disfavor and been replaced by a value-laden approach in which "science" serves as an honorific label that signifies the supposed superiority of some disciplines (such as the physical sciences) over others. Although I favor the older usage, primarily because it does not use the label "science" to pre-judge the cognitive value of a given discipline, there is little point in raising a fuss over what has become a widely accepted convention. I shall therefore use the word "discipline" instead of "science" as a generic label for any cognitive, or knowledge-seeking, enterprise.

articulated and specified in advance. It is more akin to a loosely structured discussion group in which people with similar interests come together to discuss ideas, and which develops spontaneously after that point. If an outsider were to inquire about the fundamental purpose and agenda of these meetings, he or she might receive different answers from different members, depending on their particular values and points of view.

Similarly, even those who share the same general *concept* of political philosophy may differ in their particular *conceptions* of this discipline. Ideological factors play a role here, as we shall see.

IV

Our word "political" derives from the Greek word *polis*, which is often translated as "state." This is misleading, at least if we equate "state" with "government," because the *polis* (Greek city-state) encompassed every kind of social relationship and institution – familial, economic, educational, religious, and so forth. As Andrew Vincent explains,

> The *polis* was seen to embrace the entire life of the citizen – religion, culture, politics and personal activity interpenetrated each other.... This was a totally integrated life, much admired by later generations of scholars and thinkers. The good of the individual was inseparable from the good of the society. Ethics was integral to politics. This led to another important dimension of the *polis* which is hard to compare with the modern State. There was no recognition whatsoever of either "society" or individualism. Nothing existed apart from the *polis*. There was no realm of privacy, personal rights or freedoms. Individuals only had claims as full citizens and there could be no conception of any distinction between public or private law. Law (*nomos*) was integral to religion, morality, and the constitution. The city was prior to any individual. Man had a natural need for the *polis*. He existed within it as a cell or organ within a body.[119]

Neither Plato nor Aristotle recognized the distinction between state and society that would become a mainstay of later political thought.[120] When

---

[119] Andrew Vincent, *Theories of the State* (Oxford: Basil Blackwell, 1987), 12–13.

[120] See the discussion by Ernest Barker, introduction to *The Politics of Aristotle*, trans. Ernest Barker (Oxford: Oxford University Press, 1952), xlvii: "The assumption of Aristotle, as of Greek thought generally down to the days of Zeno and the Stoic doctrine of the *cosmopolis*, is that of the small state or civic republic whose citizens know one another personally, and which can be addressed by a single herald and persuaded by a single orator when it is assembled in its 'town meeting'. It is a small and intimate society: it is a church as well as a state: it makes no distinction between the province of the state and that of society; it is, in a word, an integrated

Thomas Aquinas repeated Aristotle's celebrated dictum that "man is by nature a political animal,"[121] he expanded it to say that "man is by nature a social and political animal," explaining that it is "natural for man to live in fellowship with many others."[122] As the term "political" became more firmly associated with matters pertaining to government and law, philosophers sometimes dropped the word altogether in favor of the claim that man is naturally a *social* animal.

According to Aristotle, "A state [*polis*] is an association of similar persons whose aim is the best life possible." Aristotle regarded the state as a "perfect" association because it is "self-sufficient for the purposes of life"; it is only within a small, closely knit political community that a person can fully develop and exercise those virtues necessary for a happy, fulfilling life. Similarly, when Aristotle claims that the state is "both natural and prior to the individual," he means that a person can develop his natural potential only through active participation in a political community. The state is prior to the individual in the sense that a whole is prior to its parts, which can be defined, qua parts, only in terms of their functional relationship to the whole. Just as an acorn will not develop into an oak tree without the proper nourishment and environment, so a person cannot become fully human outside the context of a political community. Only a beast or a god can flourish without the state.[123]

The inclusive nature of the *polis* led to an expansive notion of politics. When Aristotle speaks of the "master art" that teaches people how to achieve their "chief good," he is referring not to ethics but to politics. Politics is a practical science, not a theoretic science: Its purpose is not knowledge per se but rather the betterment of action. Its function is to make people good by teaching the legislator how to instill in citizens the virtues necessary for a good political community. This is achieved through education, which is a basic and indispensable function of government. Indeed, the ideal states of both Plato and Aristotle may be called educational institutions in the broadest sense.

Since politics is a practical science that deals with the contingent and variable aspects of human affairs, it cannot achieve the same degree of precision and certainty that we find in the theoretical sciences: "We must be content [in political science] to indicate the truth roughly and in outline, and in speaking about things which are only for the most part true and with premises of the same kind to reach conclusions that are no better." Politics deals with probable

---

system of social ethics, which realizes to the full the capacity of its members, and therefore claims their full allegiance."

[121] Aristotle, *The Politics*, trans. T.A. Sinclair, rev. Trevor J. Saunders (London: Penguin Books, 1992), 1253a1.

[122] Thomas Aquinas, *On the Government of Princes*, in *St. Thomas Aquinas: Political Writings*, ed. and trans. R.W. Dyson (Cambridge: Cambridge University Press, 2002), 6.

[123] Aristotle, *Politics*, 1328a33, 1328b15, 1253a18.

reasoning, and "it is the mark of an educated man to look for precision in each class of things just so far as the nature of the subject matter admits."[124]

Aristotle's contention that political science subsumes other practical sciences, such as economics (the art of household management) and rhetoric (the art of persuasion), leads to the conclusion that ethics is a subset of politics. Although many modern philosophers would disagree with the technical implications of this classification (among other things, any attempt to bestow the honorific label of "science" on a normative discipline is frowned upon nowadays), Aristotle's approach has survived in the common contention that political philosophy is concerned with the nature of a "good society." Consider these remarks by Alan Brown:

> Ethics is concerned with the individual: how ought he to live his life; what values and ideals ought he to adopt, what rules ought he to observe? Political philosophy is concerned with the social side of this question or, more precisely, with the problem of how society ought to be organized.[125]

To say that political philosophy is concerned with the "social side" of individual ethics is a misleading way of putting the matter. Friendships, for example, are social relationships, and moral issues pertaining to friendships, such as whether it is morally wrong to deceive a friend, are concerned with the "social side" of ethics. Nonetheless, it would be peculiar to classify such issues under the rubric of political philosophy. (To assert that political philosophy is concerned with "how society ought to be organized" is even more problematic; for one thing, it presupposes that "society" is properly described as an "organization" – a dubious assumption at best.)

Brown's schema has an Aristotelian flavor to it, as he acknowledged later in his discussion:

> Politics does, in a sense, govern every aspect of our lives – for even those things left to the private concern of individuals are, as it were, conceded by the political realm. This was clearly observed by Aristotle, who identified the object of our practical inquiries as the good life for man and proposed politics as the science of the good.[126]

If to say that politics governs every aspect of our lives is true "in a sense," it is also untrue in a more important sense. Consider once again the subject of friendships. It is true that justice – a key concept in political philosophy –

---

[124] Aristotle, *Nicomachean Ethics*, trans. W.D. Ross, in *The Basic Works of Aristotle*, ed. Richard McKeon (New York: Modern Library, 1941), 1094b19–26.
[125] Alan Brown, *Modern Political Philosophy: Theories of the Just Society* (London: Penguin Books, 1986), 11.
[126] Ibid., 17.

pertains to friendships, as it pertains to every kind of social relationship; friends, for example, should not steal from one another. But the uniquely *political* notion of justice, however we might parse that notion, scarcely exhausts the moral dimensions of friendship, which may, after all, transcend all political boundaries. On the contrary, since the principles of justice that apply to friendships apply equally to *all* forms of social relationships (the prohibition of theft applies as much to strangers as it does to friends), the precepts of political justice are unable even to identify what we mean by "friendship." The unique moral features that define a friendship and set it apart from other kinds of relationships are of a social, not political, character.

The foregoing analysis depends on a particular meaning of "justice." Suppose it is said that I ought to display a higher degree of benevolence to a good friend than I do to strangers. Some people would characterize my obligation as a matter of justice; they might even say that my friend has a "right" to expect such treatment at my hands. But few who speak this way would maintain that benevolence is an *enforceable* moral claim, that is, a moral claim that should be coercively imposed.

This brings us to a distinction that was crucial to individualistic theories of justice during the seventeenth and eighteenth centuries. Adam Smith exemplified this tradition when he distinguished between "perfect" and "imperfect" rights during one of his lectures on jurisprudence:

> Perfect rights are those which we have a title to demand and if refused to compel another to perform. What they call imperfect rights are those which correspond to those duties which ought to be performed to us by others but which we have no title to compel them to perform; they have it entirely in their power to perform them or not. Thus a man of bright parts or remarkable learning is deserving of praise, but we have no power to compel any one to give it [to] him. A beggar is an object of our charity and may be said to have a right to demand it; but when we use the word right in this way it is not in a proper but in a metaphorical sense.[127]

Smith expanded on this theme in *The Theory of Moral Sentiments*, where he referred to "that remarkable distinction between justice and all the other social virtues." The obligations of justice "may be extorted by force," whereas the social virtues of beneficence – those affiliated with friendship, charity, generosity, and the like – should depend solely on "advice and persuasion." Indeed, "for equals to use force against one another" in an effort to compel

---

[127] Adam Smith, "Report of 1762–3," *Lectures on Jurisprudence*, ed. R.L. Meek, D.D. Raphael, and P.G. Stein (Indianapolis: Liberty Fund, 1982), 9. (This is a reprint of the Oxford University Press ed., 1978.) I have made some minor corrections in spelling.

the observance of imperfect rights and duties "would be thought the highest degree of insolence and presumption."[128]

This distinction between perfect and imperfect rights, according to which only perfect (i.e., enforceable) rights fall within the domain of justice, strictly construed, has important implications for the nature of political philosophy. Alan Brown, in asserting that political philosophy is concerned with the nature of "the good society,"[129] adopted an Aristotelian perspective that was significantly modified, if not rejected altogether, by those liberal individualists who distinguished between a *just* society and a *good* society.

According to Adam Smith, when the members of a society practice the social virtues of beneficence, "the society flourishes and is happy." However, even if "among the different members of the society there should be no mutual love and affection, the society, though less happy and agreeable, will not necessarily be dissolved."

> Society may subsist among different men, as among different merchants, from a sense of its utility, without any mutual love or affection; and though no man in it should owe any obligation [apart from justice], or be bound in gratitude to any other, it may still be upheld by a mercenary exchange of good offices according to an agreed valuation.[130]

Justice, in contrast to other virtues, is essential to the very existence of society:

> Society may subsist, though not in the most comfortable state, without beneficence; but the prevalence of injustice must utterly destroy it.... [Beneficence] is the ornament which embellishes, not the foundation which supports the building, and which it was, therefore, sufficient to recommend, but by no means necessary to impose. Justice, on the contrary, is the main pillar that upholds the whole edifice. If it is removed, the great, the immense fabric of human society...must in a moment crumble into atoms.[131]

From this perspective, political philosophy is concerned with the nature of a good society only insofar as it establishes conditions that are necessary, but not sufficient, for a good society. Political philosophy addresses the nature of a *just* society; whether the members of this society practice other moral virtues that render the society good rather than merely tolerable will depend on their

---

[128] Adam Smith, *The Theory of Moral Sentiments*, ed. D.D. Raphael and A.L. Macfie (Indianapolis: Liberty Fund, 1982), 80–81. (This is a reprint of the 1976 edition by Oxford University Press.)

[129] Brown, *Modern Political Philosophy*, 15.

[130] Smith, *Theory of Moral Sentiments*, 85–86.

[131] Ibid., 86.

voluntary decisions and actions. These issues fall within the purview of ethics in the broadest sense; they are not matters of *political* philosophy per se.

Unlike Aristotle (and Plato before him), many modern political philosophers have distinguished between state and society: "The one is the area of politics proper, of obligatory rule and involuntary obedience: the other is the area of voluntary co-operation, conducted in and by a variety of societies, educational, ecclesiastical, economic."[132] A good deal of modern political philosophy has thus focused on the proper spheres of state and society, that is, between those areas of human activity that should fall within the coercive jurisdiction of law and government versus those that should be left to the voluntary decisions and associations of individuals.

This approach was vital to liberal individualists, according to whom a fundamental task of political philosophy is to establish the moral boundaries of force and persuasion. As John Milton put it, "here the great art lies, to discern in what the law is to bid restraint and punishment, and in what things persuasion only is to work."[133] Similarly, John Locke insisted that "it is one thing to persuade, another to command; one thing to press with arguments, another with penalties."[134] And, according to Adam Smith, "We must always carefully distinguish what is only blamable, or the proper object of disapprobation, from what force may be employed either to punish or to prevent."[135]

This theme, which recurs throughout the history of liberal individualism, stresses the need for a bright line to separate the political sphere of coercive laws from the social sphere of voluntary cooperation. Where and how to draw this bright line are normative problems that cannot be resolved without a theory of justice. If the liberal conception of justice was typically expressed in terms of individual rights – along with cognate concepts, such as consent and a social contract – this was largely because of an overriding desire to establish moral boundaries between the spheres of coercive and voluntary interaction.

It would of course be absurd to maintain that the distinction between force and persuasion originated with liberalism, or that only liberals were concerned with the moral implications of this distinction. The distinction is obvious, as is the fact that governmental laws are ultimately backed by physical punishment, so we would expect to find discussions of this issue long before the emergence of liberal theories of government. What sets liberalism apart is the priority it places on this distinction.

[132] Barker, *The Politics of Aristotle*, lv.
[133] John Milton, *Areopagitica*, in *The Student's Milton*, rev. ed., ed. Frank. A. Patterson (New York: F.S. Crofts & Co, 1946), 741.
[134] Locke, *A Letter Concerning Toleration*, 128.
[135] Smith, *Theory of Moral Sentiments*, 80.

Plato expressly rejected the notion that "violence or consent" constitutes a "real criterion" for assessing the desirability of governments. Governance is an art for which only a "select few" are qualified, and if these elite philosopher-rulers happen to be in power, then it "makes no difference whether their subjects be willing or unwilling." To illustrate this point, Plato appealed (as he often did) to the analogy of a physician: "We do not assess the medical qualification of a doctor by the degree of willingness of our part to submit to his knife or cautery or other painful treatment." Doctors are deemed "good" so long as their work has a scientific basis and they "act for the good of our bodies to make them better instead of worse." Likewise, the "distinguishing mark of true authority" in politics is whether a ruler has the "disinterested scientific ability" to know what is objectively good for the community and acts to achieve that goal.[136]

The point here may be simply stated: If $x$ is objectively good for a community, then it is inconsequential, from a *moral* point of view, whether a ruler uses force or persuasion to achieve $x$. The object of legislation is "the welfare of the society as a whole," and the legislator "uses persuasion or compulsion" to attain this object.[137] The choice between these alternative means is a matter of expediency rather than ethics, as we see in *The Laws*. In this (his last) dialogue, Plato revises his earlier physician analogy by distinguishing between two kinds of patients. The physician who treats a slave "simply prescribes what he thinks best . . . with the self-confidence of a dictator" and is not concerned with persuading the slave that his treatment is desirable. In contrast, the physician who treats a free man "gives no prescription until he has somehow gained the invalid's consent; then, coaxing him into continued cooperation, he tries to complete his restoration to health."[138]

In accordance with the analogy of a doctor who ministers to free men, Plato recommends that governmental laws should contain "preambles" in which the reasons for these laws are spelled out in the hope of persuading people to obey them willingly. But these preambles are solely a matter of expediency, since the unconvinced will be punished for disobedience in any case. Compliant subjects are more easily ruled than subjects who must be coerced, so Plato urges rulers to include rhetorical tools in their political toolbox. A bandit may attempt to persuade his victims to surrender their money voluntarily before he brandishes a gun and threatens them with violence, but this does not mean

[136] Plato, *Statesman*, trans. J.B. Skemp, in *The Collected Dialogues of Plato*, ed. Edith Hamilton and Huntington Cairns (New York: Pantheon Books, 1964), 291e–293b.

[137] Plato, *The Republic*, 2nd ed., rev., trans. Desmond Lee (London: Penguin Books, 1987), 520a.

[138] Plato, *The Laws*, trans. Trevor J. Saunders (London: Penguin Books, 1975), 720.

that the bandit views persuasion as morally preferable to coercion; it simply means that he thinks that "coaxing" may prove a more efficient method of getting what he wants.

The indifference with which Plato views the use of force, so long as rulers possess "scientific understanding of the art of government," is dramatically illustrated in passages like the following:

> They may purge the city for its better health by putting some of the citizens to death or banishing others. They may lessen the citizen body by sending off colonies like bees swarming off from a hive, or they may bring people in from other cities and naturalize them so as to increase the number of citizens. So long as they work on a reasoned scientific principle following essential justice and act to preserve and improve the life of the state so far as may be, we must call them real statesmen according to our standards of judgment and say that the state they rule alone enjoys good government and has a real constitution.[139]

In none of Plato's writings do we find a serious interest in establishing *moral* boundaries to the use of coercion. The same may be said of Aristotle (whose writings exercised an immense influence on political philosophy after the thirteenth century). Although one can easily find passages in *The Politics* that exhibit a more individualistic attitude than anything found in Plato's writings, this is a matter of degree. Plato was so trenchantly anti-individualistic that virtually anything might seem more "liberal" by comparison. In contrast, Aristotle's *Politics* is an ideological warehouse in which both liberals and their opponents found ideas to support their agendas; moreover, liberals sometimes used Aristotle's ideas in a manner that he would have repudiated.

Some of these issues are discussed later in this book; for now, I will rest content with the summary observation that the modern liberal concern with drawing a bright line between force and persuasion owed nothing to Aristotle. If we fail to find a notion of individual rights in either Plato or Aristotle, this can partially be explained by the fact that neither had a need for this concept, which serves a function only for those who wish to determine the moral boundaries of coercion.

Plato and Aristotle "looked with alarm on the instability of Greek political life and on the moral anarchy which they believed to be its cause."[140] Since both found this cause in the excessive personal freedom spawned by democracy, it should come as no surprise that neither was inclined to limit the power of the

---

[139] Plato, *Statesman*, 293d.
[140] T.A. Sinclair, *A History of Greek Political Thought* (Cleveland: Meridian Books, 1967), 209.

state and thereby hinder its ability to mold virtuous citizens. As Ernest Barker put it,

> The "limit of state-interference" never suggested itself to the Greek philosophers as a problem for their consideration. They seek to regulate the family and the most intimate matters of family life, no less than art and music. Plato's austerities are famous; but even Aristotle can define the age for marriage and the number of permissible children. Whatever has a moral bearing may come under moral regulation.[141]

Whenever we find the claim that virtue outranks freedom in the hierarchy of political values, we are unlikely to find a keen interest in drawing a bright moral line between force and persuasion. This involves more than the fear that a bright line, however drawn, will prove disadvantageous to state power; more fundamental is a deep suspicion of the enterprise itself. As with any normative enterprise, the quest for a bright line will generate the concepts needed to make fine moral distinctions; such concepts will tend to take on a life of their own, suggesting additional distinctions and conclusions that were not intended or foreseen by their originators. Here are the words of Arthur Lovejoy:

> It is one of the instructive ironies of the history of ideas that a principle introduced by one generation in the service of a tendency or philosophic mood congenial to it often proves to contain, unsuspected, the germ of a contrary tendency – to be, by virtue of its hidden implications, the destroyer of that *Zeitgeist* to which it was meant to minister.[142]

I have contended that the quest for a bright line that delimits the moral spheres of force and persuasion was regarded as integral to the "great art" of political philosophy, as conceived by Milton, Locke, Smith, and others in the liberal tradition. I have also pointed out that this focus was far from universal, that classical political philosophers in particular (especially Plato and Aristotle) showed little or no interest in this problem. So how did this shift in perspective come about?

This and similar questions call for answers that are at once complex, controversial, and conjectural. One aspect that I shall explore in this book pertains to evolutionary developments within the discipline of political philosophy itself, specifically in the conceptual vocabulary that political philosophers employed

---

[141] Barker, *The Politics of Aristotle*, li.
[142] Arthur O. Lovejoy, *The Great Chain of Being: A Study of the History of an Idea* (1936; New York: Harper Torchbooks, 1960), 288.

to address the fundamental questions of their discipline. The most interesting question in this regard is known as the "problem of political obligation." Here we can see how concepts that were originally developed for one purpose resulted in unintended consequences.

When philosophers pressed the notion of state sovereignty into the service of political obligation, this inevitably if unintentionally invited other philosophers to develop the countertheory of *self*-sovereignty in response – and it is in this latter trend that we find the seeds of modern liberalism. As Otto Gierke (one of the greatest historians of natural law and natural rights) put it in his discussion of ideological developments during the early modern era,

> The Sovereignty of the State and the Sovereignty of the Individual were steadily on their way towards becoming the two central axioms from which all theories of social structure would proceed, and whose relationship to each other would be the focus of all theoretical controversy. . . . On the one hand, therefore, proclamation was made of the original Sovereignty of the Individual as the source of all political obligation.[143]

V

One way to understand a philosophic discipline is to view it as a problem-solving enterprise, an attempt to answer fundamental questions. One such question was formulated by Isaiah Berlin as follows: "Why should anyone obey anyone else?" This, according to Berlin, "is perhaps the most fundamental of all political questions."[144]

Berlin summarizes, in a refreshingly uncomplicated manner, the problem of political obligation while calling attention to its crucial role in political philosophy. The problem is more complicated than Berlin's question might suggest, though, since it is not immediately apparent what kind of obedience is relevant to political obligation. We might say that a soldier is obligated to obey the orders of a superior officer or that a worker is obligated to do a job assigned by her or his boss, but these would not ordinarily be classified as instances of *political* obligation. The same might be said of ordinary moral obligations, such as one's obligation not to steal from other people or otherwise violate their rights.

---

[143] Otto Gierke, *Political Theories of the Middle Ages*, trans. F.W. Maitland (1900; Boston: Beacon Press, 1958), 87, 90.
[144] Isaiah Berlin, "Does Political Theory Still Exist?," in *Philosophy, Politics, and Society (Second Series)*, ed. Peter Laslett and W.G. Runciman (Oxford: Basil Blackwell, 1969), 7.

Any attempt to differentiate political obligations from other kinds of obligation will run afoul of the same problem we discussed earlier, namely the different meanings that have been assigned to the word "political." In the liberal tradition (and in much of political thought generally), a political obligation was regarded as an enforceable moral obligation, or duty,[145] that we owe to a political authority – namely, a state, government, or some department thereof. Since an obligation of this kind presupposes another moral agent to whom the duty is owed and who may coercively enforce it, this latter agent is said to have a "right" to compel obedience.

To say that we have a duty to obey a government may therefore be reworded to say that this government has the *right* to use coercive means to enforce this duty with coercion. Since we obey commands rather than requests, entreaties, pleas, wishes, and the like, the problem of political obligation may be expressed as follows: How can the *right* of a government to issue commands, and to enforce those commands by coercive means, be justified?

How individualists have responded to this question will be discussed in a subsequent chapter. I raise the issue now to emphasize a crucial point about the role of "rights" in political philosophy. In recent decades, historians have traced the notion of individual rights (or what are technically known as "subjective" rights[146]) to late medieval philosophers (such as William of Ockham and Jean Gerson) and to certain principles contained in the canon law of the Catholic Church. As these studies have demonstrated, the modern notion of individual rights (such as defended by John Locke) emerged from currents within the classical tradition of natural law. Hence, contrary to the

---

[145] Although the terms "obligation" and "duty" are often used interchangeably, I will use "duty" to signify only those "perfect" obligations that are enforceable by coercive means. (This is solely a matter of linguistic convenience and economy.) A "duty" and a "right" are therefore correlative concepts; one is the flip side of the other, so to speak. If I have a right to do *x*, then you have a duty not to interfere with this activity. Conversely, if I have a duty to pay you $100 (perhaps because of a prior contractual agreement), then you have a right not only to demand that I pay this amount, but also to use coercive means (e.g., by seeking a legal judgment) to get it.

[146] The Latin word *jus* (or *ius*) traditionally meant "right" in an objective sense – a *rule* of right action, as when we say "*x* is the right thing to do." Over time, however, *jus* also came to signify "a right" in the sense of the moral power to choose among alternatives, as when we say "I have a right to do *x* or *y* or *z*, and I choose *z*." This is called the subjective meaning of *jus*, because "a right" was conceived as a moral ability that inheres in the individual *subject*, or moral agent, rather than as an external rule of behavior to which he or she must conform. For a seminal treatment of the history of subjective rights, see Richard Tuck, *Natural Rights Theories: Their Origin and Development* (Cambridge: Cambridge University Press, 1979). Among the many worthwhile treatments of this topic, my favorite overall is Brian Tierney, *The Idea of Natural Rights*.

claims of Leo Strauss[147] and other critics, the emergence of natural rights did not necessarily involve a rejection of the natural-law perspective, according to which justice can (and should) be grounded in objective moral principles knowable to reason.

Whatever the origin of individual rights[148] may be, the general notion of a political right to compel obedience is implicit in the notion of political obligation. To ponder our duty to obey a political authority is also to ponder the *right* of that authority to compel obedience. Whether this authority was historically conceived as secular or religious is irrelevant to this point, as is the specific language that was used to express this right. So long as political philosophers were concerned with the justification of political obligation, they were also concerned with the justification of political rights.

I have discussed this rather obvious point in order to clear the path for another point that is less obvious, one that pertains to the justification of rights theory. If the problem of political obligation is fundamental to the discipline known as "political philosophy" – and if this problem cannot be expressed, much less resolved, without invoking the concept of "a right" – then this concept is essential to the discipline itself. If we view political philosophy as an activity, then rights are indispensable conceptual tools; without which the activity cannot proceed. If we view political philosophy as a mode of discourse focused on the justification of claims to authority, then rights are essential components of its vocabulary; without them, nothing meaningful can be said.

## VI

I previously claimed that "political relationships and institutions" are the subject matter of political philosophy. This is consistent with Norman Barry's observation that "the history of political theory has been mainly concerned with the state."[149] It is also consistent with those attempts to define political

---

[147] See Leo Strauss, *Natural Right and History* (Chicago: University of Chicago Press, 1965). I should note that Strauss is always worth reading, however much one may disagree with some of his conclusions.

[148] Although the label "subjective rights" is commonly used by scholars in this field, it tends to convey the false impression that such rights cannot be rationally justified, or that they are a matter of subjective caprice. I will therefore speak of "individual rights" instead of "subjective rights." The former label is less apt to mislead; from a philosophical perspective, it matters not in the least whether we say that this kind of right is a moral power of an "individual" or a "subject." In both cases we are referring to a moral agent.

[149] Norman P. Barry, *An Introduction to Modern Political Theory* (New York: St. Martin's Press, 1981), 46.

philosophy in terms of the state. Consider the following remarks by Robert Paul Wolff:

> Politics is the exercise of the power of the state, or the attempt to influence that exercise. Political philosophy is therefore, strictly speaking, the philosophy of the state. If we are to determine the content of political philosophy, and whether indeed it exists, we must begin with the concept of the state.[150]

Why should we devote an entire discipline to the state and related matters? What is so important or unique about this institution that renders it worthy of such intense scrutiny? This is not a difficult question for the political scientist to answer. Given the enormous influence of governments, past and present, it is understandable why inquisitive people would undertake a systematic investigation of this ubiquitous institution. We want to know what makes the state tick, and we are naturally curious how this institution is able to command such widespread respect and compliance.

The enduring interest of political philosophers, who are concerned with the normative aspects of the state, is a bit more difficult to explain. Although their interests will often overlap with that of political scientists, they are uniquely concerned with how the state can be *justified*. Those who regard this normative task (which is merely the problem of political obligation stated in different terms) as pointless or meaningless will have no use for political philosophy, so we should take a closer look at the nature of this problem.

A good place to begin is with another, more basic question: Why is it necessary to "justify" the state in the first place? This enterprise would strike many people as absurd; to ask whether the state *should* exist reflects a curiosity and skepticism that are foreign to the popular mind. The state is a normal part of our daily lives, and it seems to require no more justification than any other institution.

In addition, some philosophers have looked with deep suspicion upon any attempt to justify the state. After all, there is no guarantee that such an attempt will succeed, and should it fail the consequences for social order could be catastrophic. As David Hume put it in 1739,

> No maxim is more conformable, both to prudence and morals, than to submit quietly to the government, which we find establish'd in the country where we happen to live, without enquiring too curiously into its origin and first establishment. Few governments will bear being examin'd so rigorously.[151]

---

[150] Robert Paul Wolff, *In Defense of Anarchism* (New York: Harper Torchbooks, 1976), 3.
[151] David Hume, *A Treatise of Human Nature*, 2nd ed., ed. L.A. Selby Bigge and P.H. Nidditch (Oxford: Clarendon Press, 1978), 558.

Any person who concludes that the government under which he or she lives cannot be morally justified, and who should therefore deny that government's right to allegiance, would, according to Hume, be "justly thought to maintain a very extravagant paradox, and to shock the common sense and judgment of mankind."[152] That this kind of philosophic speculation would undermine the legitimacy of all governments and thereby promote anarchy was (as we shall see) a recurring theme among critics of the Lockean paradigm. This approach began by positing the natural rights of individuals and then sought to explain how the legitimate powers of a government are derived from the consent of the governed through a social contract.

Critics of this approach (which included liberals as well as absolutists) cautioned that a political philosophy based on natural rights, though able to justify the right of revolution, cannot justify government itself. If the theory that a legitimate government must be based on the consent of the governed serves as a rationale to overthrow tyrannical governments, it simultaneously undermines the legitimacy of *all* governments, good as well as bad.

Those liberals who feared the anarchistic implications of the Lockean approach (a fear that seemed to be confirmed by the horrors of the French Revolution) sought to justify government by other means, such as utility. This gave rise to a fascinating battle within the ranks of liberalism, which I shall discuss later. The important point now is to understand the nature of the problem. To repeat: Why is it necessary to justify the state in the first place?

It is obvious that the state is a coercive institution, one that deals with people by means of physical force and threats of force. But the state is also a *normative*, or moral,[153] institution – one that claims to use coercion as a matter of *right*.

When, in the seventeenth century, Algernon Sidney differentiated between de facto power and de jure power, he was appealing to a principle with a distinguished provenance in the history of political philosophy. To possess de facto power may be sufficient to compel obedience, according to Sidney; however, only de jure power – power exercised as a matter of *right* – can claim moral legitimacy and thereby create a moral obligation to obey. De jure power, in short, is a matter of *justice*.[154]

Augustine, writing in the early fifth century, gave us the classic formulation of this issue. In a question that would be quoted for many centuries

---

[152] Ibid.
[153] The term "moral," in this context, stands in contrast to "nonmoral," not "immoral."
[154] Algernon Sidney, *Discourses Concerning Government*, ed. Thomas G. West (Indianapolis: Liberty Classics, 1990), 506.

thereafter, Augustine asked, "Remove justice, and what are kingdoms but gangs of criminals on a large scale?" He then illustrated his point with a story:

> For it was a witty and a truthful rejoinder which was given by a captured pirate to Alexander the Great. The king asked the fellow, "What is your idea, in infesting the sea?" And the pirate answered, with uninhibited insolence, "The same as yours, in infesting the earth! But because I do it with a tiny craft, I'm called a pirate: because you have a mighty navy, you're called an emperor.[155]

Both the pirate and the prince use coercion to accomplish their goals (e.g., to expropriate the property of other people), and both threaten violent retaliation (which might result in death) against those who disobey their decrees. So what is the essential *moral* difference between the pirate and the prince – where "prince" represents any legitimate political authority? What moral principle or argument can bestow legitimacy on the actions of a prince when those selfsame actions, if undertaken by anyone else, would result in his condemnation as a pirate (or other type of criminal)?

Our search for a *moral* distinction between prince and pirate is what places our investigation within the realm of political philosophy, in contrast to political science. The political scientist, who claims to be engaged in a purely descriptive, value-free enterprise, will encounter no serious problems when distinguishing between prince and pirate: She will simply point out that the actions of a prince are generally accepted as morally legitimate in a given society, whereas the actions of a pirate are not. Whether this public perception can be justified in some abstract, philosophical sense is not her concern, nor (she might add) would such a justification tell us much about the *sociological* causes of political legitimacy, which depend far more on the unquestioned assumptions of custom and convention than on the systematic and critical reasoning of philosophy.

Political philosophers have set a more difficult goal for themselves. They are concerned not merely with what people happen to believe, but with whether those beliefs can be justified. This means that philosophers are haunted by the possibility of a catastrophic failure, should they fail to find the justification they seek. If (for whatever reason) political philosophers cannot justify political

---

[155] Augustine, *Concerning the City of God Against the Pagans*, trans. Henry Bettenson (London: Penguin Books, 1972), 139. The pirate's riposte to Alexander is similar to a remark attributed to Diogenes, a leading proponent of the Cynic school of moral philosophy in ancient Greece. Upon observing the arrest of a man who had stolen a bottle, Diogenes quipped: "Lo, the big thieves taking the little one to jail!"

obligation, then Augustine's pirate will be vindicated, and the sociological notion of legitimacy will be the last word in this matter. A government will be "legitimate" to the extent that those within its jurisdiction believe it to be legitimate, and obey accordingly.

The claim to use coercion as a matter of right, if justified, would indeed generate an obligation to obey on the part of those who are the targets of this coercion, but the state makes a moral claim that is far stronger than this, a claim that is responsible for the uniquely "political" aspect of this obligation. This is the claim that the state is the final arbiter in matters involving coercion within a given jurisdiction. The state does not merely claim to use legitimate force; rather, it makes the much stronger claim that it, and it alone, has the right to determine when force is morally legitimate and when it is not. As Max Weber put it, a state claims "the *monopoly* of the *legitimate* use of physical force in the enforcement of its order."[156] (emphasis added)

This claim of a moral monopoly, of an *exclusive right* to determine when the use of physical force is and is not legitimate, is the foundation of political sovereignty. It is properly characterized as a *right*, because it is said to impose an enforceable duty on individuals to obey the decisions of a sovereign; and it is an *exclusive* (monopolistic) right, because it is a right that no individual (within the jurisdiction of that government) can be said to possess.

This claim of an exclusive right creates an obvious problem for any political theory premised on the notion that all individuals possess equal and reciprocal rights, for we must wonder how some people – namely those who claim to act on behalf of the state – come to possess a right denied to everyone else. Lockean liberals offered a solution to this problem by positing individual rights that had supposedly been transferred to government voluntarily through the mechanism of a social contract. Critics of this approach not only rejected this approach but also claimed it was a catastrophic failure, one that demolished the moral foundations of all governments and thereby paved the way to anarchy.

---

[156] Max Weber, *Economy and Society*, ed. Guenther Roth and Claus Wittich (Berkeley: University of California Press, 1978), 1: 54.

# 4

## Sovereign State, Sovereign Self

### I

In his article "On Secular Authority," Martin Luther follows the common practice of citing two biblical passages by Paul to find "a firm grounding for secular law and the Sword, in order to remove any possible doubt about their being in the world as a result of God's will and ordinance."[157] The first passage is from Romans 13.1–2 (Revised Standard Version):

> Let every person be subject to the governing authorities. For there is no authority except from God, and those that exist have been instituted by God. Therefore he who resists the authorities resists what God has appointed, and those who resist will incur judgment.

The second passage appears in I Peter 2. 13–14:

> Be subject for the Lord's sake to every human institution, whether it be to the emperor as supreme, or to governors as sent by him to punish those who do wrong and to praise those who do right.

Until the eighteenth-century Enlightenment, when appeals to divine revelation fell into disfavor, these passages exerted more influence on Western political thought than any other writings on politics, whether ancient or modern. Their effect was to render the legitimacy of government axiomatic – a premise that was not seriously questioned, except by the members of a few religious sects who believed that salvation restored people to a perfect prelapsarian condition that rendered governments unnecessary.

Even those pre-Enlightenment philosophers who did not ground their political theories on revelation did not seriously question the need for government.

---

[157] *Luther and Calvin on Secular Authority*, ed. and trans. Harro Höpfl (Cambridge: Cambridge University Press, 1991), 6.

When debates over absolute sovereignty arose after the sixteenth century, they dealt with the nature of sovereignty and the proper limits of governmental authority, not with the need for government itself. The primary question was not so much the problem of political obligation per se, but the more specific problem of political *allegiance*. Granting that people owe obligation to a government of some kind, the problem remained of which *particular* government (or kind of government) can lay claim to that allegiance.

This approach interjected, if only implicitly, the idea of rights into the discipline of political philosophy, for it meant that governments have a right to demand obedience from their subjects. Even when the moral status of government was no longer accepted as axiomatic, the notion of "a right" (an enforceable moral claim) remained essential to the enterprise of political philosophy, insofar as this discipline addressed the problem of political obligation. As I pointed out in Chapter 3, the state is a normative institution, one that claims (1) the right to use coercion to attain its goals, and (2) the right to pass final judgment on all matters pertaining to coercion within its jurisdiction. These rights are formulations of political obligation. To say that a person has a duty to obey the state is merely another way of saying that the state has the right to compel obedience. Hence if political institutions and relationships comprise the subject matter of political philosophy, and if political obligation is the chief normative problem investigated by political philosophy, then this discipline is wedded to this notion of "a right" and cannot function without it.

This political right, which is the flip side of political obligation, is generated from within political philosophy and must be taken into account (in some form and to some degree) whenever we undertake a normative investigation of political institutions and relationships. We may therefore characterize it as an endogenous right, so long as we keep in mind that we are speaking from a disciplinary perspective rather than a philosophic one. It may turn out that the "problem of political obligation" cannot be resolved at all (at least to the satisfaction of most political philosophers), in which case the corresponding "right" of the state to compel obedience would be unjustified. Nonetheless, the eventual fate of this right is not germane to its methodological role in political philosophy.

This endogenous political right stands in contrast to various exogenous conceptions, such as a theory of rights that a libertarian or socialist might defend. These latter are theories that compete in the arena of political philosophy by appealing to the justificatory criteria of this discipline itself. By calling these exogenous rather than endogenous conceptions of "a right," I mean that they are not inherent in the discipline itself. Particular theories of "a right" (such as that expressed in the Declaration of Independence) are not inherent in the discipline of political philosophy; rather, they are introduced from the outside, so to speak, and then evaluated according to the normative criteria of that discipline.

This distinction may strike some readers as needlessly pedantic. Even if it is true that some conceptions of "a right" are inextricably linked to the discipline of political philosophy, whereas others are not, what is the significance of this insight? One way to answer this question is to imagine an argument about rights between two philosophers, so that we can get some idea of who has the burden of proof. Suppose a natural-rights liberal claims that a government has no right to do *x* (say, to enact and enforce a particular law). Since her claim presupposes a theory of rights, it might seem that she has the burden of proof; in other words, this liberal must justify the theory of rights on which her rejection of *x* depends.

Although I agree that our libertarian philosopher has *a* burden of proof, I reject the claim that she has *the* burden of proof. The state, as I have pointed out, is a normative institution. This means that a moral claim (specifically, a claim about rights) is implicit in every coercive measure it takes. The law (*x*) that our libertarian philosopher condemns as unjust is not merely an exercise in brute force. It is a measure with a moral imprimatur – an official sanction of moral legitimacy that affirms the duty of obedience and the corresponding right of the state to enforce it by coercive means. And this is a rights claim that requires *justification*. At the very least, therefore, we are dealing with a situation in which both sides of a dispute (those who defend the justice of a law *and* those who reject it) have a philosophic obligation to justify the theory of rights on which their assessment of a particular law depends.

This may seem an uncontroversial point, but it carries broader implications that are easily overlooked. The general point, simply stated, is as follows: People who invoke the principle of "a right" to evaluate laws and other coercive measures by the state have not thereby introduced a novel element into political discourse. On the contrary, they have simply used a concept that is endogenous to political philosophy. Their rights claim is a response to a previously existing rights claim, one that is implicit in every coercive action by the state. Therefore, although our libertarian philosopher has a burden of proof insofar as her *specific* theory of rights is concerned, she does not have the sole obligation to justify rights talk in general, for this rights talk was introduced, if in a muted form, by the state. It was the state, not the rights philosophers, who first affirmed a right – namely its right to compel obedience – so those who defend the state have a responsibility to justify this right.

It therefore will not do for a defender of the state to roll his eyes whenever a natural-rights liberal (or other critic of governmental measures) appeals to rights, as if all such appeals should be taken with a grain of salt. Nor will it do for a defender of the state to hit the rights philosopher with a barrage of demands and questions about rights, as if she, and she alone, has the burden to justify rights. Again, this will not do because it is the state (via its agents and defenders) that first invokes the conception of "a right" in passing coercive laws for which it claims moral authority. Nor can we dispense with this moral aspect of the state – if, that is, we wish to distinguish the state from an association of common criminals.

There is more at stake here than a polemical point. An appreciation of the fact that a rights claim is inherent in the enterprise of political philosophy, insofar as this discipline is concerned with the normative nature of the state, can enhance our understanding of the historical function of rights theory in the Lockean tradition. I previously called attention to the relationship between state sovereignty and self-sovereignty, and how arguments defending the absolute rights of the state provoked responses that were framed in terms of the absolute rights of the individual. It is scarcely coincidental that both notions gained momentum during the same period of time, and that both notions were offered as solutions to the same problems (such as religious conflict).

When liberals argued for their conception of individual rights, they were not introducing a novel idea – something called "rights" – into the political debates of their time. Rather, they were simply using and adapting a thematic concept that was already in play, one that was indispensable to the enterprise of political philosophy. Long before the inalienable rights of individuals became a prominent theme in liberal thought, the defenders of absolutism had been speaking of the inalienable rights of an absolute sovereign.

Moreover, the insistence of Bodin and other absolutists that sovereignty is necessarily absolute and indivisible – that it is an all-or-nothing affair, so to speak – led to the mirrored response on behalf of the moral sovereignty of the individual. What has aptly been described as the "logic of sovereignty"[158] could push in one of two directions: either to the absolute and inalienable rights of the state, or to the absolute and inalienable rights of the individual.

This historical dialectic is relevant to the common complaint that we rarely find systematic attempts to justify rights by early liberals. Although we some-times find elaborate classifications of rights (e.g., alienable versus inalienable), many liberals take rights for granted, offering little in the way of justification other than general references to the rational and social nature of human

---

[158] For an account of the "logic of sovereignty," see Alexander P. d'Entrèves, *The Notion of the State: An Introduction to Political Theory* (Oxford: Clarendon Press, 1967), 96–103.

beings. We certainly do not find the technical and highly detailed discussions of rights by early liberals that are common in modern philosophic works.

One explanation for this is that such justifications were not especially relevant during the seventeenth and eighteenth centuries, when works on political philosophy were often written to defend a political cause. Such justifications were not relevant because *all* sides worked from *some* theory of rights, including those who defended the right of government to compel obedience in particular spheres. Thus, in invoking rights to defend a particular cause, each side was simply *doing* political philosophy. In the eyes of these participants, to reject all appeals to rights would have meant the destruction of political philosophy as a coherent discipline.

## II

The idea of sovereignty is "the idea that there is a final and absolute political authority in the community."[159] Although the term was used in political philosophy before the sixteenth century, the French philosopher Jean Bodin is credited with giving it the prominence that it would enjoy thereafter. Indeed, in focusing on sovereignty as the essential characteristic of the state, Bodin was well aware that he was breaking new ground: "We must now formulate a definition of sovereignty because no jurist or political philosopher has defined it, even though it is the chief point, and the one that needs most to be explained, in a treatise on the commonwealth."[160]

Sovereign power, according to Bodin, is "absolute and perpetual"; a sovereign authority "is not limited in power, or in function, or in length of time."[161] This stress on the absolute nature of sovereign power is what links Bodin and others in his school to the political approach called "absolutism." For our purpose, the important aspect of absolutism is its claim that absolute sovereignty must reside *somewhere* in any political community. The notion of divided sovereignty is a contradiction in terms.

This "logic of sovereignty" argument was directed against various theories of a mixed constitution (or a separation of powers), according to which sovereign

---

[159] F.H. Hinsley, *Sovereignty*, 2nd ed. (Cambridge: Cambridge University Press, 1986), 17. Although sovereignty is a relatively straightforward idea, any attempt to trace its history, even in a cursory manner, can easily get entangled in a Gordian knot of technical controversies. Hence, as with other key concepts discussed in this book, I can often do little more than call attention to some of these controversies, and then move on.

[160] Jean Bodin, *On Sovereignty*, ed. and trans. Julian H. Franklin (Cambridge: Cambridge University Press, 1992), 1. This volume consists of four chapters from Bodin's lengthy work, *The Six Books of the Commonwealth* (1576).

[161] Ibid., 1, 3.

power should be distributed among different branches of government, each of which serves to check the power of the other branches. Those "constitutionalists" who advocated a mixed sovereignty were often accused by absolutists (e.g., Robert Filmer) of promoting anarchy under another name, for the very nature of a political community logically demands that someone, be it one person or a group of persons, have the authority to render a final judgment in matters involving coercion. And whoever has that final authority is the de facto sovereign of the political community.

Because philosophers of sovereignty were affiliated with absolutism, and because absolutist theories of government were at odds with theories that were affiliated with constitutionalism, there is a natural tendency to simplify the historical picture by envisioning absolutists as forerunners of modern totalitarianism. This would be an inaccurate and unfair caricature. Bodin, for example, was no defender of the omnipotent state; on the contrary, he insisted that rulers were morally bound by the precepts of divine and natural law, and that they should respect the customary laws of their country. He was an advocate of religious toleration who also argued that rulers should not impose taxes without the consent of the governed.

Bodin's essential point about sovereignty was made from the perspective of a political scientist; he was pointing out, descriptively, what must be the case in a political community, allegedly as a matter of logic, if a government is to maintain peace and social order. In the case of conflicts that might otherwise erupt in violence, there must be a sovereign authority whose judgment is accepted by all parties as the final court of appeal. It is in this sense that sovereignty cannot be divided – for suppose we say that two persons or institutions in a political community share this sovereignty equally, and suppose that these two sovereign bodies arrive at different judgments. This situation is no better than an anarchistic state of nature, a condition in which there is no appeal to a common judge to resolve disputes.

It is helpful to understand the historical context in which disputes over sovereignty arose. During the Middle Ages, most political debates focused on conflicts between the *sacerdotium* and *regnum*. The *sacerdotium* was the realm of the priestly, or spiritual power, whereas the *regnum* was the realm of the kingly, or secular, power. It is misleading to view these realms as analogous to church and state in the modern sense, for *sacerdotium* and *regnum* were conceived as aspects of the same universal society – the *Ecclesia*, a single community composed of all Christians.

It was commonly argued that the pope receives his authority directly from God, but there was considerable disagreement over the extent of this power, and whether the pope's authority to intervene in purely secular matters was "direct" or "indirect." Also a point of controversy was the source of secular authority. Defenders of papal absolutism maintained that the authority of the secular rulers descends from the pope, whereas their opponents either maintained that God originally vested this political authority directly in secular rulers or in the people, who then transferred it to a secular ruler. Thus, although both sides agreed that political power originates with God, defenders of the *regnum* wished to omit the pope from the chain of authority by defending either divine rights of secular rulers or the notion of *popular* sovereignty, according to which the people transfer their authority to a secular ruler.

The logic of sovereignty was clearly set forth by Marsilius of Padua in the fourteenth century. What I previously described as the monopolistic feature of state power is characterized by Marsilius as the need for a "numerical unity" of a government. According to Marsilius, "there must be only a single government" in a given political community; or, when multiple governments are necessary in a large community, "then there must be among them one in number which is supreme, to which all the other governments are reduced, by which they are regulated, and which corrects any errors arising in them."[162] That this supreme power is necessary for the administration of justice is explained by Marsilius as follows.

Suppose there are several governments in one political community. If a government is to administer justice, it must be able to summon a person suspected of breaking the law to a tribunal where the charges against him or her can be examined. If we assume "a plurality of governments not reduced to some one supreme government," it would be possible for a person to receive different summons to appear before different rulers simultaneously. However, since it is impossible for a person to "appear before all the rulers at one and the same time," this would mean that the person would be held in contempt by at least one ruler for failing to fulfill a moral and legal obligation that no one could possibly fulfill. Moreover, the accused

> will perhaps be convicted by one ruler and be acquitted by another, of the same crime; or if convicted by both, with different penalties. Hence he will be both required and not required to make amends; or, if required by both, it will be to such a degree by one, and to a greater or lesser degree by another, and thus both to such a degree and not to such a degree. Hence he will either do contradictory things at the same time, or else will make no amends at all. For he must obey one ruler's command for the same reason as another's.... The only remaining course, consequently, is for the man who is summoned to

---

[162] Marsilius of Padua, *The Defender of the Peace*, trans. Alan Gewirth (New York: Harper Torchbooks, 1967), 80.

appear before no ruler at all; therefore justice will be incapable of being done in his case. It is impossible, therefore, for the city or state to have a plurality of such governments not subordinated one to another, if civil justice and benefit are to be conserved.[163]

In a community with a plurality of governments, "some of the citizens would wish to obey one government, and some another," and from this "there would result the division and opposition of the citizens, their fighting and separation, and finally the destruction of the state."

> There would also be strife between the governments themselves because one of them would want to be superior to the other; in addition, the governments would war against the citizens who refused to be subject to them. Moreover, when the rulers disagreed or quarreled among themselves, since they would lack a superior judge, the above-mentioned scandals would also arise.[164]

Thus does Marsilius, writing over two centuries before Bodin, present a clearly reasoned case for sovereignty. Although Marsilius wished to uphold the secular power of the *regnum* over the spiritual power of the *sacerdotium*, his discussion illustrates the point that certain concepts are inherent in the discipline of political philosophy, and that certain themes based on these concepts will recur from time to time, depending on the particular problem that is being addressed.

I previously discussed two normative features of the state. The first is the claim to use legitimate coercion; the second is the claim to be the final arbiter in matters involving coercion. Both claims invoke "a right" to compel obedience; however, it is the latter claim that is a distinctive characteristic of the "state," in contrast to a "government" (which may signify only a governing agency that makes no claim to territorial sovereignty). This is why "the problem of the birth of the modern State is no other than the problem of the rise and final acceptance of the concept of sovereignty."[165]

The word "state" derives from the Latin *status*, which means a condition, situation, or way of existence. In the twelfth century, a kingship was called the *status regis*; this "condition of the king" originally referred to his personal possessions and fortune, but over time it was expanded to include his functions and power. In the fourteenth century, *status* was used as a synonym for "power," "rule," or "governance." When medieval writers wished to express what we mean (roughly) by "state," they used the words *regnum* (kingdom) and

---

[163] Ibid., 82.
[164] Ibid., 83.
[165] A.P. d'Entrèves, *The Notion of the State*, 97.

*respublica* ("that which is public"). Not until the end of the fifteenth century do we find "state" used in the modern sense to designate the abstract notion of a government and body of laws.

In his influential discussion of the state, Max Weber contended that we cannot define the state in terms of its ends, or what it attempts to do, because virtually every task has been undertaken by a state at one time or another, and no one task has ever been pursued exclusively by the state. "Ultimately, one can define the modern State sociologically only in terms of the specific *means* peculiar to it, as to every political association, namely, the use of physical force."[166] Weber was careful to point out that force is not the only method employed by states, but force is their distinctive mode of operation:

> [W]e have to say that a state is a human community that (successfully) claims the *monopoly of the legitimate use of physical force within a given territory.* Note that "territory" is one of the characteristics of the state. Specifically, at the present time, the right to use physical force is ascribed to other institutions or to individuals only to the extent to which the state permits it. The state is considered the sole source of the "right" to use violence.[167]

The state is the legal sovereign of a territory. "Legal" refers to the realm of legitimate coercion. "Sovereign" refers to an ultimate judge or arbiter. "Territory" refers to a geographical area. Hence the state is the ultimate judge and enforcer of legitimate coercion within a given geographical area. The state renders the final verdict on the legitimate use of violence and executes that verdict.

The claim to exercise a *monopoly* on the use of legitimate coercion is one thing that distinguishes a "state" from a "government."[168] As the legal pluralism of medieval society – a complex network of feudal law, the king's law, canon law, and so forth – was supplanted by the modern absolutist state, the notion of state sovereignty came to the fore as a central concept in political philosophy. And the victory of the sovereign state brought with it a tendency to level all other institutions to the same dependent legal status; jealous of its powers, the sovereign state was loathe to acknowledge the independent political authority of those corporate groups that had flourished during the Middle Ages.

From a liberal perspective, the demise of these "intermediate institutions" had mixed results. On the one hand, the emergence of the sovereign state led to what is often called the "atomization" of society. No longer could the individual find refuge from the abuse of governmental power by appealing to

---

[166] Max Weber, "Politics as a Vocation," in *From Max Weber: Essays in Sociology*, trans. and ed. H.H. Gerth and C. Wright Mills (New York: Oxford University Press, 1958), 77–78.
[167] Ibid., 78.
[168] See Weber, *Economy and Society*, 1: 54.

competing institutions with independent authority; no longer was there the competition among different institutions to which Lord Acton attributed the growth of individual freedom. Now there was only the state and the individual.

On the other hand, the sovereign state tended to eliminate the class distinctions that had characterized medieval society. Individuals, in their role as citizens, were viewed as legally equal to other citizens. Most significant for our purpose was the stress on the rights of the individual. In their liberal manifestation, these rights challenged state sovereignty on a fundamental level. Against the sovereignty of the state emerged the sovereignty of the individual.

## III

When Aristotle pointed out that "people are generally bad judges where their own interests are involved,"[169] he was calling attention to a problem that would be repeated many times throughout the history of political philosophy. The problem of acting as judge in one's own case is raised by philosophers from every point on the political spectrum, so it qualifies as a common lens through which to view the topic of sovereignty. Even those philosophers (such as John Locke) who claimed that objective principles of justice, knowable to reason, should be used to resolve interpersonal conflicts, and that every individual has the natural right to enforce the principles of justice, emphasized the need for an impartial arbiter. There were two basic reasons for this.

First, there is (as Aristotle noted) a natural bias in human beings where their own interests are involved; even well-intentioned people will tend to view a conflict selectively, giving undue weight to their own motives and reasons for acting. Second, even when a person who judges his or her own case reaches a just conclusion, that decision will be viewed with suspicion by the public at large (owing to the presumption of bias), and this will render the decision difficult to enforce. The enforcement of a just decision requires the cooperation of others; it requires an institutional mechanism that commands the respect of public opinion, and an individual who judges his or her own case will be unable to command this respect.

The need for a judge to resolve disputes between individuals was admitted by every camp of political philosophers, and this generated a consensus about a minimal function of government. A government, whatever the range of its legitimate powers may be, should at least provide a judicial authority to which subjects and citizens can appeal to resolve conflicts that might otherwise result in perpetual violence.

[169] Aristotle, *Politics*, 1280a7.

To concede the general need for a government to adjudicate disputes leaves unanswered the question of who *in particular* has the right to exercise this power. Locke was insightful, and perfectly correct, when he identified this as a fundamental problem of political philosophy. It is a relatively easy matter to show that a political right of this kind must reside somewhere; it is far more difficult to show who in particular has this right, and how he or she came by it. Locke's contemporary, Algernon Sidney, was emphatic on this point:

> I cannot know how to obey, unless I know in what, and to whom: Nor in what, unless I know what ought to be commanded: Not what ought to be commanded, unless I understand the original right of the commander.... [170]

Of crucial importance here, as in other matters pertaining to the rights of government, is the function of "political reductionism" in the Lockean paradigm. By "political reductionism," I mean the doctrine that all rights are ultimately the rights of individuals, and that all rights and powers claimed by government must be reducible, in principle, to the rights and powers of individuals. As Locke put it, "no Body can transfer to another more power than he has in himself." [171] However much Lockeans may have dissented from Hugo Grotius in some respects, his individualistic approach to rights included reductionism as a basic method of political reasoning, a method that became increasingly common among natural-rights philosophers. Here I quote Richard Tuck:

> The rights enjoyed by the atomic individuals in the Grotian state of nature filled out the moral world: the state possessed no rights which those individuals had not formerly possessed, and was the same kind of moral entity as them. This was true too of his theory of property: private individuals and states were interchangeable with respect to property, and a state's boundaries were the same kind of thing as the boundaries of a private estate. In some ways, such an assimilation of the private and public realms was characteristic of all rights theorists from Gerson [1363–1429] onwards; for by attributing rights of *dominion* or a kind of sovereignty to individuals in a state of nature, they immediately made the distinction between the two realms fluid and in effect purely a question of numbers. [172]

Statements of political reductionism abound after the seventeenth and eighteenth centuries. Algernon Sidney wrote that "whatsoever is done by delegated powers, must be referred to the principals; for none can give to any a power

---

[170] Sidney, *Discourses Concerning Government*, 15.
[171] Locke, *Two Treatises*, II: §135.
[172] Tuck, *Natural Rights Theories*, 63.

which they have not in themselves."[173] Furthermore, "no man can confer upon others that which he has not in himself: If he be originally no more than they, he cannot grant to them or any of them more than they to him."[174] According to Gershom Carmichael (a seminal figure in the early Scottish Enlightenment who brought a Lockean perspective to his commentaries on Pufendorf), "civil power is in fact nothing but the right which belonged to individuals in the state of nature to claim what was their own or what was due to them, and which has been conferred upon the same ruler for the sake of civil peace."[175] And Thomas Jefferson affirmed political reductionism in no uncertain terms when he said that "the rights of the whole can be no more than the sum of the rights of individuals."[176]

Although political reductionism did not necessarily lead to liberal conclusions, it had a definite tendency to establish limits to the power of the state. For one thing, it demanded that the right of political sovereignty be reducible to the moral sovereignty of the individual, and this in turn stimulated the elaboration of a theory of individual rights. We must proceed with caution, however, for even those who began with a theory of individual rights often ended up with anti-liberal conclusions.

The lesson here is that we cannot isolate one element in political theory that necessarily leads to liberal conclusions. The Lockean paradigm is an integrated system of elements, and its liberal conclusions result from how those elements are integrated.

IV

The distinction between perfect and imperfect rights (and their corresponding obligations), which we discussed in Chapter 3 in connection with Adam Smith, was an important feature of the Lockean paradigm. Although the basic distinction is found in Grotius, as Stephen Buckle explains, it found its definitive expression in Pufendorf:

> Pufendorf's way of drawing this distinction [between perfect and imperfect rights and obligations] is a hint in the direction of modern distinctions between law and morals: between what we can be compelled to do by others,

[173] Sidney, *Discourses Concerning Government*, 103.

[174] Ibid., 304.

[175] Gershom Carmichael, *Supplements and Observations upon The Two Books of Samuel Pufendorf's On the Duty of Man and Citizen* (1724), in *Natural Rights on the Threshold of the Scottish Enlightenment: The Writings of Gershom Carmichael*, ed. James Moore and Michael Silverthorne (Indianapolis: Liberty Fund, 2002), 158.

[176] Letter to James Madison (Sept. 6, 1789), in *Life and Selected Writings*, 489.

on the one hand, and, on the other, what our own humanity should compel us to do, without external enforcement.... Imperfect obligation arises only *within* the agent, unaccompanied by an external power to compel action.... Imperfect obligation is centrally a matter of the conscience....[177]

To delimit a sphere of conscience exempt from coercion was by no means a seventeenth-century innovation; as we shall see (in the discussion of "conscience liberalism"), it has roots deep in the history of Western moral and political thought. What was new was the effort to specify the precise boundaries of this sphere of conscience by distinguishing "perfect" from "imperfect" rights. Only those actions that violate the rights of another person are the proper subject of coercion. When the nineteenth-century libertarian Lysander Spooner distinguished between vices and crimes,[178] he was merely elaborating upon a theme that had already been affirmed by John Locke and others in his tradition. As Locke wrote,

> Laws provide, as much as possible, that the goods and health of subjects be not injured by the fraud and violence of others; they do not guard them from the negligence or ill-husbandry of the possessors themselves. No man can be forced to be rich or healthful whether he will or no. Nay, God himself will not save men against their wills.[179]

In his response to those who argued that idolatry is a sin and so ought to be prohibited by law, Locke called attention to the fact that not all sins violate the rights of other people:

> Covetousness, uncharitableness, idleness, and many other things are sins, by the consent of men, which yet no man ever said were to be punished by the magistrate. The reason is, because they are not prejudicial to other men's rights, nor do they break the public peace of societies.[180]

To limit the sphere of justice to perfect rights, that is, to *enforceable* moral claims, was an important aspect of the Lockean paradigm, since it linked individual rights to the coercive functions of government. To defend political reductionism by insisting that all rights are ultimately the rights of individual moral agents made it possible to determine the legitimate boundaries of governmental power by determining the scope of individual rights.

---

[177] Buckle, *Natural Law and the Theory of Property*, 86.
[178] See *Vices are Not Crimes*, in *The Lysander Spooner Reader*, ed. George H. Smith (San Francisco: Fox and Wilkes, 1992), 25–52.
[179] Locke, *A Letter Concerning Toleration*, 137.
[180] Ibid., 148.

In opposition to the state sovereignty defended by absolutists, liberal individualists defended some version of self-sovereignty, offering it as the core right
on which other rights are based. As Locke put it, "every Man has a *Property* in
his own *Person*. This no Body has any Right to but himself."[181] In this broad
conception, to have "property" (or "propriety") *in x* is to have moral dominion
over *x*, that is, the right to determine how *x* shall be used.

Various terms have been used to express the same basic idea. In 1646, for
example, the Leveller Richard Overton wrote this of "self-propriety":

> To every individual in nature is given an individual property by nature not
> to be invaded or usurped by any. For every one, as he is himself, so he has
> a self-propriety, else could he not *be* himself; and of this no second [person]
> may presume to deprive any of without manifest violation and affront to the
> very principles of nature and of the rules of equity and justice between man
> and man.[182]

This broad conception of property made it possible to speak of the ownership
of one's liberty and even (as we find in James Madison) of property in one's
time. It is not difficult to find passing references to moral dominion over one's
person throughout the history of political thought. For instance, in his account
of the funeral oration of Pericles, Thucydides wrote that "each single one of
our citizens, in all the manifold aspects of life, is able to show himself the
rightful lord and owner of his own person."[183]

Similar statements are especially common in discussions of slavery. Since
a "slave" is defined as a person who is owned by another person, discussions
of this subject brought the notion of self-ownership into clear relief as the
defining characteristic of a free person. According to Aristotle, to say a person
is free is to say he (or she) "exists for his own sake and not for another's."[184]
Similarly, Thomas Aquinas described slavery as a condition in which a person
"forfeits something which otherwise would belong to him, namely the free
disposal of his person."[185]

In the late thirteenth century, Henry of Ghent (a master at the University
of Paris) spoke of a property right (*proprietas*) in one's own person, using
this concept to analyze the tricky issue of whether a criminal who has been

[181] Locke, *Two Treatises*, II: §27.
[182] Richard Overton, "*An Arrow Against all Tyrants*," in *The English Levellers*, ed. Andrew Sharp
(Cambridge: Cambridge University Press, 1998), 55.
[183] Thucydides, *The Peloponnesian War*, trans. Rex Warner (Harmondsworth: Penguin Books,
1954), 119.
[184] Aristotle, *Metaphysics*, trans. W.D. Ross, *Basic Works of Aristotle*, 982b25.
[185] Aquinas, *Summa Theologica*, IIa, Iae, 189, 7.

captured and condemned to death has the right to escape.[186] The doctrine that a person has moral jurisdiction over his own body, faculties, labor, and the fruits thereof was expressed by various scholastic philosophers during the sixteenth century, but it was principally from Grotius that many seventeenth-century Protestant writers picked up the idea. As he put it, "A Man's Life is his own by Nature (not indeed to destroy, but to preserve it) and so is his Body, his Limbs, his Reputation, his Honour, and his Actions."[187] A century later, Gershom Carmichael explicitly linked this broad conception of ownership to the right of self-determination: "Everyone is naturally the owner of his own liberty, or the right of determining his own actions."[188]

If these and similar notions of self-sovereignty had a radical edge that threatened to cut into the sovereignty of the state, this edge was easily blunted by the stipulation that individuals possessed this moral autonomy only in a state of nature – a condition, whether real or hypothetical, that existed prior to the establishment of a civil society under the jurisdiction of a government. Libertarian conclusions flowed from the premise of self-sovereignty only when the latter managed to survive relatively unscathed through the denuding process of the social contract – and this depended on a number of factors, such as the precise nature of the social contract and whether certain rights were deemed "inalienable."

Locke himself was no radical in this regard; on the contrary, his doctrine of tacit consent was so vague as to permit a variety of plausible interpretations, including some that rendered his theory of self-proprietorship little more than the political equivalent of Schopenhauer's cab that is dismissed and forgotten after taking its occupant to his desired destination. But there were some philosophers on the fringe of the Lockean paradigm for whom self-sovereignty was more than a theoretical premise; and when this principle was applied not only to a state of nature but to a political society as well, the results were predictably radical.

One such radical was Auberon Herbert, an admirer of Herbert Spencer and a former member of Parliament who made "self-ownership" the cornerstone of his political philosophy, and who advocated "voluntary taxation" as a result:

> We hold that the one and only one true basis of society is the frank recognition of these rights of self-ownership; that is to say, of the rights of control and direction by the individual, as he himself chooses, over his own mind, his own body, and his own property, always provided, that he respects the same

---

[186] See the discussion in Brian Tierney, *The Idea of Natural Rights*, pp. 78–89.
[187] Grotius, *The Rights of War and Peace*, II: 885.
[188] Carmichael, *Supplements and Observations*, 141.

universal rights in others. We hold that so long as he lives within the sphere of his own rights, so long as he respects these rights in others, not aggressing by force or fraud upon the person or property of his neighbors, he cannot be made subject, apart from his own consent, to the control and direction of others, and he cannot be rightfully *compelled* under any public pretext, by the force of others, to perform any services, to pay any contributions, or to act or not to act in any manner contrary to his own desires or to his own sense of right. He is by moral right a free man, self-owning and self-directing; and has done nothing which justifies others, for any convenience of their own, in taking from him any part, small or great, of his self-ownership.[189]

Unfortunately, Herbert and other unterrified Lockeans of the nineteenth century (such as Lysander Spooner) are typically neglected in standard histories of political thought, even though they represent an important theoretical development within the Lockean tradition. In some respects these radical libertarians were a concrete validation of the common charge that Lockean principles, consistently applied, cannot justify government but will land us in anarchy instead.

V

We previously discussed the distinction between alienable and inalienable rights in connection with the right of revolution. Francis Hutcheson nicely summarized the function of inalienable or ("unalienable") rights in the Lockean paradigm when he described them as "essential Limitations on all Government" while noting that "wherever any Invasion is made upon unalienable Rights, there must arise either a perfect, or external Right to Resistance."[190]

Alienable rights are those which are "within our natural Power" to transfer to another person, "so that it be possible for us in Fact to transfer our Right," whereas inalienable rights are incapable of such transfer.[191] Inalienable rights

---

[189] Auberon Herbert, "The Principles of Voluntaryism," in *The Right and Wrong of Compulsion by the State, and Other Essays by Auberon Herbert*, ed. Eric Mack (Indianapolis: Liberty Fund, 1978), 370–71.

[190] Francis Hutcheson, *An Inquiry Concerning Moral Good and Evil*, in *British Moralists*, ed. L.A. Selby-Bigge (Indianapolis: Bobbs-Merrill, 1964), 1: 170, 171. The Irish-born Hutcheson (1694–1746), a teacher of Adam Smith who succeeded Gershom Carmichael in the chair of moral philosophy at Glasgow University, was a leading proponent of moral sense theory. More important for our purpose is his essentially Lockean exposition of natural rights, an approach that he shared with Carmichael. The work of both men contradicts the misconception of F.A. Hayek and other historians that philosophers of the Scottish Enlightenment did not engage in "rationalistic" moral theory. Few Enlightenment philosophers discussed natural rights in the detail that we find in Hutcheson.

[191] Ibid., I: 163.

had a crucial function in the Lockean paradigm, because they were rights that could never have been transferred or surrendered in a social contract, even with the supposed consent of the governed. This means that no government can possibly claim legitimate jurisdiction over this sphere of free activity. As Jefferson put it, rulers can claim authority only over those natural rights that "we have submitted to them," and the rights of conscience (which were widely regarded as the quintessential inalienable rights) "we never submitted, we could not submit."[192]

Inalienable rights were justified in various ways, even within the Lockean paradigm. A common argument for the inalienability of the right of conscience in religious matters was based on cognitive determinism, according to which our beliefs are not a matter of free choice but instead are determined by the evidence available to us. We cannot will to believe, or not to believe, something apart from our understanding of the evidence for or against a belief, so our beliefs cannot be altered by coercion. As the Leveller William Walwyn wrote in 1644,

> Of what judgment soever a man is, he cannot choose but be of that judgment. [N]ow where there is necessity there ought to be no punishment, for punishment is the recompense of voluntary actions, therefore no man ought to be punished for his judgment.[193]

This is the same argument that John Locke presented several decades later, when he wrote that "it is absurd that things should be enjoined by laws which are not in men's power to perform. And to believe this or that to be true, does not depend upon our will."[194]

This argument (which has a long ancestry) illustrates the historical connection between inalienable rights and religious freedom – or "liberty of conscience," as it was often called. Although the ideological origins of liberal individualism were complex and multifaceted, this concern with the inalienable rights of conscience was the foundation from which many other features of the Lockean paradigm arose. Liberty of conscience, as J.S. Mill noted, was "first of all the articles of the liberal creed."[195] Emerging from the

---

[192] Thomas Jefferson, *Notes on Virginia*, in *Life and Selected Writings*, 274–75. In an interesting aside, Jefferson notes that "Was the government to prescribe to us our medicine and diet, our bodies would be in such keeping as our souls are now."

[193] "The Compassionate Samaritane," in *The Writings of William Walwyn*, ed. J. McMichael and B. Taft (Athens: University of Georgia Press), 1989, 103.

[194] Locke, *A Letter Concerning Toleration*, 150.

[195] John Stuart Mill, *Auguste Comte and Positivism* (Ann Arbor: University of Michigan Press, 1961), 73.

centuries-long struggle for religious freedom, the idea of conscience was gradually expanded by liberals to include other areas of social interaction. As one
historian of liberalism explained,

> At first, freedom of conscience is considered essential to [man's] personality;
> this implies religious liberty and liberty of thought. Later is added all that con-
> cerns his relations to other individuals: freedom to express and communicate
> his own thought, personal security against all oppression, free movement,
> economic liberty, juridical equality, and property.[196]

Essential to the development of conscience liberalism was the distinction
between two spheres of activity: the external and the internal. External activity
(our physical actions and interactions with other people) can adversely affect
another person when they interfere with his or her freedom to pursue values,
so the external sphere is the proper concern of government. When we violate
the rights of another person, we commit an act of injustice, and it is the proper
business of law to secure equal justice for everyone. The internal sphere of
activity is quite different. Here our actions and decisions affect only ourselves
and those who choose to deal with us voluntarily, so this sphere, which does
not touch on issues of justice, should remain outside the scope of laws and
other manifestations of state power.

Even from this brief description, it is clear that the distinction between
the external and internal realms, between the domain of justice and the
domain of conscience, is clearly connected to natural rights. This is why conscience liberalism was closely affiliated with natural-rights thinking. Rights
function as a line of demarcation between the proper sphere of governmental activity and the sphere that should be left to the voluntary choices of
individuals.

Government, according to conscience liberalism, should confine itself to
the protection of individual rights. When an aggressor initiates force against
another person, he violates the right of his victim to act according to his
own judgment. It is proper for the government to intervene in this situation,
because in so doing it is protecting the victim's liberty of conscience. However,
in situations in which this rights violation is not involved, in which a person
interacts voluntarily with another person or takes an action that affects only
himself, the government should not interfere. Indeed, to interfere in these
cases would mean the government is itself violating the rights of individuals,
by trespassing into their inner sphere of conscience.

---

[196] Guido de Ruggiero, *The History of European Liberalism*, trans. R.G. Collingwood (Boston:
Beacon Press, 1959), 26.

The idea of conscience has a long and fascinating history in Western think-ing about ethics, religion, and politics. Among ancient Greek and Roman schools of thought, it was developed most fully by the Stoics, especially Epicte-tus, who spoke eloquently of an inner freedom that was immune to external coercion. We should never sacrifice that which is within our control (our inner beliefs, values, and so forth) for external things outside our control (riches, fame, power, and the like). Freedom, for the Stoic, meant indepen-dence of the inner self from everything external. We can achieve this only through the use of "right reason," a moral faculty that enables us to distinguish good from evil and to discern the precepts of natural law.

Reason, an essential characteristic of human nature, became the foundation of the Stoic belief in the natural equality of mankind, and made Stoics the chief critics of slavery in the ancient world. Some elements of Stoic teaching, especially as formulated by Cicero and Seneca, filtered into Christian thinking; however, it was not until the seventeenth century, when there was a renewed interest in Stoicism among European thinkers, that the more liberal features of Stoic doctrines came to the fore.

Among medieval thinkers, Thomas Aquinas holds a place of pride for his discussion of conscience, and it was owing to this that Lord Action called Aquinas "the first Whig." In some circumstances, according to Aquinas, a person is justified in acting according to an erring conscience, even if this entails disobeying the state: "If error arises from some ignorance of some circumstance, and without any negligence, so that it cause the act to be involuntary, then that error of reason or conscience excuses the will that abides by that erring reason from being evil."[197]

Although it would be highly misleading to treat Aquinas as an early pro-ponent of liberalism (he did, after all, vigorously defend the persecution of religious heretics), some aspects of his political theory, if carried to their logical conclusions, have clear affinities to this tradition. We see this in his treatment of Aristotle's distinction between the "good citizen" and the "good man." Laws, for Aquinas, should enforce only those virtues, such as justice, that are neces-sary for good citizenship – laws, in other words, that are required to preserve peace and social order. One can be just, that is, one can respect the rights of others while being morally deficient in other respects, so one can be a good citizen without being a good person. It is not the proper business of govern-ment to enforce personal virtues. Why? Because the law deals in coercion – and coercion, while it can affect external behavior, cannot alter those inner qualities that are essential to virtue.

---

[197] Aquinas, *Summa Theologica*, Ia, IIae, 19: 6.

It may surprise some people to learn that Thomas Aquinas, a revered saint of the Catholic Church, opposed legal punishment of those engaged in prostitution. This was an implication of his belief that laws exist primarily to enforce the rules of justice, not to create virtuous men. As Aquinas put it,

> [H]uman law is framed for a number of human beings, the majority of whom are not perfect in virtue. Therefore human laws do not forbid all vices, from which the virtuous abstain, but only the more grievous vices, from which it is possible for the majority to abstain, and chiefly those that are to the hurt of others, without the prohibition of which human society could not be maintained; thus human law prohibits murder, theft and the like.[198]

The purpose of human law is "the upholding of the common good of justice and peace." Individuals have a sphere of action that is distinct from that of the whole, and this sphere should be left to voluntary choice, even though vice may be the result. This distinction between the private and public spheres, between voluntary interaction and unjust activities, foreshadows the fundamental tenet of conscience liberalism.

The sphere of inner liberty gradually developed into the notion of inalienable rights. As we have seen, an inalienable right cannot be surrendered or transferred by any means, including consent, because it derives from a person's nature as a rational and moral agent. For example, we cannot alienate our right to freedom of belief, because our beliefs cannot be coerced. Similarly, we cannot surrender our right of moral choice, because an action has moral significance only if it is freely chosen. Our beliefs and values fall within the sphere of inner liberty, the domain of conscience. This sphere is inseparable from our nature as rational and moral beings; it is what elevates us above animals to the status of *persons*. As Spinoza put it, "Inward worship of God and piety in itself are within the sphere of everyone's private rights, and cannot be alienated."[199] Spinoza continues:

> [N]o man's mind can possibly lie wholly at the disposition of another, for no one can willingly transfer his natural right of free reason and judgment, or be compelled so to do. For this reason government which attempts to control minds is accounted tyrannical, and it is considered an abuse of sovereignty and a usurpation of the rights of subjects, to seek to prescribe what shall be accepted as true, or rejected as false, or what opinions should actuate men

---

[198] Ibid., Ia, IIae, 96: 2.
[199] Benedict De Spinoza, A *Theologico-Political Treatise* and A *Political Treatise*, trans. R.H.M. Elwes (New York: Dover, 1951), 245.

in their worship of God. All these opinions fall within a man's natural right, which he cannot abdicate even with his own consent.[200]

It was common throughout the seventeenth and eighteenth centuries to posit liberty of conscience as the primary inalienable right. The reasoning here was clearly explained in 1744 by the Puritan minister Elisha Williams, according to whom "Every man has an equal right to follow the dictates of his own conscience in the affairs of religion." The right to judge and to follow the dictates of one's judgment in this realm is "unalienable," because it is integral to man's moral agency. By his nature man is a "reasonable being," a "moral & accountable being" who must "reason, judge and determine for himself." The right to judge for oneself in religious matters is "strictly speaking unalienable," because it is "inseparably connected" to man's moral agency: "A man can no more part with it than he can part with his power of thinking, and it is equally reasonable for him to attempt to strip himself of the power of reasoning, as to attempt the vesting of another with this right." Therefore, this original right of human nature "cannot be given up" by individuals, even "if they should be so weak as to offer it."

> A man may alienate some branches of his property and give up his right to them to others; but he cannot transfer the rights of conscience, unless he could destroy his rational and moral powers, or substitute some other to be judged for him at the tribunal of God.[201]

A significant development in liberalism occurred as the argument from conscience was applied to activities other than religion. From the distinction between the inner sphere of liberty and the external sphere of compulsion there emerged the distinction between the voluntary sphere of society and the coercive sphere of government. Perhaps the most influential proponent of conscience liberalism was Herbert Spencer. In 1842, Spencer submitted a series of articles on "The Proper Sphere of Government" to *The Nonconformist*. This periodical was edited by Edward Miall, a leader in the campaign to disestablish the Church of England (or, as Americans would say, to separate church and state). Both Miall and Spencer were actively involved in the voluntaryist effort to keep the British government out of education. In these and other areas dissenters upheld the right of conscience, that is, the right of the individual

---

[200] Ibid., 257.

[201] Elisha Williams, "The Essential Rights and Liberties of Protestants," in *Political Sermons of the American Founding Era, 1730–1805*, 2nd ed., ed. Ellis Sandoz (Indianapolis: Liberty Fund, 1998), 1: 61–62.

freely to follow his or her own judgment, so long as he or she does not commit acts of injustice against others.

The most interesting aspect of these early articles by Spencer is how they extend the right of conscience to areas other than religion. The following passage illustrates the concern of conscience liberals to keep government out of the social sphere altogether, and to restrict it to the enforcement of justice. Quoting Spencer:

> The chief arguments that are urged against an established religion, may be used with equal force against an established charity. The dissenter submits, that no party has a right to compel him to contribute to the support of doctrines, which do not meet his approbation. The rate-payer may as reasonably argue, that no one is justified in forcing him to subscribe towards the maintenance of persons, whom he does not consider deserving of relief. The advocate of religious freedom, does not acknowledge the right of any council, or bishop, to choose for him what he shall believe, or what he shall reject. So the opponent of a poor law, does not acknowledge the right of any government, or commissioner, to choose for him who are worthy of his charity, and who are not. The dissenter from an established church, maintains that religion will always be more general, and more sincere, when the support of its ministry is not compulsory. The dissenter from a poor law, maintains that charity will always be more extensive, and more beneficial, when it is voluntary. The dissenter from an established church can demonstrate that the intended benefit of a state religion, will always be frustrated by the corruption which the system invariably produces. So the dissenter from a poor law, can show that the proposed advantages of state charity, will always be neutralized by the evils of pauperism, which necessarily follow in its train. The dissenter from an established church, objects that no man has a right to step in between him and his religion. So the dissenter from an established charity, objects that no man has a right to step in between him and the *exercise* of his religion.[202]

---

[202] Herbert Spencer, "The Proper Sphere of Government," in *The Man Versus the State*, 196–97.

# 5

## The Anarchy Game

### I

In *Anarchy, State, and Utopia*, Robert Nozick wrote the following:

> The fundamental question of political philosophy, one that precedes questions about how the state should be organized, is whether there should be any state at all. Why not have anarchy? Since anarchist theory, if tenable, undercuts the whole subject of *political* philosophy, it is appropriate to begin political philosophy with an examination of its major theoretical alternative.[203]

Nozick goes on to explore the explanatory function of state-of-nature theories in political philosophy. Investigating the problems that would arise in a state of nature (a society without government) "is of crucial importance to deciding whether there should be a state rather than anarchy."[204] This perspective places Nozick squarely within the Lockean tradition; what makes him different is his determination to take anarchism seriously. Although Nozick's approach is commendable as a theoretical model, it is not typical of how Locke and others in his tradition used the state-of-nature model. Virtually no one in this tradition took anarchism seriously. Contrary to Nozick's approach, the need to justify government was a *premise* of political debates during the seventeenth and eighteenth centuries. If one's theory was unable to sustain this premise, then it was the theory, not the need for government, that was condemned and rejected.

Whenever a political theory posits a state of nature (or "natural society"), we may confidently assume that this is the onset of an argument for government, not anarchism. A state of nature has proved a popular starting point for political philosophers, but those philosophers who begin with a state of nature never end

[203] Robert Nozick, *Anarchy, State, and Utopia* (New York: Basic Books, 1974), 4.
[204] Ibid., 5.

there. Hypothetical state-of-nature models are designed for a specific purpose: to present the problems of an anarchistic society in such a way that only a government can solve them. More specifically, they are designed so that the particular kind of government favored by the designer (and no other) can be justified.

In the next chapter we shall examine the radical edge of the Lockean paradigm, namely, its justification of the rights of resistance and revolution. It was this aspect in particular that caused critics to condemn the Lockean paradigm as a recipe for anarchy. This charge was leveled by critics of all political persuasions. Edmund Burke and Jeremy Bentham may have agreed on very little, but both condemned the anarchistic implications of the Lockean paradigm, as we see in their remarks about the French Declaration of Rights (1789), which begins with this statement: "Men are born and remain free and equal in rights." What for Burke was a "digest of anarchy" was for Bentham chock-full of "anarchical fallacies."[205]

Anarchy has always been an important theme in political philosophy, but Nozick is a rare exception in treating it as a serious alternative to a political society. Instead, anarchy has functioned as the political equivalent of hell, a model of unending and unendurable social agony – a perpetual war of every man against every man, as Thomas Hobbes put it in his famous account of the state of nature. Most political philosophers react to the prospect of anarchy with theatrical horror, but they love to talk about it. Anarchy is to political philosophers what original sin is to Calvinists – a pervasive, fundamental evil that is at once repellent and fascinating. A society without government has often been depicted as so horrific and destructive that virtually any kind of government, however brutal or despotic, is preferable to the social poison of anarchy.

Plato, like many enemies of individualism after him, defended his authoritarian measures as a preventative remedy for anarchy: "*Anarchy* – the absence of the commander – is what we should expel root and branch from the lives of all mankind."[206] The fundamental principle of military discipline should therefore be applied to all aspects of human life. It is essential to social order that

> no man, and no woman, be ever suffered to live without an officer set over
> them, and no soul of man to learn the trick of doing one single thing of its

[205] See Élie Halévy, *The Growth of Philosophic Radicalism*, trans. Mary Morris (New York: Macmillan, 1928), 175.

[206] Plato, *The Laws*, trans. A.E. Taylor, in *The Collected Dialogues of Plato*, ed. Edith Hamilton and Huntington Cairns (New York: Pantheon Books, 1964), 942d.

own sole motion, in play or in earnest, but, in peace as in war, ever to live with the commander in sight, to follow his leading, and to take its motions from him to the least detail. . . . in a word, to teach one's soul the habit of never so much as thinking to do one single act apart from one's fellows, of making life, to the very uttermost, an unbroken consort, society, and community of all with all.[207]

For centuries the epithet "anarchy" served the same function in political debates that "atheism" served in religious debates. If one could show that the theory defended by one's adversary logically ended in anarchy, then that theory stood condemned and nothing more needed to be said against it. During the Middle Ages, defenders of papal authority charged that "secular governments are the anarchical powers," and the defenders of secular authority responded in kind. In the seventeenth century, after decades of wars and revolutions, it was the unanimous opinion of all sides that "anarchy at all costs must be prevented."[208] It thus became a popular tactic to accuse one's political opponents of promoting anarchy – not explicitly, of course, but implicitly, through the logical implications of their political theories.

This led to what I call the Anarchy Game. In the seventeenth century the principal contestants in this game were the defenders of absolutism versus those who worked within what I have broadly described as the Lockean paradigm.

## II

If scholars were asked to compile a list of the most influential Western political thinkers of the modern era, the name of Sir Robert Filmer (1588–1653) would not likely be included. A prosperous Kentish squire who defended monarchical absolutism against parliamentarians and others who sought to limit the power of the Stuart kings, Filmer's writings didn't exert much influence until a quarter century after his death, and even this vogue was short lived. Today he is viewed by many intellectual historians as a mediocre thinker who would deserve little attention had not John Locke devoted his *First Treatise of Government* to refuting Filmer's arguments. Even this indication of Filmer's significance is commonly passed over, as Locke's *First Treatise* is dismissed as a period piece whose importance cannot compare to the *Second Treatise*, which is one of the most important works on political theory ever written.

Moreover, Filmer's case for patriarchalism (a popular method of defending the divine right of kings, based on the natural authority of fathers over their

---

[207] Ibid., 942a–c.
[208] J.N. Figgis, *The Divine Right of Kings* (New York: Harper Torchbooks, 1965), 228, 245.

children) was not very persuasive, even to many seventeenth-century readers who were sympathetic to biblical arguments. In short, Filmer was not a first-rate political philosopher, and his positive theories were soon dismissed as a historical curiosity.

But there was a more impressive aspect to Filmer, namely his criticism of the notion that a legitimate government must be based on the consent of the governed, a theory that was grounded in a premise that Filmer characterized as "the natural liberty and equality of mankind." Although this nascent libertarian doctrine had roots in ancient Greek and Roman philosophy (especially Stoicism) and had survived in the writings of various Catholic philosophers, its explosive potential was not fully realized until after the Reformation, when both Catholics and Protestants searched for a rationale to strip heretical or tyrannical princes of their legitimacy and thereby justify the rights of resistance and revolution.

According to Filmer, the "supposed natural equality and freedom of mankind" is a "desperate assertion, whereby kings are made subject to the censures and deprivations of their subjects." If this "first erroneous principle" is refuted and exposed for the sham it is, "the whole fabric of this vast engine of popular sedition would drop down of itself."[209]

This is the primary *critical* task that Filmer undertook in *Patriarcha* and other tracts.[210] In the process he articulated arguments against a consent theory of

---

[209] Sir Robert Filmer, *Patriarcha*, in *Patriarcha and Other Writings*, ed. Johann P. Sommerville (Cambridge: Cambridge University Press, 1991), 3. All references to Filmer's tracts are to this volume.

[210] Filmer had also taken Grotius to task for seeming to argue that consent was the foundation for property, to which Filmer responded that, "Certainly it was a rare felicity that all the men in the world at one instant of time should agree together in one mind to change the natural community of things into private dominion. For without such an unanimous consent, it was not possible for community to be altered. For if but one man in the world had dissented, the alteration had been unjust, because that many by the law of nature had a right to the common use of all things in the world, so that to have given a property of any one thing to any other had been to have robbed him of his right to the common use of all things." (See "The Originall of Government," *Patriarcha and Other Writings*, 234.) That powerful criticism was the occasion for Locke's argument grounding property in estate on property in one's person. "If such a consent as that was necessary, Mankind had starved, notwithstanding the Plenty God had given him" (*Two Treatises*, II: §28). By asserting property in one's person, Locke managed to avoid the trap set by Filmer, for "Though the Earth, and all inferior Creatures be common to all Men, yet every Man has a *Property* in his own *Person*. This no Body has any Right to but himself. The *Labour* of his Body, and the *Work* of his Hands, we may say, are properly his. Whatsoever then he removes out of the State that Nature hath provided, and left it in, he hath mixed his *Labour* with, and joyned to it something that is his own, and thereby makes it his *Property*" (ibid., II: §27). It is property in one's person that justifies the appropriation of that to which everyone earlier had a right.

government (especially against social contract theory, which is the traditional form in which consent theory has manifested itself) that would later be repeated by a host of more famous philosophers, such as David Hume, Edmund Burke, and Jeremy Bentham.

It is scarcely coincidental that two of the most influential libertarian works of the seventeenth century – Algernon Sidney's *Discourses Concerning Government* and John Locke's *Two Treatises of Government* – specifically targeted Filmer as their primary opponent. Although both writers criticized Filmer's patriarchalism in detail, both also appreciated the devastating implications of Filmer's attack on the consent theory of government. It was not enough merely to demolish Filmer's positive theory; more important was to rebut his negative arguments by demonstrating the logical force and coherence of consent as the moral basis for political obligation. The former task was not difficult, but the latter task has proved to be one of the most controversial and intractable problems in the history of political philosophy.

Although some version of the Anarchy Game had been played for centuries, Filmer deserves primary credit for using this game against the Lockean paradigm, and his method of play was imitated well into the nineteenth century. The Anarchy Game is a variant of the *reductio ad absurdum* argument. If you can show that the premises employed by your opponents logically entail a conclusion that even they would reject as absurd, then you have delivered a powerful, and perhaps decisive, blow to their position.

In this context, the absurd conclusion was anarchy, or society without government. No prominent thinker in the seventeenth century (or for a long time thereafter) viewed anarchy as a respectable philosophical position. Hence if Filmer could show that the premises employed by his opponents would logically end in anarchy, then those premises, as well as any arguments based upon them, would lack credibility.

Filmer challenged consent theorists to show how *any* sovereign government can be justified if we begin with the supposition that people are naturally free and equal. He repeatedly asserted that the doctrine of natural liberty and equality, which was commonly called upon to limit the powers of government, actually destroys the foundation of government itself and will land us in anarchy instead. Those who begin their political reasoning with a state of nature – a society without political authority or dominion in which every person enjoys equal rights – are logically doomed to remain in that anarchistic condition.

Filmer's criticism of consent theory raises the obvious historical point that no government was ever established with the unanimous consent of the governed, but his criticism reaches deeper than this. His principal objection (which he presented in a couple of tracts) pertains to how separate and sovereign commonwealths can legitimately be formed if "the entire multitude or whole people have originally by nature power to choose a king." All the people in the world, according to the premises of consent theory, are born equally free from political subjection, so it follows that "a joint consent of the whole people of the world" would be required to establish a government, and "there cannot be any one man chosen a king without the universal consent of all the people of the world at one instant."[211]

Defenders of consent theory, such as the Jesuit philosopher Suarez, had considered this problem, and they replied that it was inexpedient for every person in the world to come together in one community. It was therefore necessary for people to separate into separate commonwealths, each with the power to choose its own ruler.

This is the concession that Filmer needed to raise his specter of anarchy. If different people somehow acquired the right to break away from the community of all mankind and form separate political societies on their own accord, then what is to prevent even smaller groups of people – say, a single family – from likewise seceding from the larger group and forming its own little commonwealth? Indeed, no valid objection could be raised if each individual were to decide to be his or her own king, which is the essence of anarchy. And "thereby a gap is opened for every petty factious multitude to raise a new commonwealth, and to make more commonweals than there be families in the world."[212] Here is Filmer's most complete statement of this argument:

> Since nature hath not distinguished the habitable world in kingdoms, nor determined what part of a people shall belong to one kingdom and what to another, it follows that the original freedom of mankind being supposed, every man is at liberty to be of what kingdom he please. And every petty company hath a right to make a kingdom by itself; and not only every city but every village and every family, nay, and every particular man, a liberty to choose himself to be his own king if he please. And he were a madman that being by nature free would choose any man but himself to be his own governor. Thus to avoid the having but of one king of the whole world, we shall run into a liberty as having as many kings as there be men in the world, which upon the matter is to have no king at all, but to leave all men to their natural liberty [i.e., in a condition of anarchy] – which is the mischief the pleaders for natural liberty do pretend they would most avoid.[213]

---

[211] Filmer, *The Anarchy of a Limited or Mixed Monarchy*, 140.
[212] Filmer, *Patriarcha*, 20.
[213] Filmer, *The Anarchy of a Limited or Mixed Monarchy*, 141.

Filmer examines various ways to get around this kind of problem, including the appeal to tacit consent that would later be used by John Locke. Filmer's remarks in this area are quite perceptive, and later critics of consent theory did little to improve upon them.

If it is said that the minority tacitly consents to abide by the will of the majority, then Filmer demands to know when and in what manner the minority agreed to this arrangement. In addition, if it is argued that "silent acceptation of a governor by part of the people" constitutes tacit consent by those people, then Filmer points out that this would effectively mean that *every* government in the history of the world has ruled with the consent of the governed – an inference, he adds, that is "too ridiculous" to be taken seriously.[214]

Thus, according to Filmer, a specter of anarchy haunts every attempt to justify government by appealing to the consent of the governed. This version of the Anarchy Game became the most formidable objection to consent theory, one that would be repeated many times by more illustrious critics of the social contract (some of whom acknowledged their debt to Filmer). On this basis alone a case can be made for including Sir Robert Filmer on a list of the most influential political philosophers of the modern era. He formulated a key problem that captured the attention of every major political philosopher for over two centuries, a problem that has not been satisfactorily resolved to this day.

### III

John Locke was more than willing to play the Anarchy Game in his extensive critique of Filmer's patriarchalism. It was as obvious to Locke as it was to Filmer that "there ought to be Government in the World"; however, even if we grant Filmer's contention that absolute monarchy is the form of government decreed by God, this does not solve the problem of political obligation – for we must also know the *specific* person or persons to whom we owe political allegiance. Indeed, for practical purposes the most significant issue in political philosophy is not whether political power can be justified (Locke, like his adversaries, accepted this as a premise), but *who* has the right to exercise this power. As Locke states in his *First Treatise*,

> The great Question which in all Ages has disturbed Mankind, and brought on them the greatest part of those Mischiefs which have ruin'd Cities, depopulated Countries, and disordered the Peace of the World, has been, Not

[214] Filmer, *Patriarcha*, 21.

whether there be Power in the World, nor whence it came, but who should
have it.[215]

A political theory that cannot answer this Great Question serves "very little
purpose," except to generate contention and disorder. Power can be dressed
up with "all the Splendor and Temptation Absoluteness can add to it," but
if a theory fails to indicate the *particular* individual or individuals who have
a right to exercise this power, then it cannot protect us against the perils of
anarchy.

> 'Tis in vain then to talk of Subjection and Obedience, without telling us
> whom we are to obey. For were I never so fully persuaded, that there ought to
> be Magistracy and Rule in the World, yet I am nevertheless at Liberty still, till
> it appears who is the Person that hath Right to my Obedience: since if there
> be no Marks to know him by, and distinguish him, that hath Right to Rule
> from other Men, it may be my self, as well as any other. And therefore though
> Submission to Government be every ones duty, yet that signify nothing but
> submitting to the Direction and Laws of such Men, as have Authority to
> Command, 'tis not enough to make a Man a Subject, to convince him that
> there is *Regal Power* in the World, but there must be ways of designing,
> and knowing the Person to whom this *Regal Power* of Right belongs, and
> a Man can never be oblig'd in Conscience to submit to any Power, unless
> he can be satisfied who is the Person, who has a Right to Exercise that
> Power over him. If this were not so, there would be no distinction between
> Pirates and Lawful Princes. . . . To settle therefore Mens Consciences under
> an Obligation to Obedience, 'tis necessary that they know not only that there
> is a Power somewhere in the World, but the Person who by Right is vested
> with this Power over them.[216]

After presenting a number of arguments that we need not examine here,
Locke concluded that Filmer's patriarchalism, even if we concede its initial
premise, cannot identify the legitimate heirs of Adam's monarchical authority.
This means that patriarchalism cannot answer the Great Question of who
should exercise political power. By leaving us in the dark about this crucial
matter, "it will destroy the Authority of the present Governours, and absolve
the People from Subjection to them, since they having no better a Claim than
others to that Power, which is alone the Fountain of all Authority, can have
no Title to Rule over them."[217]

---

[215] Locke, *Two Treatises*, I: §106.
[216] Ibid., I: §81. In emphasizing the need to establish a moral distinction between pirates and
princes, Locke harkens back to Augustine's illustration, which I discussed in the preceding
chapter.
[217] Ibid., I: §83.

Locke repeatedly drove this point home. Filmer's system "dissolves the Bonds of Government and Obedience"; "there would be an end of all Civil Government"; "it destroys the present Governments and Kingdoms, that are now in the World"; "instead of establishing civil government and order in the World [Filmer's system] will produce nothing but confusion"; it "cuts up all Government by the Roots."[218]

Thus did Locke turn Filmer's challenge against the challenger. In his eagerness to defend absolute sovereignty, Filmer fails "to make out any Princes Title to Government,"[219] so *he* is the unwitting anarchist. Locke placed great emphasis on this point, so it is surprising how often commentators overlook it. It is an error to dismiss the *First Treatise* as a period piece with little or no theoretical significance; it is misleading to assert, as does Peter Laslett, that Locke "refuse[d] to meet Filmer on his own ground."[220] The Anarchy Game was the principal weapon used by Filmer in his assault on consent theory, and Locke launched his counterattack on the same ground by means of the same tactic.

Having completed the *critical* phase of the Anarchy Game in the *First Treatise* by showing that the arguments of his opponent could not justify political allegiance to any particular government, Locke embarked on the *constructive* phase of the game by attempting to demonstrate that a consent theory of government does not suffer from the same fatal defect. Locke telegraphed the importance of this task in the *First Treatise*. Since Filmer's patriarchalism would effectively destroy the legitimacy of all existing governments, "we must seek out some other Original of Power" for governments, "or else there will be none at all in the world."[221]

The *Second Treatise* opens with a victory lap during which Locke again stressed that Filmer lost the Anarchy Game. It is "impossible that the Rulers now on Earth, should make any benefit, or derive any the least shadow of Authority" from patriarchalism (even if we grant, which Locke does not, that Adam had the absolute political power that Filmer attributed to him). We are

---

[218] Ibid., I: §105, §126, §142, §143, §126.

[219] Ibid., I: §21.

[220] Peter Laslett, introduction to *Two Treatises of Government*, 69. Somewhat more justified is Laslett's allegation that Locke "persistently ignored the searching counter-criticisms which are the strength of Filmer's case" (69), but even this is an exaggeration. Locke did not ignore Filmer's "skeptical commentary" about the consent theory of government; on the contrary, the entire *Second Treatise* is Locke's attempt to deal with it. Of course, whether or not Locke *succeeded* in this endeavor is another matter entirely. The debate between Locke and Filmer was not an either/or contest in which there must be a winner and a loser. Locke and Filmer were playing the Anarchy Game, and in this game the real adversary who must be defeated is the bogeyman of anarchy. It is quite possible that neither Locke nor Filmer bested this hypothetical opponent, in which case both would be losers.

[221] Locke, *Two Treatises*, I: §83.

therefore at a crossroads. One road – that of anarchy – leads to the conclusion "that all Government in the World is the product only of Force and Violence, and that Men live together by no other Rules but that of Beasts, where the strongest carries it, and so lay a Foundation for perpetual Disorder and Mischief, Tumult, Sedition and Rebellion."[222] Locke claimed that this anarchistic nightmare – which is what the advocates of absolute monarchy "so loudly cry out against" – is logically entailed by Filmer's defense of absolutism, owing to its inability to specify who in the present day can claim legitimate title to the absolute monarchical authority that God supposedly bestowed upon Adam.

In the *Second Treatise*, Locke continued to play the Anarchy Game, but this time he leveled the charge of anarchy against all forms of absolutism rather than confining it to the patriarchal version defended by Filmer. This gives it a broader theoretical significance.

An essential element in all defenses of absolute monarchy was the claim that the sovereign is accountable to none but God. Although absolutists conceded that the sovereign is *morally* obligated to obey both divine and natural law, they also insisted that the sovereign is "above" the jurisdiction of man-made law. As Filmer put it, "For as kingly power is by the law of God, so it hath no inferior law to limit it." Consequently, sovereigns cannot rightfully be punished, deposed, or otherwise held accountable by their subjects if they violate the same laws that govern them. Even the most tyrannical of rulers cannot be forcibly opposed, no matter how unjust his or her actions may be. Defenders of absolutism did not say that kings have a license to commit immoral or unjust acts, but only that "it is right for them to go unpunished by the people" if they do commit such acts.[223] (Words such as "unconditional" and "arbitrary" were also used by Filmer and others to describe this kind of power.)

Locke exploited this notion of absolutism to argue that absolute monarchy is not a legitimate form of government at all, since it effectively leaves the sovereign in a state of anarchy vis-à-vis his or her subjects. In an anarchistic state of nature, a people may act as judges in their own cases, and they may enforce their judgment. This natural right generates a serious problem, however, since we are partial to our own interests and therefore unlikely to possess the objectivity required for just procedures and decisions. According to Locke, a solution to this problem lies in the establishment of a civil (or political) society in which the individual's right to judge and punish is placed in the hands of a government that, guided by impartial laws, functions as an arbiter to resolve disputes and conflicts.

---

[222] Locke, Ibid., II: §1.
[223] Filmer, *Patriarcha*, 35–36.

Suppose a sovereign ruler acts illegally or unjustly toward his or her subjects. To whom can these subjects appeal for an impartial adjudication and resolution of their complaints? According to absolutists, the sovereign must function as judge and jury in his or her own case. The sovereign, and the sovereign alone, will decide the outcome, and this decision cannot be appealed to a higher tribunal. Even victims of tyranny have no legal recourse or appeal, no means of attaining redress or relief from an impartial judge. For Locke, this absence of an impartial judge – a common arbiter who will resolve disputes between ruler and ruled – means that subjects are in a state of nature relative to the sovereign.

> So that such a Man, however intitled, *Czar,* or *Grand Signior,* or how you please, is as much *in the state of Nature,* with all under his Dominion, as he is with the rest of Mankind. For where-ever any two Men are, who have no standing Rule, and common Judge to Appeal to on Earth for the determination of Controversies of Right betwixt them, there they are *still in the state of Nature,* and under all the inconveniences of it.[224]

One of the "inconveniences" in a state of nature is the lack of impartiality that results when a person acts as judge in his or her own case. A chief requirement of civil society is that people relinquish this right and agree to have their disputes settled by a disinterested judge, according to laws that apply equally to every member of that society. Hence if a sovereign has the exclusive right to act as judge in his or her own case, these decisions will be vitiated by the same natural bias and lack of impartiality that people seek to avoid by submitting themselves to a government in the first place.

Locke at this point introduced a novel twist to the Anarchy Game. He noted that absolute monarchy has some of the characteristics of a civil society, since there does exist a common judge to resolve disputes among subjects themselves. Consequently, this is not a condition of pure anarchy; subjects are in a state of nature only in relation to the sovereign, not in relation to their fellow subjects. But Locke went on to argue that this quasi-anarchical condition is actually *worse* than a pure state of nature.

> [W]hereas, in the ordinary State of Nature, [a man] has a liberty to judge of his Right, and according to the best of his Power, to maintain it; now whenever his Property is invaded by the Will and Order of his Monarch, he has not only no Appeal, as those in Society ought to have, but as if he were degraded from the common state of Rational Creatures, is denied a liberty to judge of, or to defend his Right, and so is exposed to all the Misery and

---

[224] Locke, *Two Treatises,* II: §91; cf. II: §13.

Inconveniences that a Man can fear from one who being in the unrestrained state of Nature, is yet corrupted with Flattery, and armed with Power.[225]

In contrast to the absolutist doctrine (which had been defended by Thomas Hobbes, as well as by Robert Filmer) that a sovereign cannot be held legally accountable or otherwise punished for his or her actions, Locke insisted that *"No Man in Civil Society can be exempted from the Laws of it."* If a sovereign may do as he or she pleases, and if his or her subjects have "no Appeal on Earth, for Redress or Security against any harm he shall do," then the sovereign is not in fact a member of that civil society but remains in a state of nature vis-à-vis everyone else. Then, as if to announce that he has scored yet another point in the Anarchy Game, Locke stated that his conclusion can be contested only by someone who says that "the State of Nature and Civil Society are one and the same thing, which I have never yet found any one so great a Patron of Anarchy as to affirm."[226]

Locke's argument touches on a question that was frequently discussed in the Anarchy Game: Which is worse – tyranny or anarchy? Absolutists, however much they condemned tyranny, regarded tyranny as preferable to a society with no government at all. According to Jean Bodin (whose theory of absolute sovereignty greatly influenced Filmer), "licentious anarchy . . . is worse than the harshest tyranny in the world."[227] This opinion was echoed by Thomas Hobbes, according to whom the state of nature is "much worse" than whatever evil consequences might result from the exercise of "unlimited power."[228]

Locke, as we have seen, gave a different answer. For him (as for other constitutionalists who wished to apply the rule of law to sovereigns and subjects alike), it is absurd to suppose that people would join a civil society to become worse off than they would have been in a state of nature – and worse off they would certainly be, if in a civil society their property, liberty, and lives would be at the mercy of an absolute sovereign and his or her arbitrary decrees.[229]

The question of which is worse, tyranny or anarchy, serves as a focal point that enables us to appreciate the significance of a number of elements in the Anarchy Game. These include the meaning of "sovereignty" (which was widely regarded as a defining characteristic of government), the rights of resistance and revolution (which were widely condemned as anarchical principles), and

---

[225] Ibid., II: §91.
[226] Ibid., II: §94.
[227] Quoted in Quentin Skinner, *The Foundations of Modern Political Thought*, vol. 2, *The Age of Reformation* (Cambridge: Cambridge University Press, 1978), 285.
[228] Thomas Hobbes, *Leviathan*, ed. Michael Oakeshott (Oxford: Basil Blackwell, 1957), 136.
[229] Locke, *Two Treatises*, II: §137.

descriptions of what life would be like in an anarchistic state of nature. These were among the most hotly debated issues in seventeenth-century political philosophy, and they retain their theoretical significance to this day.

IV

If Locke emerged victorious in his debate with Robert Filmer (which was rather one-sided, since Filmer had died years before Locke wrote his critique), this had little to do with Locke's equating of absolutism with anarchy. Patriarchalism was a feeble theory at best, and it depended too heavily on interpretations of biblical texts – a method of argument that was out of sync with the Enlightenment appeal to reason. Nevertheless, the Anarchy Game continued to be played throughout the eighteenth century, and Filmer's basic arguments against the Lockean paradigm were adopted and improved upon by philosophers of the first rank.

Two events in particular – the American Revolution and the French Revolution – precipitated interest in the Anarchy Game as a means of criticizing the Lockean defense of the rights of resistance and revolution. Unlike the previous century, when this tactic was used by absolutists, the new critics often had strong liberal sentiments, and they played the Anarchy Game with greater sophistication than anything seen in the previous century.

One strategy was that employed by the liberal English clergyman Josiah Tucker, who trenchantly observed that "the Lockian System is an universal Demolisher of all Civil Governments, but not the Builder of any."[230] If Locke's principles "were to be executed according to the Letter, and in the Manner the *Americans* pretend to understand them, they would necessarily unhinge, and destroy every Government upon Earth."[231] Tucker complained that the wise maxim in politics – "Not to be very inquisitive concerning the *original Title* of the reigning Powers"[232] – had been destroyed by John Locke and other defenders of natural rights and the social contract. According to the Lockean system, consent is the basis of legitimate government, but this is a test that no real government can pass.

Americans had accused the British of violating their rights by imposing taxes and other measures without the consent of colonial assemblies. The Americans had appealed to Lockean principles in their effort to rid themselves

---

[230] *A Treatise Concerning Civil Government* (1781), in *Josiah Tucker: A Selection from His Economic and Political Writings*, ed. Robert Schuyler (New York: Columbia University Press, 1931), 459.
[231] *A Letter to Edmund Burke*, 2nd ed. (1775), in ibid., 378.
[232] Tucker, *Treatise*, 452.

of an old government, but would they remain true to those same principles in establishing new governments? Would those inalienable rights of mankind, which had supposedly been ravished by the British, remain sacred and pristine when the Americans were in control?

No, argued Tucker, this was an impossible task. The Lockean system can justify the demolition of an established government, but it does not provide a secure foundation for establishing a new government. Did the victorious Americans give their citizens the choice of living in a state of nature without any government at all? No – Americans were given only one choice: "Who should govern, *Americans* or *Englishmen?*"[233] Neither the states nor the Continental Congress truly ruled by the consent of the people:

> Was any one of these Civil Governments at first formed, or is it now adminis-tered, and conducted according to the Lockian plan? And did, or doth any of their Congresses, general or provincial, admit of that fundamental Maxim of Mr. Locke, that every Man has an *unalienable* Right to obey no other Laws, but those of his own making? No; no – so far from it, that there are dreadful Fines and Confiscations, Imprisonments, and even Death made use of, as the only effectual Means for obtaining that Unanimity of Sentiment so much boasted of by these new-fangled Republicans, and so little practiced.[234]

Americans well versed in the Lockean paradigm were painfully aware of the appearance of hypocrisy. James Madison, referring to the anarchistic implica-tions of consent theory, wrote of "pestilent operation of this doctrine in the unlimited sense," and he sought refuge in another feature of the Lockean paradigm, namely *tacit* consent:

> I can find no relief from such embarrassments but in the received doctrine that a *tacit* assent may be given to established Governments and law, and that this assent is to be inferred from the omission of an express revocation. . . . Is it not doubtful whether it be possible to exclude wholly the idea of an implied or tacit assent, without subverting the very foundation of civil society?[235]

The most subtle and penetrating critic of the Lockean paradigm was Edmund Burke, who played the Anarchy Game with great skill in his *Reflec-tions on the Revolution in France* (1790). However, Burke displayed his games-manship years before this masterpiece was written. In *A Vindication of Natural Society* (1756), a young Burke, writing anonymously, presented himself as a

---

[233] Ibid., 445.
[234] Ibid., 461.
[235] Letter to Thomas Jefferson (Feb. 4, 1790), *The Complete Madison: His Basic Writings*, ed. Saul K. Padover (New York: Harper and Brothers, 1953), 29.

radical champion of the Lockean paradigm who argues against the violence, wars, and other brutalities of governments. Governments originate in violence and conquest, not in consent; so, according to the "sure and uncontested Principles" of that great philosopher, Mr. Locke, "the greatest Part of the Governments on Earth must be concluded Tyrannies, Impostures, Violations of the Natural Rights of Mankind, and worse than the most disorderly Anarchies."[236]

Burke, of course, intended this as satire; by embracing the anarchistic implications of consent theory, he was attempting to illustrate its absurdity. This was a classic strategy in the Anarchy Game, but Burke's *Vindication* was so well done that some readers took it seriously, thus making it, unintentionally, the first modern defense of anarchism. In 1765, as Burke thought of entering Parliament, he wanted to remove all doubt about his satire, so he prefaced the second edition with a disclaimer: His defense of "natural society" (i.e., anarchy) was nothing more than a lesson in "the abuse of reason" as practiced by consent theorists – those who live in the "fairyland of philosophy."[237]

While a member of Parliament, Burke defended the American protests against British taxation, which he viewed as a defense of traditional American liberties. His "Speech on American Taxation" contains a remarkable objection to the notion of "abstract rights" that would later play a prominent role in his *Reflections on the Revolution in France.* He warned fellow members of Parliament that their insistence on asserting the sovereign right of Parliament to tax the colonies would only provoke the Americans to respond with their own theory of rights, and this in turn would deepen the fissure between the two countries:

> Again, and again, revert to your own principles – *Seek Peace, and ensue it* – leave America if she has taxable matter in her, to tax herself. I am not here going into the distinctions of rights, not attempting to mark their boundaries. I do not enter into these metaphysical distinctions; I hate the very sound of them. Leave the Americans as they anciently stood, and these distinctions, born of our unhappy contest, will die along with it.... Do not burthen them by taxes; you were not used to do so from the beginning. Let this be your reasons for not taxing. These are the arguments of states and kingdoms. Leave the rest to the schools; for there only they may be discussed with safety. But, if intemperately, unwisely, fatally, you sophisticate and poison the very source of government, by urging subtle deductions, and consequences odious to those you govern, from the unlimited and illimitable nature of supreme

---

[236] Edmund Burke, *A Vindication of Natural Society*, ed. Frank N. Pagano (Indianapolis: Liberty Fund, 1982), 49.
[237] Ibid., 7.

sovereignty, you will teach them by these means to call that sovereignty into question. When you drive him hard, the boar will surely turn upon the hunters. If that sovereignty and their freedom cannot be reconciled, which will they take? They will cast your sovereignty in your face. Nobody will be argued into slavery.[238]

It was in his *Reflections on the Revolution in France* – a rambling mixture of maudlin sophistry and stunning brilliance unique in the history of political thought – that Burke played the Anarchy Game with a skill that remains unmatched to this day. In targeting not natural rights per se but the entire notion of "abstract rights," Burke repudiated the rationalistic foundation on which the Lockean paradigm depended. The Lockean paradigm had emerged from the conviction that it is possible to formulate abstract principles by rational methods that could be used to determine the proper functions of government, and set limits to its power. This enterprise struck Burke – who agreed with Aristotle that politics is a practical rather than a theoretic science – as not only futile, but as intrinsically anarchistic and therefore extremely dangerous. Speaking of those revolutionaries who had embraced the Lockean paradigm, Burke wrote:

> They despise experience as the wisdom of unlettered men; and as for the rest, they have wrought under-ground a mine that will blow up at one grand explosion all examples of antiquity, all precedents, charters, and acts of parliament. They have "the rights of men." Against these there can be no prescription; against these no agreement is binding: these admit of no temperament, and no compromise: any thing withheld from their full demand is so much of fraud and injustice. Against these their rights of men let no government look for security in the length of its continuance, or in the justice and lenity of its administration. The objections of these speculatists, if its forms do not quadrate with their theories, are as valid against such an old and beneficent government as against the most violent tyranny, or the greenest usurpation. They are always at issue with governments, not on a question of abuse, but a question of competency, and a question of title.[239]

I have given only the briefest indication of how Burke played the Anarchy Game to defeat the Lockean paradigm. Although Burke's *Reflections* was the most skillful example of this tactic, the argument itself was exceedingly common. We also find it in the writings of Jeremy Bentham, who assailed natural rights and other elements of the Lockean paradigm as "anarchical fallacies."

---

[238] Edmund Burke, "Speech on American Taxation," in *Select Works of Edmund Burke*, ed. Edward Payne (Indianapolis: Liberty Fund, 1999), 1: 215.

[239] Edmund Burke, *Reflections on the Revolution in France*, in *Select Works*, 2: 149–50.

As Bentham, Burke, and many other critics saw the matter, the Lockean paradigm, in its attempt to justify the rights of resistance and revolution, cut the ground from under political obligation itself and thereby opened the door for anarchy.

Although many historians of political thought have called attention to the decline of natural-rights thinking after the French Revolution, relatively few have given sufficient emphasis to the role played by the Anarchy Game in this decline. We are sometimes told that social contract theory could pass muster only during an age that was historically naïve, and that as the discipline of history matured during the post-Enlightenment era, social contract theory died a well-deserved death. A similar explanation attributes the decline of the Lockean paradigm to the rejection of natural-law ethics in general, which was regarded as too naïve and simplistic to satisfy the more sophisticated demands of philosophers who had become sensitive to sociological and cultural variations.

All such explanations tend to view the Lockean paradigm as the product of an unsophisticated mind-set, a rationalistic approach that was rejected as various disciplines, such as history and sociology, revealed its shortcomings. This is obviously a complex issue; all I can do here is to note my disagreement with the ideological bias of these explanations. It is a bit too smug for a critic of the Lockean paradigm to accuse it (or any other political ideology with which one disagrees) of lacking in sophistication, as if its rejection was virtually inevitable with the progress of knowledge. Objections that would be raised by later critics of the Lockean paradigm (such as the historical implausibility of a social contract) were nothing new; on the contrary, we find them forcefully stated by Filmer and other early critics. Nor is it the case that defenders of the Lockean paradigm subscribed to an unrealistically static conception of human nature, one that failed to take historical and cultural variations into account.

We thus see that, contrary to the assertions of some historians, the Lockean paradigm was not a conservative ideology; on the contrary, it was radical to the core, and this radical edge was the primary aspect that eventually led to its decline. For example, after Britain defeated France in 1815, the Lockean paradigm was linked in the popular mind, if unfairly, to Robespierre, Saint-Just, and other Jacobins; any British philosopher who spoke of natural rights, a social contract, and other features of the Lockean paradigm ran the risk of being branded as a subversive revolutionary.

It is scarcely controversial to point out that the Lockean paradigm (especially its stress on the right of revolution) faced an inhospitable environment after the French Revolution; this is common knowledge among intellectual historians, including those nineteenth-century historians who spoke of the "spirit" of an age. But we are not dealing solely with a hostile climate of public opinion; in addition to this "external" factor, there was also the "internal" factor of how the Lockean paradigm fared within the discipline of political philosophy. This is where it is crucial to understand how the Anarchy Game was used against the Lockean paradigm. The defenders of natural rights were repeatedly accused of endorsing an approach to political philosophy that could not satisfactorily solve the problem of political obligation. This was condemned as a catastrophic failure that paved the way to anarchy.

# 6

## The Radical Edge of Liberalism

I

Line for line, probably no passage in the history of political thought has been subjected to more intense scrutiny than the second paragraph of the Declaration of Independence.[240] In this paragraph Thomas Jefferson brilliantly summarized the radical edge of natural-rights liberalism. Fully to appreciate this paragraph – to understand its historical precedents, presuppositions, and unstated implications – requires a good deal of reading and study. Every sentence, and virtually every phrase within every sentence, has a distinct significance and ancestry. It is indeed accurate to say that Jefferson "outlined a whole system of philosophy in a few sentences."[241] He summarized a radical ideology that is at once revolutionary and restrained. Violent revolution is justified, but only under special conditions that are carefully laid out.

Many eighteenth-century writers, such as Josiah Tucker, pointed to John Locke as the principal architect of the ideas that were used to justify the American Revolution.[242] Other writers, however, descried a line of "republican" thinkers who preceded Locke. For example, in his defense of the French Revolution, James Mackintosh claimed that Locke deserves praise not because

---

[240] Jefferson titled his rough draft, A *Declaration by the Representatives of the United States of America, in General Congress Assembled.* This title was used in all copies except the engrossed parchment copy, which Congress decreed should bear the title, *The Unanimous Declaration of the thirteen united States of America.* See Carl Becker, *The Declaration of Independence: A Study in the History of a Political Idea* (1922; New York: Vintage Books, 1970), 4–5.

[241] Dumas Malone, *Jefferson the Virginian* (Boston: Little, Brown, and Co., 1948), 224.

[242] See A *Treatise Concerning Civil Government,* 407–553. Tucker (407) intended his *Treatise* to be a reply to those admirers of John Locke "who think it impossible, that such a Man as Mr. Locke, ever meant to patronize those dangerous Consequences, which his Followers... have deduced from his Principles. They wish, therefore, that all the Censure might fall on the Disciples, not on the Master." Tucker argued that Locke was in fact largely responsible for the reckless and revolutionary ideas that had animated the American Revolution.

he was especially "bold and original" but because he explained and defended republican principles in a manner that was "temperate, sound, lucid, and methodical." Locke "deserves the immortal honor of having systematized and rendered popular the doctrines of civil and religious liberty."[243]

Differences of opinion about Locke's originality continue to this day, but his influence on the ideas expressed in the Declaration is difficult to deny.[244] Richard Henry Lee charged that Jefferson had copied some of the Declaration from Locke's *Second Treatise* and one critic charged that he "stole from *Locke's Essays*."[245] Jefferson denied this allegation, stating that he had "turned to neither book nor pamphlet while writing." It was not his intention "to invent new ideas altogether, and to offer no sentiment which had never been expressed before." Instead, the Declaration "was intended to be an expression of the American mind."[246]

These accounts are not necessarily incompatible. Lee was right in the sense that some passages in the Declaration can be found, nearly verbatim, in Locke's *Second Treatise*. Nevertheless, this doesn't mean that Jefferson consulted this book while drafting the Declaration. Jefferson was probably so familiar with the *Second Treatise* – which he once described as "perfect as far as it goes"[247] – that he unconsciously duplicated some of its wording. This, far more than if Jefferson had borrowed deliberately, testifies to the tremendous influence of John Locke on Jefferson and other eighteenth-century Americans.

II

The second paragraph of the Declaration is an excellent vehicle for exploring the radical edge of Lockean liberalism. But before we move to that paragraph, some remarks about the first paragraph will help us establish a context for the remainder of this discussion.

> When in the Course of human events, it becomes necessary for one people
> to dissolve the political bands which have connected them with another, and

---

[243] James Mackintosh, *Vindiciae Gallicae and Other Writings on the French Revolution*, ed. Donald Winch (Indianapolis: Liberty Fund, 2006), 135–36.

[244] The most ambitious attempt to deny Jefferson's influence in favor of Francis Hutcheson and other philosophers of the Scottish Enlightenment is Garry Wills, *Inventing America: Jefferson's Declaration of Independence* (Boston: Mariner Books, 2002). For a defense of the more traditional view, according to which Locke was a dominant influence, see Michael P. Zuckert, *The Natural Rights Republic: Studies in the Foundation of the American Political Tradition* (Notre Dame: University of Notre Dame Press, 1996).

[245] See Pauline Maier, *American Scripture: Making the Declaration of Independence* (New York: Vintage Books, 1988), 124–25, 171.

[246] "To Henry Lee" (May 18, 1825), in *Life and Selected Writings*, 719.

[247] "To Thomas Randolph" (May 30, 1790), in ibid., 497.

to assume among the Powers of the earth, the separate and equal station to which the Laws of Nature and of Nature's God entitle them, a decent respect to the opinions of mankind requires that they should declare the causes which impel them to the separation.

It should be kept in mind that the Declaration did not actually "declare" the independence of the American colonies from Great Britain; this occurred on July 2, 1776 (two days before the Declaration was approved by the Second Continental Congress), following a resolution by Virginia's Richard Henry Lee. It fell to Jefferson, as part of a five-man committee, to explain and justify this momentous decision, and this was his purpose in writing the Declaration. It declares, not the political separation per se, but "the causes which impel" Americans to make the separation.

Jefferson's use of the word "impel" is significant, as is his use of "necessary." Jefferson didn't feel the need to justify the Lockean paradigm, since he believed it was already the prevailing ideology in America, but many Americans were either undecided about independence or opposed it outright. The Declaration was addressed as much to these people as it was to "mankind" at large. Jefferson wished to convince fence sitters and skeptics that, contrary to assertions of critics, independence was not a reckless scheme hatched by hotheaded, seditious radicals who were eager to grab power for themselves, but was rendered necessary by the despotic actions of the British government.

This was not an easy case to make. Jefferson was writing a century after Locke had written his *Second Treatise*, and though Locke believed that revolution is theoretically warranted against any form of government that had degenerated into tyranny, his primary target was Sir Robert Filmer and other champions of absolute monarchy. Jefferson faced a different situation. Theories of absolute monarchy were a spent force in Britain after the "Glorious Revolution" of 1688, and they were never popular in the colonies. Even the most radical of American revolutionaries didn't claim that Britain was an absolute monarchy; on the contrary, in the years leading up to independence, their complaints were directed against the British Parliament, not against the King, and they frequently petitioned the King to protect them against a corrupt and predatory Parliament.

Because the British government was a constitutional monarchy of the sort that Locke himself had defended (the Glorious Revolution of 1688 was sometimes hailed as a triumph of Lockean principles), Jefferson had to adapt the Lockean paradigm accordingly. He needed to demonstrate that "The history of the present King of Great Britain is a history of repeated injuries and usurpations, all having in direct object the establishment of an absolute Tyranny over these States." Jefferson speaks of absolute *tyranny*, not of absolute

*monarchy* – thereby stressing a point that Locke had also made but not emphasized, namely that the people may overthrow *any* "Form of Government" that
has lapsed into tyranny.

This is why the most relevant part of the Declaration, so far as Jefferson's contemporaries were concerned, was not the second paragraph that commands
our attention today but rather the list of grievances. The Lockean paradigm
was widely accepted in both America and Britain, so Jefferson (unlike Locke)
didn't need to mount a philosophical defense of its principles. But even those
who work within the same theoretical paradigm will often disagree about
*how* its principles should be applied to a concrete problem. This was the
most serious problem that Jefferson faced. Unlike Locke, he didn't need to
convince his readers that revolution is justifiable in principle; instead, Jefferson needed to show that the relationship between America and Britain had
degenerated to the point where a revolution was justified – indeed, *necessary* – in this *particular* case, according to criteria spelled out in the Lockean
paradigm.

We now turn to the second paragraph:

> We hold these truths to be self-evident, that all men are created equal,
> that they are endowed by their Creator with certain unalienable Rights,
> that among these are Life, Liberty and the pursuit of Happiness. That to
> secure these rights, Governments are instituted among Men, deriving their
> just powers from the consent of the governed. That whenever any Form of
> Government becomes destructive of these ends, it is the Right of the People to
> alter or to abolish it, and to institute new Government, laying its foundations
> on such principles and organizing its powers in such form, as to them shall
> seem most likely to effect their Safety and Happiness. Prudence, indeed,
> will dictate that Governments long established should not be changed for
> light and transient causes; and accordingly all experience hath shown, that
> mankind are more disposed to suffer, while evils are sufferable, than to right
> themselves by abolishing the forms to which they are accustomed. But when
> a long train of abuses and usurpations, pursuing invariably the same Object,
> evinces a design to reduce them under absolute Despotism, it is their right, it
> is their duty, to throw off such Government, and to provide new Guards for
> their future security. Such has been the patient sufferance of these Colonies;
> and such is now the necessity which constrains them to alter their former
> Systems of Government. The history of the present King of Great Britain is
> a history of repeated injuries and usurpations, all having in direct object the
> establishment of an absolute Tyranny over these States. To prove this, let
> Facts be submitted to a candid world.

Let us now consider some key ideas in this paragraph.

*We hold these truths to be self-evident . . .*

As with every other clause in the second paragraph, historians have explored in painstaking detail what Jefferson meant by "self-evident." One possibility is that Jefferson was referring to propositions that are *epistemologically* self-evident. Such propositions do not stand in need of demonstration (indeed, they are incapable of it), because their truth can be grasped immediately by any person who understands what they mean. All reasoning must start somewhere – not all truths can be proven, for this would lead to an infinite regress – and these starting points, or epistemological axioms, are self-evident truths.

Those commentators who defend this interpretation often invoke the fact that Jefferson subscribed to the "moral sense" theory that had been defended by Francis Hutcheson and other luminaries of the Scottish Enlightenment, and they go on to argue that Jefferson believed that certain moral truths can be immediately apprehended by means of this moral sense.

We needn't examine the details of moral sense theory to appreciate the implausibility of this account. It is true that some philosophers before Jefferson (including some who did not believe in a moral sense) had defended the notion of self-evident truths in ethics (e.g., the maxim that we should pursue good and avoid evil), and some extended this notion into the realm of political theory. According to Algernon Sidney, the doctrine of the natural freedom of mankind (the "principle of natural liberty") is an "evident truth as seems to be planted in the hearts of all men"; this truth has "its roots in common sense." In addition, "nothing can be more evident, than if many had been created, they had been all equal, unless God had given a preference to one." These are among "the common notions agreed by all mankind."[248]

Likewise, John Locke (who was not a moral sense theorist) characterized the doctrine of natural equality as "evident in it self,"[249] so this might support the claim that Jefferson was making an epistemological claim. This interpretation might be credible if Jefferson had confined his self-evident truths to the inalienable rights to "Life, Liberty and the pursuit of Happiness," but he doesn't stop here. He extends the list to include the purpose for which "Governments are instituted among Men," the doctrine that governments derive their "just powers from the consent of the governed," and "the Right of the People to alter or to abolish" an unjust government. It transcends the limits of credibility to contend that Jefferson viewed *all* of "these truths" as epistemologically self-evident, as if they should be accepted without argument.

[248] Sidney, *Discourses Concerning Government*, 12, 11, 9, 24, 52.
[249] Locke, *Two Treatises*, II: §5.

Perhaps the most compelling argument against the interpretation we are here considering has nothing to do with philosophy. It has to do with the probable fact that Jefferson wasn't even responsible for the term "self-evident." In the original draft of the Declaration, Jefferson wrote, "We hold these truths to be sacred & undeniable. . . . " In this draft the words "sacred & undeniable" are crossed out and "self-evident" substituted in their place. Since this editorial change appears to be in the handwriting of Benjamin Franklin (who served on the five-man committee responsible for drafting the Declaration), most historians credit him with the term "self-evident."[250]

Jefferson later characterized alterations made by other committee members as "merely verbal" and insisted that they did not fundamentally change the meaning of what he wished to say.[251] This indicates that Jefferson didn't view the change from "sacred and undeniable" to "self-evident" as anything more than a stylistic improvement, which doesn't make a lot of sense if we interpret "self-evident" in a technical philosophical sense.

The most plausible interpretation is rather mundane. In stating that "We hold these truths to be self-evident" (or "undeniable," as in the original version), the Declaration was offering these as the premises on which the case for independence was based; they were principles shared not only by revolutionaries but by Americans at large. "These truths" were therefore taken for granted so far as the Declaration was concerned; this was the point of saying *We hold* these truths to be self-evident.

*that all men are created equal . . .*

This clause refers to *moral* equality. As it pertains to political theory, the doctrine of natural equality means that no person has a natural right to rule over others. When John Locke claimed that *"all Men by Nature are equal,"* he was referring to a state of nature "wherein all the Power and Jurisdiction is reciprocal, no one having more than another."[252]

The doctrine of natural equality has a long ancestry in Western political thought and is by no means unique to the Lockean paradigm. According to A.J. Carlyle, the emergence of this doctrine marks "the dividing-line between the ancient and the modern political theory."

---

[250] For an authoritative version of the "original Rough draught," see *The Papers of Thomas Jefferson*, ed. Julian P. Boyd (Princeton: Princeton University Press, 1950), 1: 423–24.

[251] See Zuckert, *Natural Rights Republic*, 53.

[252] Locke, *Two Treatises*, II: §54, §4. In view of some feminist criticisms of the Lockean paradigm, it should be noted that "men," as used by Locke and Jefferson, refers to the human species, not to males specifically. Lockeans did not invest females with fewer *natural* rights than males; such differences as they did defend were conceived as civil (or political), not natural.

There is no change in political theory so startling in its completeness as the change from the theory of Aristotle to the later philosophical view represented by Cicero and Seneca. Over against Aristotle's view of the natural inequality of human nature we find set out the theory of the natural equality of human nature.[253]

The doctrine of the natural equality of humankind is far more than a pleasant platitude. It has profound implications for political theory generally and political obligation specifically, for it places the burden of proof on anyone who claims a right that is denied to others. The relationship between ruler and ruled, wherein a sovereign has a right to command and his or her subjects a duty to obey, appears to establish a condition of *unequal* rights, and this raises the question: How did a sovereign acquire an *exclusive* right to act as the final arbiter in matters pertaining to coercion?

There are two basic ways to approach this problem: The first is to assert that the superior–subordinate relationship is *natural.* It may be that some people, by virtue of their superior strength or intelligence, are naturally entitled to command others. (This is a variant of the "might makes right" theory that Plato attributed to some sophists.) Or it may be that God has *directly* authorized some people to rule over others. (This was the essence of the "divine right of kings," as defended by Sir Robert Filmer.)

The second approach (which typifies classical liberalism), denies the natural status of political obligation and contends instead that the natural political condition of humankind is one of equality. Hence, if there is no such thing as a natural right to rule, we must explain how, beginning from this condition of equality, we can justify a political society in which some people have a right to command and others have a duty to obey. This is the role played by *consent* in the Lockean paradigm. Consent, when manifested in a "social contract," is the vehicle that takes us from the natural equality of a state of nature to the political obligations of a civil society.

*that they are endowed by their Creator with certain unalienable Rights . . .*

That God is the ultimate source of moral principles (in some sense) was as true for a deist like Thomas Jefferson as it was for conventional Christians. Earlier in the Declaration, in a display of vintage deistic rhetoric, Jefferson refers to "the laws of nature and of nature's God." Moreover, in his original draft, after stating that "all men are created equal and independent," Jefferson adds that "from that equal creation they derive rights inherent and inalienable." This

---

[253] A.J. and R.W. Carlyle, *A History of Medieval Political Theory in the West* (Edinburgh: Blackwood, 1950), 1: 8.

formulation (which Jefferson probably changed for stylistic reasons) is more philosophically precise than the final version, because it expresses the common deistic belief that God, in his role as the creator of nature, is the remote (or ultimate) source of moral principles, whereas nature itself, as revealed by reason, is the proximate source.

Jefferson subscribed to a theory of natural law that was exceedingly popular among the "enlightened" intellectuals of his day, and he did so in a manner that would not alienate or offend most Christians. When, over a century earlier, the Christian Hugo Grotius suggested that the fundamental principles of justice "would have a degree of validity even if we should concede that which cannot be conceded without the utmost wickedness, that there is no God, or that the affairs of men are of no concern to him,"[254] he was not breaking new ground. For many rationalistic theologians (especially the Catholic followers of Thomas Aquinas), this was a logical implication of a belief in natural laws discernible by reason alone, without the aid of the Bible and other appeals to special revelation.

Let us now consider Jefferson's mention of "unalienable rights." Unalienable (or "inalienable"[255]) rights stood in contrast to alienable rights, so we might wonder why Jefferson found it necessary to refer to this rather technical distinction, especially in a political document that was intended for popular consumption. Why didn't Jefferson simply speak of "rights" in general, instead of focusing on inalienable rights?

Inalienable rights were regarded as fundamental corollaries of a person's essential nature, especially his or her reason and volition, so these rights could never be surrendered or transferred to another person (including a government), even with the agent's consent. People can no more transfer their inalienable rights than they can transfer their moral agency, their ability to reason, and so forth. This means that inalienable rights could never have been transferred to government in a social contract, so no government can properly claim jurisdiction over them. Consequently, any government that systematically violates inalienable rights is necessarily tyrannical and vulnerable to revolution. As Francis Hutcheson put it, "Unalienable Rights are essential Limitations to all Governments."[256]

According to this theory, legitimate disagreements may occur between subjects and rulers when *alienable* rights are involved, but no such disputes are

---

[254] Grotius, *Prolegomena*, 10.

[255] Both "unalienable" and "inalienable" were in common use during the eighteenth century. Jefferson used "inalienable" in his original draft; how and why this ended up as "unalienable" in the final parchment version is a matter of conjecture. In any case, both variations mean the same thing, and I will follow the modern practice of referring to such rights as "inalienable."

[256] Francis Hutcheson, *An Inquiry Concerning Moral Good and Evil*, in *British Moralists*, 1: 171.

possible between people of good will when *inalienable* rights are involved. No government can claim jurisdiction over inalienable rights, because they are incapable of alienation and so could never have been delegated or surrendered to a government in the first place. This means there can be no excuse for the systematic violation of inalienable rights. This is the bright-line test that enables us to distinguish the incidental or well-intentioned violation of rights, which even just governments may occasionally commit, from the deliberate and inexcusable violations of a tyrannical government.

This is why Jefferson focused on inalienable rights in his effort to fasten the charge of tyranny on the British government. The violation of inalienable rights was a defining characteristic of a tyrannical government, and only against such a government is revolution clearly justified.

*that among these are Life, Liberty and the pursuit of Happiness . . .*

The controversy over this clause, which has been considerable, is owing not to what it says but to what it fails to say. Why did Jefferson omit "property" from his trinity of rights? Could it be, as some historians have argued, that Jefferson was a proto-socialist who did not hold property rights in the same esteem as many of his American contemporaries?

The first thing to note is that Jefferson did mention "property," along with "life" and "liberty," in his other writings, such as these: "The End of Government would be defeated by the British Parliament exercising a Power over the Lives, the Property, and the Liberty of the American Subject; who are not, and, from the local Circumstances, cannot, be there represented,"[257] and "To obtain Redress of the Grievances, which threaten Destruction of the Lives, Liberty, and Property, of his Majesty's Subjects."[258]

The second thing to note is that Jefferson refers specifically to inalienable rights, and he states that "among these" inalienable rights are the rights to life, liberty, and the pursuit of happiness – thereby indicating that his list is not exhaustive. Why he did not include property in his partial list is a matter of conjecture, but the reason probably had to do with the fact that the term "property" had two different meanings in Jefferson's day. Property was an inalienable right according to one meaning, whereas it was an alienable right according to another meaning. Given this ambiguity, to refer to property as an inalienable right would have been confusing without further explanation.

Today when we speak of property, we usually mean a thing or object that is owned, something to which we have a moral or legal right to use and dispose

[257] "Instructions by the Virginia Convention to Their Delegates in Congress, 1774," in Boyd, *The Papers of Thomas Jefferson*, I: 141–42.
[258] "Continental Association of 20 October 1774," in Boyd, *The Papers of Thomas Jefferson*, I: 150.

of, such as a car or an acre of land. This car, we say, is my property; I own it; I have a right to use it, give it away, sell it, or destroy it.

During the seventeenth and eighteenth centuries, the word "property" was often used in a broader sense to mean rightful dominion, or moral jurisdiction, over something. As the Lockean William Wollaston put it during the early eighteenth century, "To have the property of any thing and to have the sole right of using and disposing of it are the same thing: they are equipollent expressions." The broad conception permitted Wollaston to speak of a man's "*property* in his own happiness."²⁵⁹

Thus whereas we would say "This land is my property," earlier liberals were more likely to say, "I have a property in this land." When John Locke argued that the proper function of government is to protect property, he explained that, by "property," he meant a person's "Life, Liberty, and Estate."²⁶⁰ This usage is what Locke had in mind when he wrote that "every Man has a *Property* in his own *Person*."²⁶¹

In Jefferson's day both meanings of property were common; the older usage, according to which I would be said to have property *in* this land, was giving way to the modern usage, according to which this land would be said *to be* my property. This dual usage was discussed by James Madison in 1792:

> This term [property] in its particular application means "that dominion which one man claims and exercises over the external things of the world, in exclusion of every other individual."
>
> In its larger and juster meaning, it embraces everything to which a man may attach a value and have a right, and *which leave to every one else the like advantage.*
>
> In the former sense, a man's land, or merchandize, or money is called his property.
>
> In the latter sense, a man has a property in his opinions and the free communication of them.
>
> He has a property of peculiar value in his religious opinions, and in the profession and practice dictated by them.

---

²⁵⁹ William Wollaston, *The Religion of Nature Delineated*, 7th ed. (London J. and P. Knapton, 1750), 243, 252. This book, which was originally published in 1722, was a best seller in its day, going through eight editions in a few decades and selling over 10,000 copies. For additional details, see George H. Smith, "William Wollaston on Property Rights," *Journal of Libertarian Studies*, vol. 2, no. 3 (1978).

²⁶⁰ For example, see Locke, *Two Treatises*, II: §87.

²⁶¹ Ibid., II: §27.

He has a property very dear to him in the safety and liberty of his person.

He has an equal property in the free use of his faculties and free choice of the objects on which to employ them.

In a word, as a man is said to have a right to his property, he may be equally said to have a property in his rights.[262]

Property in the broad sense – that is, the right to exercise moral jurisdiction over one's person, labor, and the fruits of one's labor – was viewed as an inalienable right; to have moral jurisdiction over that which is essential to one's survival is inextricably linked to moral agency and so can never be transferred or surrendered. But this is not true of property in the narrower sense of something that is owned; one can clearly transfer one's title to land or other material goods. Indeed, the title to a certain amount of property, collected in the form of taxes, was said to have been implicitly surrendered in the Lockean version of the social contract, since this was needed for a government to function. It would thus have been confusing for Jefferson to have included "property" in his partial list of inalienable rights. He would have needed to draw the same distinction that Madison did between two meanings of "property," and this would have transformed the Declaration from a brief manifesto into a philosophical treatise.

Given other statements by Jefferson, there is no reason to think he would have disagreed with this very Lockean conclusion by Madison:

> Government is instituted to protect property of every sort; as well that which lies in the various rights of individuals, as that which the term particularly expresses. This being the end of government, that alone is a *just* government which *impartially* secures to every man, whatever is his *own*.[263]

*That to secure these rights, Governments are instituted among Men, deriving their just powers from the consent of the governed . . .*

This is perhaps the best-known part of the Lockean paradigm. It involves the notion of a "social contract," which is one of the most controversial aspects of natural-rights liberalism. The Declaration does not specifically endorse any particular version of social contract theory. In Locke, there is no reciprocal contract (or compact) per se between the people and a government. Instead of this "pact of submission" (as it was sometimes called), there is only a pact of association among the people themselves, after which a government is

---

[262] "Property," *National Gazette*, March 29, 1792, in *Madison: Writings*, 515.
[263] Ibid.

entrusted with certain powers that have been delegated to it by society in its corporate capacity. Jefferson, however, did believe that the colonies had entered into a compact with the British government. Referring to Jefferson's *Summary View*, Dumas Malone observes that Jefferson "claimed that there was a compact between the colonists and the King which was embodied, partly at least, in the early charters."[264] Hence, in the list of grievances, Jefferson attempted to show that the King had violated the terms of this agreement and thereby absolved the Americans of their duty of allegiance.

### III

Having concisely laid the foundation for the right of revolution, Jefferson continues as follows:

> That whenever any Form of Government becomes destructive of these ends, it is the Right of the People to alter or to abolish it, and to institute new Government, laying its foundations on such principles and organizing its powers in such form, as to them shall seem most likely to effect their Safety and Happiness. Prudence, indeed, will dictate that Governments long established should not be changed for light and transient causes; and accordingly all experience hath shown, that mankind are more disposed to suffer, while evils are sufferable, than to right themselves by abolishing the forms to which they are accustomed. But when a long train of abuses and usurpations, pursuing invariably the same Object, evinces a design to reduce them under absolute Despotism, it is their right, it is their duty, to throw off such Government, and to provide new Guards for their future security.

The right of revolution is the radical edge of Lockean liberalism, and this is what so disturbed its critics, even those who were sympathetic to its liberal principles in other areas. It is therefore important to explore this right in more detail.

The right of revolution differs from the right of resistance.[265] The right of resistance pertains to particular unjust laws, or to the illegal enforcement of laws, whereas the right of revolution pertains to the complete overthrow of an established government. These rights, though closely related, are conceptually distinct, and I shall first consider the right of resistance before moving on to the right of revolution.

---

[264] Malone, *Jefferson the Virginian*, 185.
[265] On this topic generally, see the account in Pauline Maier, *From Resistance to Revolution: Colonial Radicals and the Development of American Opposition to Britain, 1765–1776* (New York: W.W. Norton & Co., 1991), 27–48.

There are three traditional positions on our duty to obey the laws of a legitimate government. The first, which is called "passive obedience," is affiliated with various theories of absolute sovereignty, such as that defended by Thomas Hobbes. According to the doctrine of passive obedience, every citizen has a duty to obey every governmental law, whatever his personal opinion of that law may be. To maintain otherwise, to uphold the right of each person to decide which laws he or she will or will not obey, will, according to the absolutist, destroy the foundation of law itself and plunge society into chaos and conflict – that anarchistic state of nature which Hobbes described as a "war of every man against every man" where life is "nasty, brutish, and short."

The second position, known as "passive resistance" or "passive disobedience," was popular among seventeenth century Quakers and other religious dissenters, who traced this tactic to the early Christian community in Rome. This doctrine asserts the right to disobey an unjust law, especially in matters of religious conscience, but it further affirms one's duty to submit to the legally prescribed punishment. In other words, one may resist an unjust law by refusing to obey it, but one may not resist the enforcement of that law.

Defenders of this view had a viable response to their absolutist critics, who contended that the right of resistance undermines the authority of all laws, whether just or unjust. Passive resistance permits the individual to decide which laws are unjust without endangering the entire legal order. The individual resister, by submitting to legal punishment, is able to register his or her protest – or to give his or her testimony, as the Quakers liked to say – without undercutting the public authority of law itself. In its modern form, this approach is often called "nonviolent resistance" or "civil disobedience."

The third approach is the theory of active, or violent, resistance. This theory asserts the right of every individual to disobey unjust laws and to forcibly resist the implementation of such laws. In the American revolutionary tradition, and throughout radical republicanism generally, this is what is denoted by the term "the right of resistance."

American radicals believed that certain rights, if ignored or violated by a government, can legitimately be defended with physical force. They found a justification for this doctrine not only in the writings of John Locke but also in the writings of his contemporary, Algernon Sidney, according to whom it is "folly" to say that he who has a right or obligation to disobey an unjust law ought nevertheless to submit to punishment. If a law is just, then we ought to be punished for disobeying it. But, to quote Sidney, "no one can be obliged to suffer for that which he ought not to do, because he who pretends to command has not so far an authority."[266] A government exceeds its proper authority whenever it enacts an unjust law, so it has no legitimate right to punish those who disobey. I am no more obligated to obey an unjust law of government than I am to obey a decree of a pirate; indeed, when a government repeatedly issues unjust laws, it reduces itself to the same moral level and deserves the same lack of respect.

Opponents of the right of resistance argued that such a right will undercut the authority of all governments and legal orders. The theory that everyone may decide when a law is unjust, and so resist its enforcement, reduces to anarchy in practice, since people will simply obey laws they like and disobey laws they dislike.

Contrary to the charge that the right of resistance will foment the overthrow of governments and the dissolution of social order, defenders of this right claimed that it will often have precisely the opposite effect. There is a natural "lust for power" in all humans; this is the desire to control others so they behave as we think they should. Those in government are especially susceptible to the corruption of power, because government is institutionalized coercion. Ultimately, the only way to check the abuse of power is through active resistance. Only if rulers understand that they can go only so far, and no farther, will they curb their insatiable desire for more power.

The right of resistance therefore functions as a kind of safety valve, alerting rulers that they are overstepping their legitimate boundaries. If this right is denied, if the abuse of power is allowed to grow unchecked until it becomes tyrannical, then no remedy will be available except a complete revolution. The right of resistance provides citizens with another option. By resisting unjust laws before the onset of total tyranny, we may be able to reverse the growth of power, thereby avoiding tyranny – and the need for revolution.

This is more or less how John Locke viewed this issue. The "state of Mankind is not so miserable that they are not capable of using this Remedy, till it be too late to look for any." It does no good to tell people that "they may expect Relief, when it is too late, and the evil is past Cure." Locke continues:

> This is in effect no more than to bid them first be Slaves, and then to take care of their Liberty; and when their Chains are on, tell them, they may act like Freemen. This, if barely so, is rather Mockery than Relief; and Men can never be secure from Tyranny, if there be no means to escape it, till they are perfectly under it: And therefore it is that they have not only a Right to get out of it, but to prevent it.[267]

---

[266] Sidney, *Discourses Concerning Government*, 438.
[267] Locke, *Two Treatises*, II: §220.

The classic objection to the right of resistance – that it will undercut the authority of all law – was answered by pointing out that law can retain its authority only so long as it is generally regarded as just. When a government enacts and enforces unjust laws, it rebels against the principles of natural right and undercuts its own authority. Locke, Jefferson, and others never tired of pointing out that tyrannical rulers, not those who resist them, are the true rebels. As Locke put it, "For Rebellion being an Opposition, not to Persons, but Authority, which is founded only in the Constitutions and Laws of the Government; those, whoever they be, who by force break through, and by force justify their violation of them, are truly and properly *Rebels*."[268]

The ruler must obey the same laws that are constitutionally prescribed for everyone else. Thus, whenever a ruler exceeds his or her constitutional limits, it is that ruler who rebels against the legal order and undermines legitimate authority. The right of resistance, therefore, is essential for preserving the authority of law, because it demands that everyone must abide by it, including those in power.

John Locke and others in his tradition believed that violent resistance is inappropriate so long as citizens have recourse to an impartial judiciary, where their grievances will be fairly adjudicated. Generally speaking, seeking redress in a court of law applied to those cases where government agents (or "lesser magistrates," as Locke called them) exceeded their constitutional powers when attempting to enforce the law. Locke gives the example of a lesser magistrate who serves a writ, or warrant, to a man in the street. This may be perfectly justifiable, but the same is not true if that magistrate attempts to enforce the writ by invading a man's home. In this case, the agent may be forcibly resisted, because, so far as the homeowner can tell, his life is in imminent danger. Therefore, I may forcibly resist the invasion of a government agent, just as I may resist the actions of a housebreaking thief.

In this and other cases in which my life is threatened, resistance is justified, because there is no time for a legal appeal. As Locke repeatedly emphasizes, a court of law cannot help a dead man. Moreover, we do not have direct insight into the minds and motives of other people. According to Locke, if a man is willing to break into my home and seize my property, we may reasonably assume that he is also willing to kill me, if he deems it necessary. Any such invasion can reasonably be interpreted as a threat against my life, whatever the real intentions of the invader may be. If it should turn out that my interpretation is mistaken, then it is the invader who should bear the consequence of this mistake, for it is he who took the invasive action.

[268] Ibid, II: §226.

In contrast to resistance, revolution involves the complete overthrow of a government and its replacement by a new government. This theme dominated much of political philosophy during the seventeenth and eighteenth centuries, and its influence was profound. Those centuries witnessed the English Civil Wars of the 1640s, which overthrew the Stuart monarchy and led to the execution of Charles I; the Glorious Revolution of 1688, which again overthrew the Stuarts, but this time for good; the American Revolution of 1776; and the French Revolution of 1789.

All of these revolutions were based to some degree on the theory of natural rights, social contract, and government by consent. Together, these theories constituted the radical libertarian ideology of their day. The theory of natural rights, which was the foundation of this ideology, was widely denounced by critics as the highway to revolution and anarchy. When the utilitarian philosopher Jeremy Bentham denounced the doctrine of natural rights as "nonsense upon stilts," he did so in part because he believed that no government can survive when confronted with a doctrine that sanctions the right of revolution.

This does not mean that every natural-rights philosopher necessarily sanctioned the right of revolution. The pivotal issue was the social contract, according to which individuals in a state of nature voluntarily join together in civil society and delegate to government certain powers that are necessary to protect their rights. When a government abuses that trust, when it systematically violates rights, it becomes tyrannical and may be coercively replaced through revolution.

As John Locke explained, no person would voluntarily submit to a government in order to become worse off than he or she would be without government. This insight provides a rough test that enables us to judge the legitimacy of government activities. We submit to government in order to protect our natural rights of life, liberty, and property from other people who may wish to violate those rights. When these rights are systematically violated by a government whose only justification is the protection of rights, then that government delegitimates itself and may be overthrown. Or, as Locke said about monarchy, a tyrannical king "unkings" himself and thereby reverts to the status of a common outlaw or thug.

As used within the Lockean paradigm, social contract theory specifies criteria by which we can judge when a revolution is justified. Unless it can be shown that reasonable people would consent to particular laws as a means of protecting their life, liberty, and property, then those laws are unjust, and any government that enforces them is theoretically ripe for revolution. This is what so disturbed the opponents of contract theory. Virtually no government, as they astutely pointed out, can pass this test, so all governments will be vulnerable to revolution.

Foes of contract theory included the reactionary defenders of absolute monarchy, but they also included conservative liberals, such as David Hume, Adam Smith, and Edmund Burke, who were sympathetic to liberal principles. It is instructive to look at what some of these philosophers had to say about revolution. According to David Hume, "in the case of enormous tyranny and oppression, 'tis lawful to take arms even against supreme power. . . . But though this general principle be authorized by common sense, and the practice of all ages, 'tis certainly impossible for the laws, or even for philosophy, to establish any particular rule, by which we may know when resistance is lawful; and decide all controversies, which may arise on that subject."[269]

In other words, though Hume conceded the need for revolution in extreme cases, he did not believe that the criteria for a legitimate revolution can be specified with any degree of precision. As Hume saw the matter, our allegiance to a government is determined by its utility, or usefulness, for most members of society; so no revolution is justified, even against a corrupt government, unless that government has degenerated into a hopeless and irremediable tyranny.

Adam Smith held the same view. Government is based on utility, not on consent, so the harm caused by a government must significantly outweigh its usefulness before revolution is justified. According to Smith, "No government is quite perfect, but it is better to submit to some inconveniences than make attempts against it." Speaking of the English government, Smith says that many "foolish laws" have been made, many "improper taxes" have been imposed, and many "imprudent wars" have been entered into – but these are not sufficient to justify revolution. Indeed, "many such things may be done without entitling the people to rise in arms." When, then, is a revolution justified? Smith's answer, like that of Hume, is based on utility: "Wherever the confusion which must arise on an overthrow of the established government is less than the mischief of allowing it to continue, then resistance is proper and allowable."[270]

This criterion is rather vague, and intentionally so, but Smith does get more specific. When the abuse of power becomes "gross, flagrant, and palpable," then armed resistance is allowable. As an example of such gross, flagrant, and palpable abuse, Smith cites a tax that absorbs one-third of the people's wealth.[271] Any government that would impose such a burdensome tax has obviously crossed the line into tyranny and may be forcibly opposed.

---

[269] Hume, *Treatise of Human Nature*, 563.
[270] Smith, *Lectures on Jurisprudence*, 435, 326, 320–21.
[271] Ibid., 326.

We must remember that this one-third test, which is cited by a number of eighteenth-century writers, represented the thinking of moderate liberals on revolution. There was a good reason for this. As Herbert Spencer was to point out in the following century, feudal serfs were required to turn over one-third of their produce to their overlord. This means that any citizen who is required to pay a tax rate greater than one-third is worse off in this respect than the lowly serf.

Who has the right to judge when revolution is justified? This was the most difficult of all questions for proponents of revolution, for it seems to open a Pandora's Box of problems. Some theorists argued that a legitimate revolution against monarchy must win the approval of lesser magistrates, such as a parliament or the nobility. The position of John Locke was more radical than this. To the question, Who shall judge if the government has violated its trust and should be overthrown? Locke replied, *"The People shall be Judge."*[272]

This response is more complex than it may first appear; it is based on Locke's sociological view that most people simply prefer to be left alone and to live in peace. (This, after all, is the reason they agree to submit to government in the first place.) The vast majority of people have no desire to engage in the tumult and destruction of revolution. Therefore, as Locke puts it, "For till the mischief be grown general, and the ill-designs of the Rulers become visible, or their attempts sensible to the greater part, the People, who are more disposed to suffer, than right themselves by resistance are not apt to stir."[273] We find the same position expressed with similar words in Jefferson's Declaration: "All experience hath shown that mankind are more disposed to suffer, while evils are sufferable, than to right themselves by abolishing the forms to which they are accustomed."

This seemingly innocuous observation has important implications. It suggests that large numbers of people would never engage in revolutionary activity unless their government had pushed them beyond the limits of endurance. According to some British observers, the American Revolution had been instigated by a small band of malcontents who used propaganda to dupe many of the common people into joining their cause. Americans responded with the claim that their revolution enjoyed mass support; in the words of General Charles Lee, it was a "people's war." Locke's argument supports this claim on sociological grounds. He thinks it quite absurd to suppose that most people would uproot their lives, endanger their families, and take up arms against a

---

[272] Locke, *Two Treatises*, II: §240.
[273] Ibid., II: §230.

powerful adversary, unless they felt compelled to do so. The mere fact of mass revolution, therefore, constitutes presumptive evidence against a government.

This also relates to an important proviso that was repeatedly stressed by American revolutionaries. A revolution, however justified on moral grounds, should never be undertaken without a reasonable expectation of success. This is why mass support is necessary. Without it, a revolution is bound to fail, and a failed revolution will invariably make things even worse than they were originally. It is therefore highly irresponsible to foment a revolution without adequate preparations – most notably, gathering the support and cooperation of a sufficiently large number of people, without whom no revolution can hope to succeed.

Given this base of support, when may resistance properly turn to revolution? When may we move from resistance against particular laws and seek the complete overthrow of a government? This was a crucial problem for American radicals, who had been involved in resistance activities for thirteen years prior to the Declaration of Independence. Many Americans, even some who approved of resistance, questioned whether the situation was bad enough to justify outright revolution. Therefore, this issue was of great concern to Jefferson, who made it a major theme of the Declaration. This concern is especially evident in the second paragraph.

As we have seen, Jefferson explicitly ties the right of revolution to the violation of inalienable rights. But the violation of inalienable rights justified resistance as well as revolution, so we are still left with the problem of deciding when to turn from limited resistance to unlimited revolution. Jefferson deals with this problem as follows: After stating that governments "should not be changed for light and transient causes," Jefferson says: "But when a long train of abuses and usurpations, pursuing invariably the same object, evinces a design to reduce them under absolute despotism, it is their right, it is their duty, to throw off such government, and to provide new guards for their future security."

This passage, which closely follows a passage from Locke,[274] constituted a crucial step in justifying revolution. Radical republicans acknowledged that no government is perfect and that even the best of governments may sometimes engage in inappropriate or unjust activities. Although resistance may be appropriate in such cases, especially if inalienable rights are involved, revolution is not justified when one is dealing with incidental and unconnected violations. Government must commit unjust acts as a matter of policy in an

---

[274] Ibid., II: §225.

effort to deprive citizens of their freedom, or, as Jefferson says, "to reduce them under absolute despotism."

Here, of course, we encounter the problem of mind reading. We cannot enter into the thoughts of rulers, so how can we know if they intend to establish despotism? Jefferson summarizes the typical answer to this question when he says, "But when a long train of abuses and usurpations, pursuing invariably the same object, evinces a design to reduce them under absolute despotism. . . ." In other words, we infer the intentions of rulers from their actions. If we have empirical evidence of a continuous and systematic violation of inalienable rights, then we may reasonably infer a deliberate design by government to violate those rights. At a certain point, it simply becomes unreasonable to excuse such violations as the honest mistakes or misunderstandings of well-intentioned rulers.

We thus see how the right of revolution had been worked out in considerable detail by those who worked within the Lockean paradigm. Indeed, the justification of this right was the ultimate purpose in Locke's *Second Treatise*, which makes it a radical document even by modern standards. An appreciation of this radical edge is essential if we are to understand the outcry against natural rights and social contract theory, why the Lockean paradigm was disliked even by many liberals, and why utilitarianism emerged as the preferred alternative in nineteenth-century liberalism.

To fully appreciate how the themes of resistance and revolution were integrated into liberal thought, we need to examine the liberal conception of freedom in more detail. That is the subject of the next chapter.

# 7

## The Idea of Freedom

### I

"No word has received more different significations and has struck minds in so many ways as has liberty."[275] This passage from Montesquieu's *The Spirit of the Laws* (1748) was echoed several decades later by Edmund Burke: "Of all the loose terms in the world liberty is the most indefinite."[276] And in 1895 the liberal historian Lord Acton said that liberty "is an idea of which there are two hundred definitions, and . . . this wealth of interpretation has caused more bloodshed than anything, except theology."[277]

"Liberty" and "freedom" (the words are normally used interchangeably) have received the nominal endorsement of most political philosophers over the past several centuries. Even the defenders of absolutism have embraced these terms in an effort to exploit their positive connotations. The enemies of liberal individualism, while repudiating its notion of personal liberty as vulgar or simplistic, have represented themselves as the standard-bearers of a more sophisticated kind of authentic freedom.

When Rousseau declared that people can be forced to be free through obedience to the general will, he presented himself not as freedom's enemy, but as its friend. Hegel, another self-proclaimed champion of liberty, predicted that the "subjective freedom" of the individual would inevitably evolve into the "objective freedom" of the organismic state, which would represent the "divine idea as it exists on earth." When Marx condemned freedom of exchange

[275] Montesquieu, *The Spirit of the Laws*, trans. and ed. Anne M. Cohler, Basia Miller, and Harold Stone (Cambridge: Cambridge University Press, 1989), 154.
[276] Edmund Burke, "A Letter to M. Dupont," *Edmund Burke: Selected Writings and Speeches*, ed. Peter J. Stanlis (Washington, D.C.: Regnery, 1963), 503.
[277] Lord Acton, "The Study of History," in *Selected Writings of Lord Acton*, vol. 2, *Essays in the Study and Writing of History*, ed. J. Rufus Fears (Indianapolis: Liberty Classics, 1986), 523.

as economic slavery and the personal rights of liberal individualism as an ideological smokescreen for exploitation, he did so in the name of a new and better kind of freedom. His was the freedom of scientific socialism, a freedom that would liberate everyone from the oppressive forces of alienation, poverty, and class domination.

Thus have the terms "liberty" and "freedom" been used as a kind of linguistic imprimatur – a stamp of approval affixed by philosophers to their own political doctrines. Montesquieu was quite correct when he spoke of the many significations of the word "liberty"; so was Burke when he referred to it as a loose and indefinite term – but Acton's estimate of 200 definitions is somewhat misleading.

To define a concept is to state its *fundamental* characteristics, those that best distinguish it from other concepts – so Acton's estimate, if correct, would mean that the word "liberty" has been used to signify 200 different concepts. This is highly unlikely. True, "liberty" has been used with many different *meanings* throughout the history of political thought, but these can be reduced to a fairly small number of basic *concepts*. We should not confuse the *nominal* meaning of a word, which is stated in its definition, with its *contextual* meaning, which is determined by the meaning of cognate concepts to which it is closely related.

The meaning of "liberty" can vary considerably even among philosophers who operate from the same nominal definition. Liberty is a complex idea, one that is abstracted from other abstractions rather than from the perceptual concretes of the external world. Liberty does not refer to a physical object or an attribute, or to a relationship that can be described in physical terms. It is an analytical concept that enables us to interpret and understand social relationships from a particular point of view.

Freedom is something we understand with our minds, not something we see with our eyes. It cannot be defined ostensively: There is nothing we can point to and say "See, that is what I mean by freedom." It must be defined in terms of other concepts – such as "coercion," "property" and "rights" – so its contextual meaning will vary according to how these cognate concepts are defined within a particular theoretical system.

Suppose we agree to define "freedom" as "the absence of coercion" or as "the right to use and dispose of one's property." Such definitions will typically fragment into a variety of interpretations, depending on how we define the cognate concepts of "coercion," "property," and "rights." If, for example, a socialist considers the market transactions of capitalism to be inherently coercive (owing perhaps to unequal bargaining power of the participants), then the "absence of coercion" will mean that freedom and capitalism cannot coexist. Similarly, if we believe that every person has a right to a minimum wage or to a decent standard of living, then "the unfettered right to use and dispose of one's property" will mean that true freedom cannot exist without the coercive egalitarianism of the welfare state.

We must therefore look beyond the nominal definition of "freedom" to its contextual meaning if we wish to understand the significance of this concept within a particular theoretical system. This is why debates over the "true" meaning of freedom are usually futile. Nominal definitions are determined by linguistic conventions, not by philosophers, and the conventional meanings of "freedom" are sufficiently diverse to support a wide variety of interpretations. Even the various notions of positive freedom can find support in common usage, so they cannot be summarily dismissed by the libertarian as arbitrary and illegitimate. Thus, rather than embark on a futile quest for the true meaning of "freedom," I shall confine myself to investigating its meaning within the social and political tradition of liberal individualism.

## II

The liberal tradition is associated with the idea of negative freedom. This is freedom conceived as the absence of physical constraint and compulsion by other human beings. This negative freedom – so called because it denotes the *lack* of coercive interference by others – is often contrasted with various positive conceptions of freedom, which see freedom as a kind of personal empowerment. A person is said to be positively free to the extent that she or he possesses the *means* that are necessary to achieve a desired goal. Thus, although a poor person would be considered free to purchase a Cadillac in the negative sense (so long as she or he was not coercively hindered by others from doing so), this person would not be considered free in the positive sense, since she or he lacks the necessary means (i.e., money) to buy this expensive item.

This distinction between negative and positive freedom has value as an analytic tool, and it reflects two major ways of thinking about freedom that have emerged since the nineteenth century. But this distinction also has serious flaws, not the least of which is its tendency to distort our understanding of earlier political debates, especially those that occurred during the seventeenth-century. This kind of distortion is particularly evident in modern interpretations of Thomas Hobbes. In *Leviathan* (1651), Hobbes defines "liberty" in negative terms as "the absence of external impediments."[278] This negative definition has caused many historians to describe Hobbes as an early forefather of liberal individualism, despite the fact that he defended many absolutist

---

[278] Hobbes, *Leviathan*, 84.

measures (e.g., governmental control of religious practices) that were anathema to that tradition. Since the concept of negative liberty was essential to liberalism, we are told that Hobbes, despite his political absolutism, should be regarded as an early proponent of liberal individualism.

It is true that Hobbes cast his nominal definition of freedom in negative terms, as did John Locke and other individualists. But this was only a superficial similarity. Hobbes's definition of freedom differs fundamentally from that of Locke, but this difference has been obscured by the conventional distinction between negative and positive freedom. There is another distinction that is far more important in this context, namely the difference between freedom conceived as a *mechanistic* concept that refers to a physical relationship between *things*, and freedom conceived as a *social* concept that refers to an *interpersonal* relationship between human beings. Hobbes employed the mechanistic concept, defining freedom as the absence of physical impediments; Locke employed the social concept, defining freedom as the absence of coercion in social affairs.

To understand what is involved here, we need to understand the broad meaning that Hobbes gives to the word "power." For Hobbes, "power" means the ability to achieve our goals. To the extent that we have the means required to get what we want, we are said to have power. With this in mind, let us look at Hobbes's definition of freedom.

Freedom, for Hobbes, means "the absence of opposition," that is, of "external impediments to motion." This kind of freedom applies "no less to irrational and inanimate creatures." We may say, for example, that water is not free to flow beyond the vessel that contains it.

> For whatsoever is so tied, or environed, as it cannot move within a certain space, which space is determined by the opposition of some external body, we say it hath not liberty to go further. And so of all living creatures, whilst they are imprisoned, or restrained, with walls, or chains; and of the water whilst it is kept in by banks, or vessels, that otherwise would spread itself into a larger space, we use to say, that they are not at liberty, to move in such manner, as without those external impediments they would. But when the impediment of motion, is in the constitution of the thing itself, we use not to say; it wants the liberty; but the power to move; as when a stone lieth still, or a man is fastened to his bed by sickness.[279]

When we are restrained from achieving our goals by internal impediments, then Hobbes says that we lack power. When those impediments are external, then we lack freedom to exercise our power. For Hobbes, therefore, freedom

---

[279] Hobbes, *Leviathan*, 137.

consists of unimpeded power. In a social context, a free man *"is he, that in those things, which by his strength and wit he is able to do, is not hindered to do what he has a will to."*[280]

This physical concept of freedom differs from the social concept of freedom that we find in Locke and most other individualists. Hobbes, who proclaimed himself the father of political science, based his mechanistic concept of freedom on his understanding of Galileo's law of inertia, according to which an object will stay in motion until it is impeded or stopped by another object. Likewise, the external motions of human beings – our efforts to get what we like and avoid what we dislike – will continue until and unless they are impeded by an external object, whether that object be an inanimate thing or another human being. For Hobbes, therefore, "freedom" does not necessarily refer to a social relationship. If I desire to travel from here to there, my freedom to act can be impeded as much by a high wall or impassable river as it can by another person. Any external obstacle that prevents me from exercising my power, that keeps me from getting what I want, diminishes my liberty.

In opposition to the Hobbesian notion of mechanistic freedom, Locke viewed freedom as a *social* concept, one that refers to interpersonal relationships. In a state of perfect freedom, people can "dispose of their Possessions, and Persons as they think fit, within the bounds of the Law of Nature, without asking leave, or depending upon the Will *of any other man*" (my emphasis). Perfect freedom is also a state of equality, "wherein all the Power and Jurisdiction is reciprocal, no one having more than another."[281]

Whether one uses the mechanistic or social concept of freedom can have profound ideological implications, as we see in seventeenth-century discussions of the relationship between liberty and positive law. The mechanistic view was favored by absolutists, such as Robert Filmer and Thomas Hobbes, because it supported their contention that all laws *necessarily* restrict liberty. All governments enforce laws that restrain people from doing what they might otherwise have a will to do – so it is absurd to claim, as did the political individualists, that the primary purpose of government is to preserve liberty. It is therefore nonsensical to reject absolutism for its supposed incompatibility with freedom, for all governments, however limited they may appear to be, must necessarily restrict freedom. Robert Filmer put this argument as follows:

A great deal of talk there is in the world of the freedom and liberty that they say is to be found in popular commonweals. It is worth the inquiry how far and in what sense this speech of liberty is true: "true liberty is for every man to do what he list, or to live as he please, and not to be tied to any laws."

---

[280] Ibid.
[281] Locke, *Two Treatises*, I: §4.

But such liberty is not to be found in any commonweal, for there are more laws in popular estates than anywhere else, and so consequently less liberty; and government, many say, was invented to take away liberty, and not to give it to every man. Such liberty cannot be; if it should, there would be no government at all.[282]

If Filmer and Hobbes were correct, if the primary purpose of government is to restrain freedom, then the complaints made by individualists against absolute monarchy made little sense. True, absolute monarchies restrict freedom, but so do all forms of government, even those supposedly derived from the consent of the people. Complete liberty can exist only under anarchy; and this liberty is diminished each time a government passes or enforces a law. Therefore, to argue that the purpose of government is to maintain freedom is arrant nonsense.

Locke, in rejecting this argument, maintains that "the end of law is not to abolish or restrain, but to *preserve and enlarge freedom.*" Liberty, properly considered, is a social rather than a mechanistic concept; to be free "is to be free from restraint and violence from others. . . . "

> [F]reedom is not, as we are told [by Filmer], *A liberty for every Man to do what he lists:* (For who could be free, when every other Man's Humour might domineer over him?) But a *Liberty* to dispose, and order, as he lists, his Persons, Actions, Possessions, and his whole Property, within the Allowance of those Laws under which he is; and therein not to be subject to the arbitrary Will of another, but freely follow his own.[283]

This is the kind of contextual definition that I mentioned previously. In establishing the conceptual relationship between freedom and the cognate idea of property, Locke gives to freedom an *ideological identity* – a distinct character, so to speak, that emerges from the relationship of ideas within his theoretical system. Freedom, for Locke, is not the unimpeded *power* to do as one wills, but the *right* to do as one wills *with one's own property*. In this view, a condition of perfect freedom can be said to exist when property rights, both in one's person and in external goods, are fully recognized and protected. Thus to the extent that a legal system approximates this goal, it can be said to preserve and enhance liberty.

For Hobbes, freedom is the ability to do as one wills without external impediments of any kind. For Locke, in contrast, freedom is the ability to do as one wills *with one's own* without the coercive intervention of other people.

---

[282] Filmer, "Observations upon Aristotle's Politiques," in *Writings,* 275.
[283] Locke, *Two Treatises,* II: §57.

To clarify the difference between these two concepts, consider the case of an armed robber who says to his victim, "Your money or your life." From a Hobbesian perspective, this action by the robber is merely an exercise of his freedom. And this freedom would be curtailed if the intended victim were to resist her assailant with physical force, since this would impose an "external impediment" on the power of the robber to do as he wills. It is also the case, however, that the robber constitutes an "external impediment" to the freedom of his victim, so the same action (the robbery) is at once an exercise *and* a violation of freedom, depending on our point of view.

The same situation, when analyzed from a Lockean perspective, leads to a different conclusion. If "freedom" denotes a social condition in which every person is able to use and dispose of those things that are rightfully her own (including her person and labor), then the robber, by introducing coercion into a relationship where it did not previously exist, is the sole violator of freedom. Should the victim use force in an effort to protect her property, the victim is not similarly violating the "freedom" of the robber, but is instead attempting to restore the former condition of freedom that was violated by the robber's action. Since this notion of freedom describes a noncoercive *relationship* between two or more persons – a social state of affairs in which the rights of each person are respected – any use of defensive violence by the victim is properly construed as an effort to restore and preserve freedom, rather than as an additional violation of the robber's mechanistic "freedom" to do as he wills.

This conception of freedom as a social concept is a recurring theme of liberal individualism (though it was not always consistently upheld). In linking "a state of perfect freedom" to "a state also of equality, wherein all the power and jurisdiction is reciprocal, no one having more than another,"[284] Locke set the stage for later liberals who attempted to express social freedom in terms of a universal principle of equality. We see this in Immanuel Kant who, having defined "freedom" as "independence from the constraint of another's will," insisted that authentic freedom must be "compatible with the freedom of everyone else in accordance with a universal law."[285] Similarly, Herbert Spencer maintained that "the freedom of each must be bounded by the similar freedom of all" and that "every man may claim the fullest liberty to exercise his faculties compatible with the possession of like liberty by every other man."[286]

---

[284] Ibid., II: §4.
[285] Immanuel Kant, *The Metaphysical Elements of Justice*, trans. John Ladd (Indianapolis: Bobbs-Merrill, 1965), 43–44.
[286] Herbert Spencer, *Social Statics* (New York: Robert Schalkenbach Foundation, 1995), 69.

Edmund Burke, despite his opposition to the radical individualists of his day, preferred the liberal notion of social freedom to the mechanistic notion of "unconnected" liberty:

> The liberty I mean is *social* freedom. It is that state of things in which liberty is secured by the equality of restraint. A constitution of things in which the liberty of no one man, and no body of men, and no number of men, can find means to trespass on the liberty of any person, or any description of persons, in the society. This kind of liberty is, indeed, but another name for justice.... [287]

Although it is something of a rhetorical exaggeration to say that liberty is "but another name for justice," few individualists would have denied that freedom and justice (along with rights and property) are cognate concepts with interdependent meanings. These conceptual links account for the strong normative undercurrent that we typically find in liberal discussions of freedom. Freedom, when defined nominally as "the absence of coercion," may appear to be a purely descriptive concept with no moral components whatever. However, this misleading impression quickly dissipates when we descend from the generalities of a nominal definition to the particulars of a contextual definition. This contextual definition – the freedom to do as one wills *with one's own* – is inextricably linked to the concepts of rights and property, which in turn are essential to a theory of justice.

### III

According to John Locke, "Laws provide, as much as possible, that the goods and health of subjects be not injured by the fraud and violence of others."[288] This pairing of fraud and violence (or force) was common in seventeenth-century political philosophy. Samuel Pufendorf, whose massive treatise on the philosophy of law was praised by Locke as "the best book of that kind,"[289] wrote this: "Every man is obliged to suffer another, who is not a declared enemy, quietly to enjoy whatsoever things are his; and neither by fraud or violence to spoil, embezzle, or convert them to his own use."[290] Similarly, Algernon

---

[287] Burke, *Reflections on the Revolution in France*, 505.

[288] John Locke, *A Letter Concerning Toleration*, x.

[289] John Locke, "Some Thoughts Concerning Reading and Study for a Gentleman," in *Locke: Political Essays*, ed. Mark Goldie (Cambridge: Cambridge University Press, 1997), 352.

[290] Samuel Pufendorf, *The Whole Duty of Man, According to the Law of Nature*, trans. Andrew Tooke, ed. Ian Hunter, and David Saunders (Indianapolis: Liberty Fund, 2003), 137.

Sidney argued that "violence and fraud can create no right."[291] Even Sir Robert Filmer (whose theory of the divine right of kings was attacked by both Locke and Sidney) cautioned that an absolute monarch should not take the private property of his or her subjects "by force or fraud."[292]

Why does the duo of force and fraud appear so frequently on the stage of seventeenth-century political philosophy? Part of the answer lies in the tremendous influence of Hugo Grotius and Samuel Pufendorf, both of whom developed a rights-based theory of justice in which force and fraud served as paradigmatic examples of unjust actions.

In this approach, violence and fraud correspond to two types of obligation. One type of obligation (which Pufendorf called "natural" or "absolute") is inherent in the moral principles of natural law, whereas the other type of obligation ("adventitious" or "conditional") is not inherent but arises instead from a contract or some other voluntary arrangement.[293]

This twofold classification of obligations was based on Aristotle's discussion of justice in the *Nicomachean Ethics*. After dividing justice into two general categories – distributive and commutative[294] – Aristotle further subdivides commutative justice into "involuntary transactions" and "voluntary transactions." Involuntary transactions include "violent" acts of injustice, such as assault, forcible confinement, murder, and robbery. Voluntary transactions (so called because they originate in voluntary agreements) include purchases, loans, and other kinds of economic exchanges.[295]

According to Pufendorf, acts such as murder are absolutely unjust because they violate a right that does not arise from a previous agreement, contract, or other human institution. (Your right to life does not depend on whether I previously agreed not to kill you.) In contrast, acts such as fraud are conditionally unjust because they violate a right that was *acquired* through some voluntary transaction. Suppose that I shoot you during a robbery attempt. My violent action is naturally unjust because I violated an absolute precept of natural law, an obligation that is not contingent on human will or choice. Now suppose that I agree to sell you a diamond ring for $1,000, but that I give you a fake ring

[291] Sidney, *Discourses Concerning Government*, 31.
[292] Filmer, *Patriarcha*, in *Writings*, 36.
[293] Pufendorf, *The Whole Duty of Man*, 94–95.
[294] Aristotle did not use the term "commutative" but spoke instead of "corrective" or "rectificatory" justice. It was Thomas Aquinas who coined the expression "commutative justice," offering it as a more accurate label for the type of justice in question, and this is the term that came to be widely used. For details on this issue, including the meaning of "commutative," see John Finnis, *Natural Law and Natural Rights* (Oxford: Clarendon Press, 1980), 177–84.
[295] Aristotle, *Ethics*, 1131a1–9.

made of glass instead. This fraudulent action is adventitiously (noninherently) unjust, because my obligation depended upon, and logically presupposed, a mutual agreement. Without this agreement my action would not have been unjust, for I had no *natural* obligation to give you a ring of any kind, be it made of diamond or glass.

We can now better understand why the terms "violence" (or "force") and "fraud" appeared in tandem so frequently in seventeenth-century political thought. Violence (physical force) was linked to the violation of natural rights, whereas fraud was linked to the violation of those rights that arise from voluntary agreements. Of course, those who employed this distinction knew that matters are more complicated than this, since (to cite just one example) fraud is not the only means whereby an adventitious right can be violated. Nevertheless, force and fraud were well suited to serve as exemplars of two kinds of rights (and their correlative duties), which, taken together, comprise the sphere of justice.

The endurance and significance of Pufendorf's classification can be seen in the fact that it was routinely cited over a century later by William Paley. In *The Principles of Moral and Political Philosophy* (1785), a widely read text that was part of the curriculum at Cambridge University, Paley wrote:

Rights are natural or adventitious.

Natural rights are such as would belong to a man, although there subsisted in the world no civil government whatever.

Adventitious rights are such as would not.

*Natural rights* are, a man's right to his life, limbs, and liberty; his right to the produce of his personal labor; to the use, in common with others, of air, light, water. If a thousand different persons, from a thousand different corners of the world, were cast together upon a desert island, they would from the first be every one entitled to these rights.

*Adventitious rights* are, the right of a king over his subjects; of a general over his soldiers; of a judge over the life and liberty of a prisoner; a right to elect or appoint magistrates, to impose taxes, decide disputes, direct the descent or disposition of property; a right, in a word, in any one man, or particular body of men, to make laws and regulations for the rest. For none of these rights would exist in a newly inhabited island.[296]

---

[296] William Paley, *The Principles of Moral and Political Philosophy* (Indianapolis: Liberty Fund, 2002), 51. In the foreword to this edition (xi), D.L. Le Mahieu notes that Paley's book "played a seminal role in the dissemination of utilitarianism in England." Paley's integration of utilitarianism with natural-rights theory, which we later see in Herbert Spencer (among others), stood in stark contrast to the utilitarianism of Jeremy Bentham and his followers. Paley represented

Paley's list of natural and adventitious rights highlights the importance of this distinction for the problem of political obligation. An important feature of liberal individualism was its insistence that political sovereignty (the right to rule over others, in effect) is not a natural right. Rather, it is an adventitious right, a right that arises from human agreement. It was this belief that generated various theories that are known generically as the "social contract."

There is nothing intrinsically libertarian about social contract theory; on the contrary, it could be, and often was, pressed into service on behalf of absolutism. In Roman law, the *lex regia*, whereby the Roman people supposedly transferred their sovereignty to the emperor, was frequently interpreted by later commentators to mean that "the people had made a total and irrevocable alienation of all their powers."[297] Similarly, Hugo Grotius suggested that people might transfer all of their rights to the state and thereby contract themselves into a perpetual condition of political slavery. Thomas Hobbes is well known for his use of the social contract to show that an absolute sovereign is the only remedy for the violent conflict and turmoil in an anarchistic state of nature. In addition, J.J. Rousseau used libertarian rhetoric in his version of the social contract to justify a state with unmistakable totalitarian implications, a state in which citizens are subservient to a "general will" that can force them to be free.

In short, the social contract was a vehicle that could take political philosophers virtually anywhere they wanted to go. The only essential thing that social contract philosophers had in common was their rejection of the belief that political sovereignty is a *natural* right; all agreed that sovereignty is adventitious, that it must be acquired in some fashion through consent, contract, or some other voluntary means. This was a common theme even before the rise of liberal individualism; indeed, as Otto Gierke has noted, since the end of the thirteenth century "it was held as an axiom of political philosophy that the legal basis of all government lies in the voluntary or contractual subjection or submission of the governed."[298]

It is one thing to say that a government should protect those within its jurisdiction from force and fraud – it would be difficult to find a political philosopher from any era or tradition who disagreed with this – but it is quite

---

an older tradition in liberal thought, which saw no conflict between the two doctrines. I discuss this issue in some detail later in this book.

[297] J.W. Gough, *The Social Contract: A Critical Study of its Development*, 2nd ed. (Oxford: Clarendon Press, 1957), 22.

[298] Otto Gierke, *Political Theories of the Middle Ages*, trans. Frederic William Maitland (Boston: Beacon Press, 1958), 52.

another thing to say that this task is the *only* legitimate function of government. Consider this passage by John Locke:

> [I]f men could live peaceably and quietly together, without uniting under certain laws, and entering into a commonwealth, there would be no need at all of magistrates or politics, which are only made to preserve men in this world from the fraud and violence of one another; so that what was the end of erecting of government ought alone to be the measure of its proceeding.[299]

Whether Locke consistently adhered to this highly restrictive view of governmental functions is a controversy that needn't concern us here. Even if he did not, the notion that the basic purpose of government is to protect its citizens from force[300] and fraud was a longstanding *ideal* of *laissez-faire* liberalism, and we wish to understand the reasoning behind this ideal.

Although Locke frequently invoked natural rights in his political works, he has often been criticized for failing to provide a *theory* of rights per se. In Locke's defense, it might be said that no philosopher can do everything, but this excuse for all occasions is bound to leave us unsatisfied. Fortunately, the past several decades have witnessed an outpouring of first-rate works on seventeenth-century political thought; these have provided us with valuable information on political thinkers who, though immensely influential in their own day and for a considerable time thereafter, tended to fade, if not disappear altogether, from the radar of later historical accounts. Grotius and Pufendorf in particular wrote books that were viewed as mandatory reading for anyone who dabbled in political philosophy. Even those philosophers, such as Locke, who disagreed with some of their conclusions were indebted to Grotius and Pufendorf for their detailed treatments of rights and obligations. As Stephen Buckle wrote in 1991,

> If Grotius's star shines only feebly in the modern philosophical firmament, that of Samuel Pufendorf (1632–94) not uncharacteristically suffers a total eclipse. In the latter stages of the seventeenth century, however, things were vastly different. Pufendorf was then the best known and, by and large, the

---

[299] John Locke, *An Essay on Toleration*, in *Political Essays*, 135. This manuscript, written in 1667, should not be confused with Locke's better-known work, *A Letter Concerning Toleration* (1689). The former is historically significant, because it marks the transition from the authoritarian views that Locke held in his earlier years to the liberalism of his later works.

[300] "Force" encompassed threats of force, including threats from foreign nations. Grotius, Pufendorf, and other philosophers of law discussed threats in some detail; responding to threats was regarded as an aspect of one's right of self-defense.

most respected, writer on natural law, not least because he was recognized as an authoritative interpreter and defender of Grotius.[301]

According to Locke, those who read *The Rights of War and Peace* (Grotius) and The *Law of Nature and Nations* (Pufendorf) "will be instructed in the natural rights of men, and the original and foundations of society, and the duties resulting thence." These are "studies which a gentleman should not barely touch at, but constantly dwell upon, and never have done with."[302] Neither Grotius nor Pufendorf could be called liberal individualists; on the contrary, both reached conclusions that were more favorable to absolutism. But (as Locke indicated) Grotius and Pufendorf presented a theory of natural rights and obligations that could be used to solve the fundamental problems of political philosophy. They provided a conceptual structure, a way of *thinking* about political problems, that promised to bring system and coherence to a difficult discipline.

As Hobbes and Locke later emphasized, sovereign nations have no authoritative common judge to which they can appeal to adjudicate disputes; a nation is therefore in a "state of nature" – a condition of "pure anarchy," as Locke described it – relative to other nations. Thus, when Grotius investigated the moral principles that should govern international affairs, he was obliged, by the very nature of the subject matter itself, to develop a theory of natural law that was at once secular and minimalist.

Grotius could scarcely appeal to the Bible as a definitive moral authority, since this source would carry no weight with non-Christian nations. He needed a secular theory, a system of natural law and natural rights that could be justified by reason alone, a system that reasonable people could agree upon regardless of their religious differences.

## IV

In the Lockean paradigm, "natural liberty" refers to freedom as it would exist in an anarchistic state of nature, a condition of equal rights in which there is no political authority or subordination, a society in which all "Power and Jurisdiction is reciprocal, no one having more than another."[303]

The idea of natural liberty plays a key role in Locke's theory of political obligation. What is the origin of political authority? Why are we obligated to obey the decrees of government? By what right can a government demand

---

[301] Buckle, *Natural Law and the Theory of Property*, 51.
[302] Locke, "Some Thoughts Concerning Reading," 349.
[303] Locke, *Two Treatises*, II: §4.

our obedience and then punish us if we disobey? The political authority of government must be based on more than sheer force, on the physical power to compel obedience. The fact that a strong man can compel a weaker man to obey his will does not confer upon the former any legitimate *authority* over the latter. The weak man may obey the strong man as a matter of prudence, but he is not under any *moral* obligation to do so. Political power, unlike sheer physical power, is "a *Right* of making laws" for the public good.[304]

Government, in other words, is a *moral* institution, one that compels obedience as a matter of *right*. The moral right is what distinguishes a government from a criminal gang. But how can this right be justified? What is the moral foundation of political sovereignty? This question must be answered if we are to understand the nature and source of political obligation.

Social contract theory was regarded by Locke as a solution to the problem of political obligation (which is merely the problem of sovereignty viewed from a different angle). This background is also essential if we are to understand the significance of natural liberty for his overall approach. Locke did not philosophize in a social vacuum. Hip-deep in the revolutionary politics of his day, Locke proposed a theory that condemned the Stuart monarchy as tyrannical, illegitimate, and ripe for revolution.

Locke was keenly aware that the burden of proof in political controversies does not fall solely on the defender of natural rights. It was not as if Locke was the first to introduce moral claims into a political arena where they did not previously exist. Like most everyone else in the world, Locke was born under the jurisdiction of a government that demanded his obedience as a matter of rights. Government is the institutional embodiment of a moral argument, and its legitimacy is contingent on the validity of that argument. If there is no moral basis for sovereignty and political obligation, then government is reduced to the moral equivalent of a violent thug who exercises power without authority.

What, then, is the justification of government? As we saw in Chapter 5, after disposing of Filmer's argument for the divine right of kings, Locke pointed out that we are left with two alternatives: Either political authority "is the product only of Force and Violence, and . . . Men live together by no other Rules but that of Beasts," or we "must of necessity find out another rise of Governments, another Original of Political Power. . . . "[305]

The first alternative – the claim that no moral rights can be justified and that government has no foundation other than brute force – would bring political theory to a stand. We can never derive the normative *Ought* of

[304] Ibid., II: §3.
[305] Ibid., II: §1.

political authority from the factual *Is* of brute power. The physical capacity to coerce others can never generate a moral obligation to obey the dictates of power. Superior force can bestow "no Title to the Subjection and Obedience of the Conquered."[306] Thus does moral skepticism destroy the legitimacy of government. If no claim of right can be justified, then no claim of sovereignty can be justified – and government becomes nothing more than an instrument of force and violence.

It is in taking up the second alternative, in searching for "another original of political power," that Locke presents his theory of natural liberty and equal rights in the state of nature. Having refuted Filmer's argument that monarchs derive their authority from a special *divine* right, Locke claimed to have destroyed the only plausible argument for *unequal* rights. If God has not declared that some people are morally superior to others, this means that no person can claim to possess an inherent right which he or she denies to others. Reason does not recognize any claim of special privilege in the realm of rights, yet this is precisely the kind of claim that government appears to make. In affirming a moral monopoly on the right to pass and enforce laws, rulers are claiming to possess and exercise a right that they deny to everyone else.

If natural society may be described as a condition of moral equilibrium, wherein all rights are equal and reciprocal, then a political society may be described as a condition of moral *disequilibrium*, wherein the sovereign rights of government are denied to everyone else. Thus, if we are to justify the power of government, we must find a moral vehicle that will take us from the "here" of equal rights to the "there" of unequal sovereignty. This vehicle, for John Locke, was the social contract.

Locke's general approach to the problem of sovereignty and political obligation may be described as "political reductionism." This is the doctrine that all rights claimed by government must ultimately be reducible to the rights of individuals. Since the institution of government is itself an association of individuals, it cannot claim any rights other than those that have been delegated to it by individuals. The rights of government, in other words, are derivative rather than original. When a government exceeds its legitimate sphere of jurisdiction by claiming rights that have not been (or could not be) derived from the rights of individuals, then it reverts to the status of a common criminal and may be forcibly resisted: "Wherever violence is used, and injury done, by hands appointed to administer Justice, it is still violence and injury, however colour'd with the Name, Pretences, or Forms of Law."[307]

---

[306] Ibid., II: §176.
[307] Ibid., II: §20.

This is what it means to say that the natural laws of reason are *prior* to the positive laws of government. The priority here is theoretical, not historical; it refers to *the logical order of moral justification.* Government, in claiming an exclusive right, a right not possessed by others within society, must justify this claim. The defender of government has the burden of proof because this institution lays claim to a moral monopoly on the exercise of legitimate violence within society. The right to exercise physical force "belongs wholly to the civil magistrate" and "is the same in every place."[308] This monopolistic feature is what fundamentally distinguishes political institutions from social institutions, and it generates the philosophical need to justify government. It was this need to justify the exclusive right of political power that gave rise to the social contract theory of Locke and other individualists.

Perhaps the most significant feature of Locke's anarchistic state of nature (or natural society) is that it is *pre-political*, but not *pre-social.* This stands in contrast with the Hobbesian conception of natural freedom, which is synonymous with a "state of war," a condition of perpetual violence and conflict where life is "nasty, brutish, and short." Anarchy, according to Hobbes, is incompatible with even a minimal degree of social order. Social order is not spontaneous; it does not emerge from the voluntary interaction of individuals but requires the strong hand of an absolute sovereign. Hence the Hobbesian state of nature is not only pre-political, but pre-social as well.

Locke's state of nature is essentially peaceful and civilized. People can exercise their natural freedom in an anarchistic society without necessarily lapsing into a state of war, because they are able, through the use of reason, to discern the many benefits of social cooperation. However, this natural society, though tolerable, would not be ideal, owing to the various "inconveniences" that arise from the lack of an impartial "umpire" who can arbitrate and resolve disputes. Unlike Hobbes, therefore, Locke views government as a supplement to social order rather than its indispensable foundation. Government is a convenience rather than a necessity.

Locke, of course, was no anarchist (though Edmund Burke and some other critics accused him of harboring anarchist sentiments). Nonetheless, his contention that social order can exist in the anarchistic state of nature had profound implications for political philosophy. It was, for example, a key element in the case for revolution against tyrannical governments. For consider: If a government is overthrown through revolution, there will be a transitional period of anarchy before a new government can be established. Thus, according to Hobbes and other absolutists, a revolution can *never* be justified, because it

---

[308] Locke, *A Letter Concerning Toleration*, 3, 7.

would plunge society into a condition of chaotic warfare from which it may never recover. A government, no matter how brutal or despotic, is always better than no government at all, because nothing is more destructive than the anarchistic state of nature.

In suggesting (however obliquely) the possibility of ordered anarchy, Locke was arguing that a revolution, although it may dissolve the social contract, will not necessarily produce chaos. Indeed, the state of nature is preferable to a political society under despotism, because people in an anarchistic society at least have the right (and possibly the means) to defend themselves against violent oppression.

Locke discussed two kinds of liberty: the natural liberty of a society without government and the civil liberty of a society with government. Natural liberty is regulated by the moral law of reason, whereas civil liberty is regulated by the positive law of government. This dual meaning of "law" must be kept in mind if we are to understand Locke's assertion that "where there is no Law, there is no Freedom."[309] The term "law" refers not only to governmental legislation but to any general rule that imposes a moral obligation. Natural laws are grounded in reason, which formulates general principles of action essential to human happiness. The fundamental purpose of law, both natural and/or civil, "is not so much the limitation as the direction of a free and intelligent agent to his proper interest." Since law should promote human welfare ("the general good"), it would become a "useless thing" if people could be happier without it.[310]

Locke's discussion of natural and civil liberty stimulated an interesting debate among eighteenth-century philosophers. According to Locke, when people leave the state of nature and unanimously agree to form a political society, they exchange some of their natural liberty for the greater security of civil liberty.

Later interpretations of this transition from natural to civil liberty generally fell into one of three categories. According to the conservative interpretation, natural liberty is entirely supplanted by civil liberty, so *all* freedom under government is of the latter kind. According to the moderate interpretation, only *part* of a person's natural liberty is displaced by civil liberty, so some natural liberty continues to exist in a political society. According to the radical interpretation, a person surrenders *none* of his or her natural liberty upon entering civil society, but merely delegates to government his or her *power* to protect that liberty against encroachment by others.

---

[309] Locke, *Two Treatises*, II: §57.
[310] Ibid.

The moderate and radical interpretations of Locke, which assert that civil liberty *supplements* rather than replaces natural liberty, played a key role in the development of spontaneous order theory, such as we find in Adam Smith's famous account of the "invisible hand." Indeed, in referring to a free society as a "system of *natural* liberty," Smith was expressing his belief that a good deal of freedom depends, not on the fear of legal punishment, but on moral, economic, and social considerations that have nothing inherently to do with government.

Between the time of John Locke and Adam Smith, the idea of natural liberty underwent a subtle but profound transformation. When in 1767 Adam Ferguson asked, "Where the state of nature is to be found?," he answered, "It is here; and it matters not whether we are understood to speak in the island of Great Britain, at the Cape of Good Hope, or the Straits of Magellan."[311] It is a mistake to relegate a person's "natural" condition to a bygone Golden Age, or confine it to an abstract rational being without passion. The state of nature is people as they exist here and now, with all their virtues and vices, wisdom and folly.

Recall that, according to John Locke's theory of natural liberty, people can (and typically will) interact peacefully and harmoniously in the anarchistic state of nature. They will (to a considerable degree) respect the rights of others, even though there exists no government to compel obedience and inflict punishment. But in treating the state of nature as a self-contained model, Locke implied that natural liberty was (or should be) superseded by civil liberty. What some of Locke's successors did was to blend the natural and the political into a unified model of society, thereby assigning to natural liberty an important role in maintaining social order.

This transformation had the effect of deemphasizing the social role of government. The culture and prosperity of a society were no longer attributed to the wise edicts of a virtuous prince; they were seen as the spontaneous, unplanned products of natural liberty. Just rulers should generally leave people alone to pursue their own values, according to their own judgment, while maintaining justice through the impartial application of equitable laws. No longer was government seen as the foundation of social order; on the contrary, as Thomas Paine observed, "society performs for itself almost every thing which is ascribed to government," and "governments, so far from being always the cause or means of order, are often the destruction of it."[312]

---

[311] Adam Ferguson, *An Essay on the History of Civil Society* (New Brunswick: Transaction Publishers, 1991), 8.

[312] Thomas Paine, *Rights of Man, Part Second, in The Life and Major Writings of Thomas Paine*, ed. Philip S. Foner (Secaucus, N.J.: Citadel Press, 1948), 357, 359.

When natural society and political society, which Locke had presented as different *types* of society, came to be viewed as different aspects of the *same* society, the door was opened for an anarchistic mode of social explanation. By "anarchistic," I mean those social activities that are normally unaffected by positive laws and that would continue to function without government. These anarchistic spheres of interaction – which are "governed" by moral and religious opinions, psychological bonds, aesthetic sensibilities, personal habits, institutional incentives, customs, economic self-interest, and the like – have far more influence on social behavior (especially in a free society) than does the fear of legal punishment. These voluntary institutional relationships are enclaves of natural liberty – anarchistic *societies* (or *states* of nature) that operate within, but independently of, political society.

The idea of natural liberty came to play a major role in the development of the social sciences during the eighteenth century. This is particularly true of economics. It is scarcely coincidental that most early economists, such as the Physiocrats and Adam Smith, were highly sympathetic to *laissez-faire* and generally hostile to government intervention. Economic science was made possible by the discovery of an autonomous economic order – a society of mutually beneficial exchanges that operates through the spontaneous adjustments of natural liberty rather than through the coercive and cumbersome decrees of a legislator.

# 8

## Conflicts in Classical Liberalism

An ideological movement can have two faces, depending on whether we view it externally or internally. Classical liberalism, when viewed externally in opposition to conservatism, socialism, and other ideological competitors, may appear as a fairly unified system of principles and policies. However, when viewed internally as a loose coalition of subgroups, this appearance of unity disappears; in its stead we find a number of significant differences and tensions. One such ideological conflict occurred between the Benthamite utilitarians and the advocates of natural rights.

Natural-rights theory was *the* revolutionary doctrine of the seventeenth and eighteenth centuries, being used to justify both resistance to unjust laws and revolution against tyrannical governments. As we have seen, this is why Edmund Burke attacked natural rights – or "abstract rights," as he called them – so vehemently in his famous polemic against the French Revolution, *Reflections on the Revolution in France*. Indeed, Burke condemned the French Constitution of 1791, which exhibited a strong American influence, as a "digest of anarchy." Similarly, Jeremy Bentham, in his attack on the same document, called natural rights "anarchical fallacies," because he believed that no government can truly be based on the consent of the governed, which is precisely what the natural-rights philosophy demanded.

The fear that the defenders of natural rights would foment a revolution in Britain – just as they had in America and France – alarmed the British establishment, causing them to institute repressive measures. It is therefore hardly surprising that natural-rights theory went underground, so to speak, during the long war with France. Even after peace returned in 1815 a cloud of suspicion hung over this way of thinking. Natural rights were commonly associated with the French Jacobins – Robespierre and others who had instigated the Reign of Terror – so a defender of natural rights ran the risk of being condemned as a French sympathizer, a Jacobin, or (worst of all) an anarchist.

Thus did British liberalism take on a new face after 1815, as an atmosphere of peace resuscitated the movement for political and economic reforms, and as many middle-class liberals embraced a nonrevolutionary foundation for economic and civil liberties. The premier theory in this regard, which would later become known as "utilitarianism," was developed by Jeremy Bentham and popularized by his Scottish protégé James Mill (the father of John Stuart Mill) and many other disciples.

The utilitarian principle of "the greatest happiness for the greatest number" was not original with Bentham; on the contrary, we find this expression in a number of eighteenth-century philosophers, such as Helvetius and Beccaria. (Bentham probably borrowed the phrase from the latter.) In 1726, for example, Francis Hutcheson wrote that "that Action is best, which procures the greatest Happiness for the greatest Numbers; and that, worst, which, in like manner, occasions misery."[313] But, like many early "utilitarians," Hutcheson defended natural rights as a *standard* to determine what will in fact promote the greatest happiness for the greatest number, and this fundamentally differentiated his approach from Bentham's.

For our purpose the most significant feature of Bentham's utilitarianism is its unequivocal rejection of natural rights. Natural rights, according to Bentham, are "simple nonsense: natural and imprescriptible rights, rhetorical nonsense, – nonsense upon stilts."[314] So-called moral and natural rights are mischievous fictions – "anarchical fallacies" – that encourage civil unrest, disobedience and resistance to laws, and revolution against established governments. Only political rights, those positive rights established and enforced by government, have "any determinate and intelligible meaning" – for in asserting the existence of political rights "the existence of a certain matter of fact is asserted; namely, of a disposition, on the part of those by whom the powers of government are exercised, to cause him to possess . . . the benefit to which he has a right."[315]

Rights are, then, the fruits of the law, and of the law alone. There are no rights without law – no rights contrary to the law – no rights anterior to the law. Before the existence of laws there may be reasons for wishing that there

---

[313] Francis Hutcheson, *An Inquiry Concerning the Original of Our Ideas of Virtue or Moral Good*, in *British Moralists*, 1: 107.

[314] Jeremy Bentham, "Anarchical Fallacies," in *The Works of Jeremy Bentham*, ed. John Bowring (Edinburgh: Simkin, Marshall, & Co., 1843), 2: 493.

[315] *Bentham's Theory of Fictions*, ed. C.K. Ogden (London: Kegan Paul, 1932), 119.

were laws – and doubtless such reasons cannot be wanting, and those of
the strongest kind – but a reason for wishing we possessed a right, does not
constitute a right. To confound the existence of a reason for wishing that
we possessed a right, with the existence of the right itself, is to confound the
existence of a want with the means of relieving it. It is the same as if one should
say: Everybody is subject to hunger, therefore everybody has something to
eat. There are no other legal rights – no natural rights, no rights of man,
anterior or superior to those created by the laws. The assertion of such rights,
absurd in logic, is pernicious in morals. . . . We may feign laws of nature –
rights of nature, in order to show the nullity of real laws, as contrary to these
imaginary rights; and it is with this view that recourse is had to this fiction –
but the effect of these nullities can only be null.[316]

The significance of Bentham does not lie in his advocacy of social utility,
or the general welfare, or the common good – for this idea, by whatever name
it was called, was regarded by earlier liberals as the *purpose* of legislation,
in contradistinction to its *standard*. In other words, given that social utility
(however defined) should be the purpose of legislation, how can this goal be
attained? How can the legislator possibly know which measures will promote
the greatest happiness for the greatest number? To this key question liberals in
the Lockean tradition had, in effect, answered this: by respecting the natural
rights of individuals. Thus if social utility is the general *goal* of legislation,
natural rights are the *standard*, or rule, which must be followed if this goal is
to be achieved.

Bentham broke with this venerable tradition, in which utility and rights were
seen as different aspects of the same process, by rejecting the entire scheme
of natural rights and by proposing that social utility serve as both the goal
*and* standard of political activity. The "happiness of individuals, of whom a
community is composed . . . is the sole end which the legislator ought to have
in view [and] the sole standard, in conformity to which each individual ought,
as far as depends on the legislator, to be *made* to fashion his behaviour."[317]
Natural rights are not only a groundless fiction, one that is incompatible
with an empiricist methodology, but they are a highly dangerous fiction to
boot, because they have traditionally been used to undermine the authority
of governments. Natural rights are anarchical fallacies that undermine the
legitimacy of all governments. In maintaining that no positive law can impose
a legitimate obligation if it supposedly violates natural rights, the theory of

---

[316] Ibid., cxxvi.
[317] Jeremy Bentham, *An Introduction to the Principles of Morals and Legislation* (Amherst:
Prometheus Books, 1988), 24.

natural rights leaves it open to the discretion of each individual to decide which laws should be obeyed and which should not. Hence, if you think taxes are unjust, then you will feel justified in throwing the tax collector out the window and, when you are tried for this crime, attacking the judge with a dagger. No government, Bentham insisted, can function under these circumstances.

Thus did Bentham reject the roundabout method of natural rights, according to which the legislator should respect rights as a *means* to the end of social utility; instead, the legislator should calculate social utility *directly* by assessing the impact of a given law on the greatest happiness for the greatest number. As we have seen, this was a significant departure from earlier liberal thinking, in which natural rights and social utility were seen as complementary. Bentham severed this friendly relationship by totally rejecting natural rights. If a law promotes the greatest happiness for the greatest number, then it is legitimate and proper, regardless of how it might be evaluated from a natural-rights perspective.

Many philosophers before Bentham had considered the possibility of directly calculating social utility – that is, a method of comparing and adding up the happiness of different people – but had rejected this as an impossible task. In the early 1700s, for example, the moralist Samuel Clarke argued that only an omniscient deity could possibly know what specific measures will promote "public utility," but any such calculation is beyond the powers of the human mind.[318] Bishop Butler expressed a similar concern when he said that although God is probably a utilitarian, it is better that men not be, for they are likely to commit serious errors in calculating what will promote the greatest happiness for the greatest number.[319]

What others saw as an impossibility, however, Bentham saw as a challenge; he believed that the greatest happiness for the greatest number could be ascertained by "some calculus or process of 'moral arithmetic' by means of which we may arrive at uniform results."[320] But how? Bentham's solution came in the form of his so-called hedonic calculus, a discussion of which occupies a good deal of his most famous book, *An Introduction to the Principles of Morals and Legislation* (1789).

How can the legislator calculate the greatest happiness for the greatest number, measured in terms of maximal pleasure and minimal pain? Bentham's

---

[318] Samuel Clarke, *Discourse Upon Natural Religion*, in *British Moralists*, 2: 37.
[319] See D.H. Munroe, "Utilitarianism," in *Dictionary of the History of Ideas*, 4: 444.
[320] Jeremy Bentham, *Theory of Legislation*, trans. C.M. Atkinson (Oxford: Clarendon Press, 1914), 1: 2.

procedure, despite a veneer of exactitude, is remarkably vague on this point. After listing seven "circumstances" (intensity, duration, certainty, fecundity, etc.) that are relevant to this calculation, Bentham said that an "exact account" of a proposed legislative act can be arrived at by first determining for a given individual the sum of "all the values of all the *pleasures* on the one side, and those of all the pains on the other"; and by then taking an account "of the *number* of persons whose interests appear to be concerned" and repeating the same calculation "with respect to each."[321] He continues:

> *Sum up* the numbers expressive of the degrees of *good* tendency, which the act has, with respect to each individual; in regard to whom the tendency of it is *good* upon the whole: . . . do this again with respect to each individual, in regard to whom the tendency of it is *bad* upon the whole. Take the *balance*; which, if on the side of *pleasure*, will give the general *good* tendency of the act, with respect to the total number or community of individuals concerned; if on the side of pain, the general *evil tendency*, with respect to the same community.[322]

In presenting his detailed typology of pleasures and pains, Bentham repeatedly referred to their quantity and measurement, but nowhere did he address the serious problems of dealing with pleasure and pain quantitatively (as if they can be added together in a single sum), nor did he explain how it is possible to quantify and compare the subjective feelings of different individuals. Bentham, however, did seem uneasy with the implications of his moral arithmetic, for just after the passage just quoted he added the following proviso:

> It is not to be expected that this process should be strictly pursued previously to every moral judgment, or to every legislative or judicial operation. It may, however, be always kept in view: and as near as the process actually pursued on these occasions approaches to it, so near will such process approach to the character of an exact one.[323]

Bentham's skepticism about the feasibility of a hedonic calculus was expressed even more bluntly in an unpublished manuscript, where he had this to say about the possibility of adding up quantities of happiness among different individuals:

> Tis in vain to talk of adding quantities which after the addition will continue distinct as they were before, one man's happiness will never be another man's happiness: a gain to one man is no gain to another: you might as well pretend

---

[321] Bentham, *Principles of Morals and Legislation*, 30–31.
[322] Ibid., 31.
[323] Ibid.

to add twenty apples to twenty pears, which after you had done that could not be forty of any one thing but twenty of each just as there was before.[324]

Bentham conceded that his hedonic calculus, like the theory of natural rights, is based on a fiction, an unreal supposition, or abstraction. However, he also claimed that his fiction is "successful" because it can function as a practical guide for legislation.

> This addibility of the happiness of different subjects, however, when considered rigorously, it may appear fictitious, is a postulatum without the allowance of which all political reasoning is at a stand.[325]

When Bentham applied his principle of utility to political measures, he often appealed not to his fictional hedonic calculus but to the general principle that each individual is normally the best judge of his own interests and should therefore be left free to pursue his own happiness in his own way.[326] Furthermore, the legal recognition of this principle, as manifested in a respect for individual freedom, is the best way to further the greatest happiness for the greatest number.

That each person is normally the best judge of his own interests seemed to Bentham so obvious so as not to require much justification. But there was a serious danger lurking in this premise, as his natural-rights critics were quick to point out. They agreed that a person is usually the best judge of his own interests, but they argued further that, even when this is not the case, a person has a *right* to act according to his own judgment, so long as he respects the rights of others. So the crucial point was this: W*ho* is entitled to decide whether a given person assesses his interests correctly or not – the individual or the government? After all, Bentham conceded that people can make mistakes about what will promote their happiness, but *who* should determine when these mistakes are made and when they are not? Bentham's theory suggests such decisions should ultimately be made by a legislative authority, not by individuals for themselves, for it is the job of legislators to calculate the greatest happiness for the greatest number, and they are empowered to enforce their decisions. This was what so infuriated Bentham's liberal critics, such as Thomas Hodgskin and Herbert Spencer, and this is the key to understanding the rift in nineteenth-century British liberalism that had been precipitated by the immense influence of Benthamite utilitarianism.

---

[324] Quoted in Halévy, *Growth of Philosophic Radicalism*, 495.
[325] Quoted in ibid.
[326] See *Principles of Morals and Legislation*, 267.

The utilitarians, according to their critics, had undercut the foundation of the liberal tradition by their rejection of natural rights. True, many utilitarians had strong liberal sentiments and beliefs – Jeremy Bentham, for example, was a fairly consistent advocate of personal liberty, religious freedom, and free-market economics, and he did not hesitate to take up unpopular causes in the area of civil liberties (as we see in his opposition to capital punishment and in his call to abolish laws against homosexuality). Given these and other liberal causes, the principle of utility could indeed function as a powerful weapon in defense of individual liberty – provided, of course, that those in power agreed with Bentham's assessments of social utility. That, however, was precisely the problem.

Bentham's ideal legislator reminded his critics too much of Plato's philosopher-king, that wise and benevolent social planner who has the best interests of his subjects at heart. Bentham prided himself on his hardheaded political realism, but this lapse into fantasy was severely ridiculed by the defenders of natural rights. Again and again Thomas Hodgskin and Herbert Spencer – Bentham's most formidable liberal critics – attacked the utilitarians for their historical blindness and political naiveté. How often in human history, they asked, have political rulers actually governed with the best interests of their subjects at heart? Never, or almost never, they answered. And, given human nature, can we expect that rulers will magically lose their self-seeking inclinations immediately upon gaining power, forgoing their own interests for those of the general good? Or may we expect them to behave like other mortals, and continue to pursue their own interests through the instrumentality of government?

Bentham was aware of this problem, and he found an answer in his theory of democracy. If the franchise were extended, if the people at large were able to elect their rulers, then there would emerge an identity of interests between the rulers and the ruled. Bentham attributed much of Britain's repressive legislation to what he called the "sinister interests" operating in government (by which he chiefly meant the landed aristocracy).

Bentham's natural-rights critics, though they also favored democratic reform, were not nearly so sanguine about its prospects. Democracy is desirable, but it is not a cure-all. Like many of their American counterparts, they believed that a majority could tyrannize over a minority as surely as any despot; indeed, they regarded this kind of tyranny as more dangerous than despotism, since a despot can be resisted more easily than a majority. Only a theory of natural rights, which defines the proper limits of government, can morally empower the oppressed to demand that their rights be respected, whatever the form of a government may be.

And so went the great British debate between the two great schools of liberalism: the Benthamite utilitarians versus the defenders of natural rights. This debate, one of the most fascinating in the history of political thought, sets the stage for our discussion of Thomas Hodgskin's *The Natural and Artificial Right of Property Contrasted*, to which let us now turn.

II

The Englishman Thomas Hodgskin was born December 12, 1787. His spendthrift father, despite making decent money as a storekeeper at the Chatham naval stockyard, managed to keep his family in dire financial straits, so he sent Thomas (who was barely twelve) to serve as a cadet aboard a British warship. Although he served with distinction during the Copenhagen expedition, Hodgskin detested his twelve years as a sailor. For one thing, it deprived him of an education. His access to books was limited, so he could do little more than "reflect in the midnight watch, on the solitary deck, on the wide ocean, amidst the wildest or the most peaceable scenes of nature . . . before I had acquired a sufficient stock of material."[327]

Hodgskin's independent spirit, his intense dislike of authority, his determination "to make a powerful resistance to oppression every time I was its victim," was not well suited to the rigors and harsh discipline of naval life. Thus, when it became clear that he would be passed over for promotion, Hodgskin complained "of the injury done to me, by a commander-in-chief, to himself, in the language that I thought it merited."[328] This of course only made matters worse. Hodgskin, at age twenty-five, was forced into retirement at half-pay (first as a lieutenant, later as a captain), after which he wrote a scathing indictment of conscription and the brutal conditions endured by British sailors. The complete title of this rare tract is *An Essay on Naval Discipline, showing part of its evil effects on the minds of the officers and the minds of the men and on the community; with an amended system by which Pressing may be immediately abolished.*

Although Hodgskin's political and economic views had not been fully developed when this tract was published in 1813, it clearly displays the libertarian tendencies that would become prominent in his later works. For example, in speaking of the "absurdity of [the navy's] laws and customs," Hodgskin wrote this: "Having received so deep an injury from these laws, it has become a positive duty in me to attempt to alter *them* through the medium of public

---

[327] Quoted in Élie Halévy, *Thomas Hodgskin*, trans. A.J. Taylor (London: Ernest Benn, 1956), 30.
[328] Quoted in ibid.

*opinion.*"[329] This appeal to public opinion would become an important feature in Hodgskin's efforts to bring about political reform.

To submit to oppression, Hodgskin declared, is a vice, whereas to "resist it, is a virtue." This is a precept not only of that utilitarianism, which has "the real interest and good of society" as its goal, but also of "the most sacred kind of justice."[330] Again, this belief in the compatibility of social utility and a justice based on natural law is something that would later permeate Hodgskin's writings, especially his *Natural and Artificial Right of Property Contrasted* (1832).

Hodgskin would also elaborate upon his ideas in the pages of *The Economist*, after he became an editor of that paper in 1846. There, in addition to supporting free trade, domestic *laissez-faire*, voluntary education, and other liberal causes, he also opposed capital punishment and questioned the traditional wisdom about the efficacy of punishment as a deterrent to crime. Most crimes, he argued, are motivated by a desire to escape intolerable poverty, and such poverty is often the consequence of taxes, economic regulations, and other governmental restrictions of free-market activities. If people were allowed to pursue their own interests through voluntary interaction with others, and if they were allowed to keep the fruits of their own labor rather than having much of it expropriated by government, a good deal of poverty would be eliminated, and with it would go the chief motive for criminal acts. This theme – that governments are themselves a principal source of crime – would also dominate *The Natural and Artificial Right of Property Contrasted*.

In the preface to this book, Hodgskin explained that he intended to discuss the distinction between two kinds of property – that which flows from natural right and that which is established by governmental legislation (which he called "artificial right"). Legislators typically believe they are blessed with the moral authority to decree what is just or unjust and with the wisdom to determine the social good, but these pretensions are "arrant humbug." Hodgskin, in contrast, maintained that "society can exist and prosper without the lawmaker, and consequently without the taxgatherer."[331]

This book was originally written in 1829 as a series of eight letters to Lord Brougham (addressed to him, as Hodgskin says, "without permission") and then published in 1832 with some "verbal alterations." This selection of Lord Brougham, who became Lord Chancellor of England in 1830, was significant

---

[329] Quoted in ibid., 31.
[330] Quoted in ibid., 32.
[331] Thomas Hodgskin, *The Natural and Artificial Right of Property Contrasted* (1832; rpt. Clifton, N.J.: Augustus Kelley, 1969), ii.

for several reasons. First, he was regarded as sympathetic to Benthamite utili-tarianism (though Bentham seems to have disliked him personally). Second, Brougham had long been known as an advocate of liberal causes, such as the abolition of slavery. Third, Brougham had been appointed to spearhead a committee whose purpose was to recommend changes in the English legal system that would render it more efficient and equitable.

Thus, in criticizing Brougham, Hodgskin was addressing not a conservative Tory but a liberal reformer whose views were in some ways similar to his own. Hodgskin's real target, however, was not a single person but the theory of Benthamite utilitarianism, according to which legislators should promote the greatest happiness for the greatest number of people.

Hodgskin criticized the notion that significant improvements can be effected through the piecemeal reform of existing laws. This would do little if anything to further the cause of liberty, and it might even make things worse. Hence legislators, before undertaking reforms, should first educate themselves in the basic principles of social and economic theory.

> Never were the discrepancies between the state of the law and the condition of society greater than at present. Never was the conviction so general that the laws must now be extensively altered and amended. Rapidly therefore as the gentlemen at Westminster work, making three or four hundred laws per year, repeating their tasks session after session – actively as they multiply restraints, or add patch after patch, they invariably find that the call for their labors is continually renewed. The more they botch and mend, the more numerous are the holes. Knowing nothing of natural principles, they seem to fancy that society – the most glorious part of creation, if individual man be the noblest of animals – derives its life and strength only from them. They regard it as a baby, whom they must dandle and foster into healthy existence; but while they are scheming how to breed and clothe their pretty fondling – lo! it has become a giant, whom they can only control as far as he consents to wear their fetters.[332]

Before the lawmaker attempts to mend society with legal tinkering, he should first understand the nature of social order. But this is not what the legislator wants to hear, so he "acts before he understands." And without a comprehensive knowledge of society, "he grubs forward under the influence of his passions and animal instincts, like the mole, and is quite as blind."[333]

Hodgskin distinguished between the natural right of property, as defended by John Locke, and the artificial right of property, as defended by Jeremy

[332] Ibid., 9.
[333] Ibid., 10.

Bentham and his utilitarian followers. Natural rights flow from the characteristics of human nature and the conditions required for social cooperation,
whereas artificial rights are created by the legislative fiat of governments. The
defenders of natural rights believed that these rights exist independently of
government, and that government is justified only to the extent it protects
them. Jeremy Bentham and his utilitarian disciples, however, rejected this
notion, claiming instead that rights do not exist unless they are embodied in
law. And though Hodgskin knew that the Benthamite utilitarians were sincere
defenders of liberty, he believed their theoretical foundation was inadequate
to a proper defense of liberty and, moreover, that their doctrine of artificial
rights could easily serve to justify virtually any kind or degree of governmental
encroachments on individual liberty and property rights.

The Benthamite theory, according to Hodgskin, handed to government a
virtual blank check to pass any legislation whatever, provided the legislators
believe, or profess to believe, that such legislation promotes social utility. Contrary to traditional liberalism, which viewed government at best as a necessary
evil, the liberal utilitarians viewed government as a potentially beneficent
power that could be used to promote the greatest happiness for the greatest
number.

> Messrs. Bentham and Mill, both being eager to exercise the power of leg-
> islation, represent it as a beneficent deity, which curbs our naturally evil
> passions and desires (they adopting the doctrine of the priests, that the desires
> and passions of man are naturally evil) which checks ambition, sees justice
> done, and encourages virtue. Delightful characteristics! – which have the
> single fault of being contradicted by every page of history.[334]

Hodgskin was highly skeptical, to say the least, about the Benthamite theory
of government. The first priority of legislators is to promote their own interests, not the general good, and the Benthamites merely provide them with a
convenient rationale to do this.

> To me, this system appears as mischievous as it is absurd. The doctrines
> according too well with the practice of lawgivers, they cut too securely all
> the gordian knots of legislation, not to be readily adopted by all those who,
> however discontented with a distribution of power, in which no share falls
> to them, are anxious to become the tutelary guardians of the happiness of
> mankind. They lift legislation beyond our reach, and secure it from censure.
> Man, having naturally no rights, may be experimented upon, imprisoned,
> expatriated or even exterminated, as the legislator pleases. Life and property

---

[334] Ibid., 19.

being his gift, he may resume them at pleasure; and hence he never classes the executions and wholesale slaughters, he continually commands, with murder – nor the forcible appropriation of property he sanctions, under the name of taxes, tithes, etc., with larceny or highway robbery. Filmer's doctrine of the divine right of kings was rational benevolence, compared to the monstrous assertion that "all right is factitious, and only exists by the will of the lawmaker."[335]

Like liberals before him, Hodgskin pinpointed the chief weakness of the utilitarian agenda, namely that the greatest happiness for the greatest number simply cannot be measured or calculated. It is a vague and ultimately meaningless standard, and this is why it is so beloved by legislators, who can never be called to account for their actions.

> Much has of late been very needlessly written about the greatest happiness principle, the basis of all Mr. Bentham's philosophy. There can be no doubt that the Deity wills the greatest happiness – no doubt that the legislator, whenever he speaks of the good of the country, pretends to mean the greatest happiness of the greatest number of inhabitants; and no doubt that the faculties of individuals, admirably adapted to secure their own preservation, are not competent to measure the happiness of nations. Admitting therefore that the legislator ought to look at the general good, the impossibility that any individual can ascertain that which will promote it, leads directly to the conclusion that there ought to be no legislation. If the greatest happiness principle, be the only one that justifies lawmaking, and if that principle be suitable only to Omniscience – man, having no means of measuring it, there can be no justification of all Mr. Bentham's nicely adapted contrivances, which he calls civil and penal laws.[336]

In opposition to rights established by government decree, Hodgskin defended the natural right of property. After quoting lengthy passages from John Locke's *Second Treatise of Government*, Hodgskin goes on to say:

> I look on *a right* of property – on the right of individuals, to have and to own, for their own separate and selfish use and enjoyments, the produce of their own industry, with power freely to dispose of the whole of that in the manner most agreeable to themselves, as essential to the welfare and even to the continued existence of society.[337]

---

335 Ibid., 21.
336 Ibid., 22.
337 Ibid., 24.

Thomas Hodgskin's analysis of legislation anticipated the modern economic school known as "public choice theory," which seeks to understand political behavior as stemming from the pursuit of self-interest by those in government. As he put it, "Let us look closer at who is the legislator, and what is his object in making laws." Just as Adam Smith had posited self-interest as an explanatory principle in economics, so Thomas Hodgskin now extended this method to the realm of politics. The impulse of self-interest, in politics as in economics, is everywhere operative. It is naïve to suppose that lawmakers do not act from the same motives as other men. Although the law is often defended as necessary to maintain property rights, in fact it is designed to enable those in government to maintain their power:

> When we inquire, casting aside all theories and suppositions, into the end kept in view by legislators, or examine any existing laws, we find that the first and chief object proposed is to preserve the unconstrained dominion of law over the minds and bodies of mankind. It may be simplicity in me, but I protest that I see no anxiety to preserve the natural right of property but a great deal to enforce obedience to the legislator. No misery indeed is deemed too high a price to pay for his supremacy, and for the quiet submission of the people. To attain this end many individuals, and even nations, have been extirpated. Perish the people, but let the law live, has ever been the maxim of the masters of mankind. Cost what it may, we are continually told, the dominion of the law, not the natural right of property, must be upheld.[338]

The cry of "anarchy" is raised by those in government (and also, Hodgskin perceptively noted, by most journalists) every time a law is disobeyed, regardless of how unjust or tyrannical that law may be. The principle of self-preservation – "that holy and delightful impulse by which we cherish our happy animal existence" – is extended by "a ridiculous analogy" to corporate bodies, with the result that "men are massacred that governments may be upheld."

Government, in Hodgskin's view, is essentially an exploitative institution; and law is the mechanism by which those in government, who produce nothing, expropriate the property of others. "Our leaders invent nothing but new taxes, and conquer nothing but the pockets of their subjects."

> Actually and in fact [laws] are intended to appropriate to the law-makers the produce of those who cultivate the soil, prepare clothing, or distribute what is produced among the different classes, and among different communities. Such is law.[339]

[338] Ibid., 44–45.
[339] Ibid., 47.

Laws are made, not by those who labor to produce wealth, but by those who live off the labor of others and who expropriate what they have produced.

> Laws being made by others than the laborer, and being always intended to preserve the power of those who make them, their great chief aim for many ages, was, and still is, to enable those who are not laborers to appropriate wealth to themselves. In other words, the great object of law and of government has been and is, to establish and protect a violation of that natural right of property they are described in theory as being intended to guarantee. This chief purpose and principle of legislation is the parent crime, from which continually flow all the theft and fraud, all the vanity and chicanery, which torment mankind, worse than pestilence and famine.[340]

Given this viewpoint, it is not surprising that taxes, for Hodgskin, are "the parent theft, from which flow all other thefts." Taxes forcibly transfer wealth from producers to legislators, who justify their expropriation under cover of law. Yet Hodgskin believes that the ultimate purpose of lawmakers is not wealth per se, but the maintenance and exercise of power over others. "Those who make laws," he says, "appropriate wealth in order to secure power." Taxes, then, are a necessary means for the maintenance of political power, so the law, first and foremost, must enforce compulsory taxation.

> One of the first objects then of the law, subordinate to the great principle of preserving its unconstrained dominion over our minds and bodies, is to bestow a sufficient revenue on the government. Who can describe the disgusting servility with which all classes submit to be fleeced by the demands of the tax-gatherer, on all sorts of false pretenses, when his demands cannot be fraudulently evaded? Who is acquainted with all the restrictions placed on honest and praiseworthy enterprise; the penalties inflicted on upright and honorable exertions? What pen is equal to the task of accurately describing all the vexations, and the continual misery, heaped on all the industrious classes of the community, under the pretext that it is necessary to raise a revenue for the government?[341]

Taxes and revenue laws have inflicted more suffering on humanity than even natural disasters:

> [The legislator] has inflicted on mankind for ages the miseries of revenue laws – greater than those of pestilence and famine, and sometimes producing both these calamities. . . . Revenue laws meet us at every turn. They embitter our meals, and disturb our sleep. They excite dishonesty, and check

---

[340] Ibid., 48.
[341] Ibid., 49.

enterprise. They impede division of labor and create division of interest. They sow strife and enmity amongst townsmen and brethren; and they frequently lead to murders, not the less atrocious because they are committed in battle with smugglers, or consummated on the gallows. The preservation of government, it is said, must be purchased at whatever sacrifice; and it is impossible to enumerate the vexatious statutes and cruel penalties by which its preservation is sought to be attained. Government, as such, produces nothing, and all its revenues are exacted by violating the natural right of property. This I put down as the first point aimed at by all laws.[342]

III

The relation between school and state in American liberal thought has a checkered past. Many traditional heroes of American individualism, such as Thomas Paine and Thomas Jefferson, upheld some role for the state in education, however minor that role is by today's standard. Even William Leggett, the radical Jacksonian and *laissez-faire* advocate who opposed nearly all kinds of government intervention, made an exception in the case of education.[343]

Radical individualism in America was a different matter. Josiah Warren, often regarded as the first American anarchist, warned in 1833 that national aid to education would be like "paying the fox to take care of the chickens,"[344] and he feared the consequences of placing control of education in the hands of a single group. Gerrit Smith (a radical abolitionist who supported John Brown) upheld the separation of school and state. "It is justice and not charity which the people need at the hands of government," Smith argued. "Let government restore to them their land, and what other rights they have been robbed of, and they will be able to pay for themselves – to pay their schoolmasters, as well as their parsons."[345] William Youmans (an admirer of Herbert Spencer and editor of *Popular Science Monthly*) favored leaving education to "private enterprise."[346] And the Spencerean John Bonham vigorously attacked "the one true system" of Horace Mann that would impose a dulling uniformity and extirpate diversity in education.[347]

---

[342] Ibid., 50.

[343] See *A Collection of the Political Writings of William Leggett*, ed. Theodore Sedgwick, Jr. (New York: Taylor and Dodd, 1840), 1: 80–81.

[344] Quoted in William O. Reichert, *Partisans of Freedom: A Study in American Anarchism* (Bowling Green: Bowling Green University Popular Press, 1976), 70.

[345] Quoted in Octavius Brooks Frothingham, *Gerrit Smith: A Biography* (New York: Putnam's, 1878), 184.

[346] *Popular Science Monthly*, May, 1887, 124–27.

[347] John M. Bonham, *Industrial Liberty* (New York: Putnam's, 1888), 286–326.

The most thorough arguments against state education appeared in the writings of British liberals during the 1840s and 1850s. Calling themselves "voluntaryists," these liberals launched a sustained campaign against state education in England that, though it was doomed to failure, produced a remarkable body of literature that has been largely ignored by historians.

The voluntaryist movement grew from the ranks of dissenters, or Nonconformists (i.e., non-Anglican Protestants). After the Restoration of Charles II in 1660, dissenters who refused to subscribe to the articles of the Established Church of England faced severe legal disabilities. Oxford and Cambridge were effectively closed to them, as were other conventional channels of education. Dissenters therefore established their own educational institutions, such as the dissenting academies of the eighteenth century, which one historian has described as "the greatest schools of their day."[348]

Individual liberty was a basic concern of all voluntaryists. Religious liberty in particular was viewed as the great heritage of dissenting tradition, any violation of which must call forth "stern and indomitable resistance." Liberty should not be sacrificed for a greater good, argued the voluntaryist Richard Hamilton: "There is no greater good. There can be no greater good! It is not simply means, it is an end."[349] Education is best promoted by freedom, but should there ever be a conflict "liberty is more precious than education." "We love education," Hamilton stated, "but there are things which we love better."[350] Edward Baines agreed that education is not the ultimate good: "Liberty is far more precious." It is essential to "all the virtues which dignify men and communities."[351]

Government, an ever-present danger to liberty, must be watched with vigilance and suspicion. "The true lover of liberty," warned *The Eclectic Review* (a leading dissenting journal), "will jealously examine all the plans and measures of government."

> He will seldom find himself called to help it, and to weigh down its scale. He will watch its increase of power and influence with distrust. He will specially guard against conceding to it any thing which might be otherwise

---

[348] Irene Parker, *Dissenting Academies in England* (Cambridge: Cambridge University Press, 1914), 45.

[349] Rev. Richard Winter Hamilton, *The Institutions of Popular Education* (London: Hamilton, Adams, 1845), 266.

[350] Rev. Richard Winter Hamilton, "On the Parties Responsible for the Education of the People," in *Crosby-Hall Lectures on Education* (London: John Snow, 1848), 77.

[351] Edward Baines, Jr., *Letters to the Right Hon. Lord John Russell . . . on State Education*, 3rd ed. (London: Ward, 1847), 76.

done. He would deprecate its undertaking of bridges, highways, railroads. He would foresee the immense mischief of its direction of hospitals and asylums. Government has enough on its hand – its own proper functions, – nor need it to be overborne. There is a class of governments which are called paternal.... They exact a soulless obedience.... Nothing breathes and stirs.... The song of liberty is forgotten.... And when such governments tamper with education, the tyranny, instead of being relieved, is eternized.[352]

The voluntaryist concern for liberty can scarcely be exaggerated. Schemes for state education were repeatedly denounced as "the knell of English freedom," an "assault... on our constitutional liberties," and so forth. Plans for government inspection of schools were likened to "government *surveillance*" and "universal *espionage*" that display "the *police* spirit." Compulsory education was characterized as "child-kidnapping." Educational freedom is "a sacred thing" because it is "an essential branch of civil freedom." Declared Baines, "A system of state-education is a vast intellectual police, set to watch over the young at the most critical period of their existence, to prevent the intrusion of dangerous thoughts, and turn their minds into safe channels."[353]

Voluntaryists often drew parallels between educational freedom on the one hand and religious freedom, freedom of the press, and the like on the other hand. "We cannot violate the principles of liberty in regard to education," Baines noted, "without furnishing at once a precedent and an inducement to violate them in regard to other matters."

> In my judgment, the State could not consistently assume the support and control of education, without assuming the support and control of both the *pulpit* and the *press*. Once decide that Government money and Government superintendence are essential in the schools, whether to ensure efficiency, or to guard against abuse, ignorance, and error, and the self-same reasons will force you to apply Government money and Government superintendence to our periodical literature and our religious instruction.[354]

Baines realized that a government need not carry the principle inherent in state education to its logical extreme, but he was disturbed by a precedent that gave to government the power of molding minds. If, as the proponents of state

---

[352] *The Eclectic Review*, n.s. 20 (July–Dec., 1846): 291.

[353] *The Eclectic Review*, n.s. 13 (Jan.–June, 1843): 581; *The Eclectic Review*, n.s. 21 (Jan.–June, 1847): 507; Baines quoted in ibid., 363; Baines, *Letters to Russell*, 124; *The Eclectic Review*, n.s. 20 (July–Dec., 1846): 303; Baines quoted in *The Eclectic Review*, n.s. 21 (Jan.–June, 1847): 363; and Baines, *Letters to Russell*, 72.

[354] Baines, *Letters to Russell*, 73–74.

education had argued, state education is required in order to promote civic virtue and moral character, then "where, acting on these principles, could you consistently stop?"

> Would not the same paternal care which is exerted to provide schools, school-masters, and school-books, be justly extended to provide mental food for the adult, and to guard against his food being poisoned? In short, would not the principle clearly justify *the appointment of the Ministers of Religion, and a Censorship of the Press?*[355]

Baines conceded that there were deficiencies and imperfections in the system of voluntary education, but freedom should not be abrogated on this account. Again, he pointed to the example of a free press. A free press has many "defects and abuses"; certainly not all the products of a free press are praiseworthy. But if liberty is to be sacrificed in education to remedy deficiencies, then why not regulate and censor the press for the same reason? Baines employed this analogy in his brilliant rejoinder to the charge that he was an advocate of "bad schools."

> In one sense I am. I maintain that we have as much right to have wretched schools as to have wretched newspapers, wretched preachers, wretched books, wretched institutions, wretched political economists, wretched Members of Parliament, and wretched Ministers. You cannot proscribe all these things without proscribing Liberty. The man is a simpleton who says, that to advocate Liberty is to advocate badness. The man is a quack and a *doctrinaire* of the worst German breed, who would attempt to force all minds, whether individual or national, into a mould of ideal perfection, to stretch it out or to lop it down to his own Procrustean standard. I maintain that Liberty is the chief cause of excellence; but it would cease to be Liberty if you proscribed everything inferior. Cultivate giants if you please, but do not stifle dwarfs.[356]

Freedom of conscience was precious to liberal dissenters, and they feared government encroachment in this realm, even in the guise of "secular" education. *The Eclectic Review*, using arguments similar to those of Baines, stressed the relation between religious freedom and educational freedom. Advocates of state education claimed that parents have the duty to provide their children with education and that the state has the right to enforce this duty. But parents have a duty to provide religious and moral instruction as well. "Are we

[355] Ibid., 8.
[356] Edward Baines, Jr., "On the Progress and Efficiency of Voluntary Education in England," in *Crosby-Hall Lectures on Education*, 39.

then prepared to maintain ... that government should interpose, in this case, to supply what the parent has failed to communicate? ... If sound in the one case, it is equally so in the other."[357]

A common prediction of voluntaryists was that government would employ education for its own ends, especially to instill the habit of obedience in subjects. An earlier voluntaryist, William Godwin, put it this way:

> [The] project of a national education ought uniformly to be discouraged on account of its obvious alliance with national government. ... Government will not fail to employ it, to strengthen its hands, and perpetuate its institutions.[358]

This warning by Godwin was repeatedly stressed by nineteenth-century voluntaryists, as in this example:

> It is no trifling thing to commit to any hands the moulding of the minds of men. An immense power is thus communicated, the tendency of which will be in exact accordance with the spirit and policy of those who use it. Governments, it is well known, are conservative. The tendency of official life is notorious, and it is the height of folly, the mere vapouring of credulity, to imagine that the educational system, if entrusted to the minister of the day, will not be employed to diffuse amongst the rising generation, that spirit and those views which are most friendly to his policy. By having, virtually, at his command, the whole machinery of education, he will cover the land with a new class of officials, whose dependence on his patronage will render them the ready instruments of his pleasure.[359]

We see a similar concern with indoctrination in the work of J.S. Mill. Mill contended that education "is one of those things which it is admissible in principle that a government should provide for the people," although he favored a system where only those who could not afford to pay would be exempt from fees. Moreover, a parent who fails to provide elementary education for his or her child commits a breach of duty, so the state may compel a parent to see that his or her child receives instruction. Where and how a child is taught should be up to the parents; the state should simply enforce minimal educational standards through a series of public examinations. Thus did Mill

---

[357] *The Eclectic Review*, n.s. 13 (Jan.–June, 1843): 579.

[358] William Godwin, *Enquiry Concerning Political Justice and Its Influence on Morals and Happiness*, 3rd ed. (1797), ed. F.E.L. Priestley (Toronto: University of Toronto Press, 1946), 2: 302.

[359] *The Eclectic Review*, n.s. 13 (Jan.–June, 1843): 580.

attempt to escape the frightening prospect of state control. On this subject he sounds like an ardent voluntaryist:

> That the whole or any large part of the education of the people should be in State hands, I go as far as any one in deprecating.... A general State education is a mere contrivance for moulding people to be exactly like one another; and as the mould in which it casts them is that which pleases the predominant power in the government... in proportion as it is efficient and successful, it establishes a despotism over the mind, leading by natural tendency to one over the body.[360]

A fundamental theme in voluntaryism was the need for diversity in education. Voluntaryists warned that state education would impose a dulling uniformity that would result, at best, in mediocrity. This was a primary concern of the eighteenth-century dissenter Joseph Priestley. Education is an art, and like any art it requires many "experiments and trials" before it can approach perfection. To bring government into education would freeze this art at its present stage and thereby "cut off its future growth." Education "is already under too many legal restraints. Let these be removed." The purpose of education is not simply to promote the interests of the state but rather to produce "wise and virtuous men." Progress in this area requires "unbounded liberty, and even caprice." Life requires diversity in order to improve, and this is especially true of human life. Variety induces innovation and improvement. "From new and seemingly irregular methods of education, perhaps something extraordinary and uncommonly great may spring." The "great excellence of human nature consists in the variety of which it is capable. Instead, then, of endeavouring, by uniform and fixed systems of education, to keep mankind always the same, let us give free scope to everything which may bid fair for introducing more variety among us."[361]

Similar concerns were expressed by Godwin. State institutions resist change and innovation. "They actively restrain the flights of mind, and fix it in the belief of exploded errors." Government bureaucracies entrench themselves and resist change, so we cannot look to them for progress. State education "has always expended its energies in the support of prejudice."[362]

The deleterious effects of intellectual and cultural uniformity were also of great concern to Herbert Spencer, who developed a theory of social progress based on increasing social diversity. National education "necessarily assumes

---

[360] J.S. Mill, *On Liberty*, (London: Parker and Son, 1859), pp. 190–91.
[361] See *Priestley's Writings on Philosophy, Science, and Politics*, ed. John A. Passmore (New York: Collier, 1965), 306–09.
[362] Godwin, *Enquiry Concerning Political Justice*, 2: 298–99.

that a uniform system of instruction is desirable," and this Spencer denied. Unlimited variety is the key to progress. Truth itself – "the bright spark that emanates from the collision of opposing ideas" – is endangered by a coerced uniformity. The "uniform routine" of state education will produce "an approximation to a national model." People will begin to think and act alike, and the youth will be pressed "as nearly as possible into one common mould." Without diversity and competition among educational systems, education will stagnate and intellectual progress will be severely retarded.[363]

Baines also warned that a uniform state education would obstruct progress. It would serve to "stereotype the methods of teaching, to bolster up old systems, and to prevent improvement." If we leave education to the market, we will see continual improvements. "But let it once be monopolized by a Government department, and thenceforth reformers must prepare to be martyrs."[364] Algernon Wells made a similar point:

> How to teach, how to improve children, are questions admitting of new and advanced solutions, no less than inquiries how best to cultivate the soil, or to perfect manufactures. And these improvements cannot fail to proceed indefinitely, so long as education is kept wide open, and free to competition, and to all those impulses which liberty constantly supplies. But once close up this great science and movement of mind from these invigorating breezes, whether by monopoly or bounty, whether by coercion or patronage, and the sure result will be torpor and stagnancy.[365]

Voluntaryists prized social diversity (or what we call today a "pluralistic society"), and they were convinced that state education would impose the dead hand of uniformity. Rather than giving to government the power to decide among conflicting beliefs and values, they preferred to leave beliefs and values to the unfettered competition of the market. One must appreciate this broad conception of the free market, which includes far more than tangible goods, if one wishes to understand the passionate commitment of many liberals to competition and their unbridled hatred of governmental interference. They believed that coercive intervention, whatever its supposed justification, actually served special interests and enhanced the power of government. The various campaigns against government were therefore seen as battles to establish free markets in religion, commerce, education, and other spheres.

---

[363] Herbert Spencer, "The Proper Sphere of Government," *The Nonconformist*, Oct. 19, 1842: 700.
[364] Baines, "On the Progress and Efficiency," 42–43; and *Letters to Russell*, 53.
[365] Algernon Wells, "On the Education of the Working Classes," in *Crosby-Hall Lectures on Education*, 60.

# 9

## Individualism

### I

The term "individualism" was introduced into social and political philosophy by the French disciples of Edmund Burke. In *Reflections on the Revolution in France*, Burke assailed the Lockean theory of social contract and natural rights for its revolutionary tendencies; he condemned the liberal defense of individual reason and self-interest as incompatible with social order. If people were to view society as nothing more than a voluntary association for the pursuit of self-interest while relying upon their "private stock of reason" to assess the desirability of traditional customs, values, and institutions, then the commonwealth would "crumble away [and] be disconnected into the dust and powder of individuality."[366]

Burke, while professing love for "a manly, moral, regulated liberty," cautioned that we should not praise freedom in the abstract without taking into account its moral, social, and historical context. These circumstances "are what render every civil and political scheme beneficial or noxious to mankind."[367] Liberty, viewed abstractly, is a blessing to mankind, but we should not praise the freedom of a country until we investigate other circumstances, such as the role of its government, its respect for peace, order, and property, and the like. Liberty means that people are free to do as they wish, so we should find out what they wish to do with their freedom before we offer our congratulations and support. Freedom in a democracy translates into political *power*, and such power can be used for evil purposes, whatever its source and justification may be.

Like Filmer, Hume, and others before him, Burke repudiated the individualistic theory of natural rights because of its revolutionary implications.

---

[366] Burke, *Reflections on the Revolution in France*, 86–87.
[367] Ibid., 90.

Significantly, however, Burke condemned not natural rights per se but what he called "abstract rights." By this he meant that such rights are applied in the abstract to every government as a test of legitimacy, without regard for particular circumstances. Since no government can possibly meet these abstract standards, every government becomes theoretically ripe for revolution. "Against these . . . rights of men let no government look for security in the length of its continuance, or in the justice and lenity of its administration." The abstract rights of revolutionaries "are as valid against such an old and beneficent government as against the most violent tyranny, or the greenest usurpation."[368]

Burke upheld "the *real* rights of men." These rights are historical, not abstract; they are embodied in the traditional institutions of society and government and represent the accumulated wisdom of past ages. The rights of revolutionaries, in contrast, are purely metaphysical. They are extremes that do not permit the many gradations and compromises that are essential to the real world of politics. Revolutionaries "are so taken up with their theories about the rights of man, that they have totally forgot his nature."[369]

Traditional institutions and sentiments have been "dissolved by this new conquering empire of light and reason." Philosophical rationalists – those defenders of individual reason and abstract rights – profess scorn for irrational traditions, such as the customs of ancient chivalry, and in so doing they dissolve the civilizing tendencies that hold society together. According to this "barbarous philosophy," law has no basis other than narrow self-interest, so government has no option except to rule through the terror of punishment. Pure reason, unable to replace the traditional sentiments of respect and veneration, can offer no motive for obedience except fear. Furthermore, since governmental power will always exist in some form or other, rulers will quickly learn that they must rule through fear, or not at all.

This style of criticism became popular among French conservatives who hoped to counteract the evil effects of individualism by restoring the social and political authority of the Catholic Church. Indeed, we may owe the word "individualism" itself to one such theocrat, Joseph de Maistre, who, in 1820, assailed the diversity of religious and political opinions that had replaced the uniformity of an earlier age. This "absolute individualism," – this "infinite fragmentation" of doctrines – was frightening because it had undermined the uniformity of belief that is so essential to peace and social harmony. Nine years later the theocrat Lamennais issued a similar warning: The same

---

[368] Ibid., 149.
[369] Ibid., 156.

individualism that causes "anarchy among minds" will inevitably produce political anarchy and thereby overturn the "very bases of human society." Individualism, according to Lamennais, is "power without obedience" and "law without duty."[370]

The term "individualism" was first used systematically in the mid-1820s by the disciples of Saint-Simon. For the Saint-Simonians, as for their theocratic predecessors, "individualism" was a term of opprobrium, one that characterized the Enlightenment stress on political liberalism, freedom of conscience, individual rights, and the pursuit of economic self-interest. According to the Saint-Simonians, the Enlightenment defenders of individualism, in reviving the egoism of Epicurus and the Stoics and in upholding the right of individual judgment, had denied the legitimacy of any organization that sought to direct the moral interests of mankind.

Some nineteenth-century liberals, such as William Graham Sumner, also condemned individualism. Sumner argued that individualism is an offshoot of rationalism. The rationalist, secure in his own judgment and moral autonomy, "tears off from himself the restraints of tradition and custom and asserts his absolute independence."[371] He starts anew, as if there was nothing to learn from the past, and questions every customary belief, moral principle, and law that comes his way. The rationalist favors the new, however superficial it may be, and spurns the old. Upon detecting flaws in a traditional institution, he cries for abolition rather than reform. The rationalist spurns as irrational or unjust anything that cannot be demonstrated or justified, thereby pitting his own feeble reason against traditional wisdom. Thus does rationalism lead to the individualism of social isolation and selfish independence.

> Thus it is that rationalism, in its practical manifestations, is individualism. It teaches men to say: "Every one for himself," and so regard life as a great scramble, in which each one must use strength and cunning to get and to keep as much as he possibly can. No one is to give quarter, none is to ask it. To every question that would call me to account for neglect of another or for harm done to him, to every obligation which is asserted to bind men together in mutual interest and responsibility, they answer with the question of Cain: "Am I my brother's keeper?"[372]

---

[370] See Robert Nisbet, "Conservatism," in *A History of Sociological Analysis*, ed. Tom Bottomore and Robert Nisbet (New York: Basic Books, 1978), 80–117.

[371] William Graham Sumner, "Individualism," in *On Liberty, Society, and Politics: The Essential Essays of William Graham Sumner*, ed. Robert C. Bannister (Indianapolis: Liberty Fund, 1992), 5.

[372] Ibid., 7.

Individualism isolates the singular human being from the rest of society by rejecting all social obligations. This pure egoism breeds moral anarchy, makes the individual "in some sense hostile to all the rest of society,"[373] and thereby leads to the dissolution of social order. Society becomes a collection of hostile individuals, where no one is willing to curtail her selfish pursuits for the sake of social harmony. Individualism rejects the idea of *duty* on which society depends; it does not accept the idea that each person is obligated to forgo some of his own rights, interests, and pleasures for the common good. It rejects the need for mutual concessions, teaching instead that the individual should assert his interests and enforce his rights, whatever the social consequences may be.

Individualism, according to Sumner, contends that happiness is the supreme goal of life. In society, however, people are mutually interdependent; the interests of one person cannot be totally separated from the interests of others, so the pursuit of happiness by one person may significantly affect the happiness of others. But the individualist cares for no one except himself. He chases happiness, demanding change when discontented, without taking the interests of others into account. By stressing rights over duties, individualism "threatens the greatest dangers to society."[374]

Another liberal, Alexis de Tocqueville, was somewhat more sympathetic to individualism. Individualism differs from egoism – that "passionate and exaggerated love of self which leads a man to think of all things in terms of himself and to prefer himself to all."

> Individualism is a calm and considered feeling which disposes each citizen to isolate himself from the mass of his fellows and withdraw into the circle of family and friends; with this little society formed to his taste, he gladly leaves the greater society to look after itself.[375]

Unlike the "depraved feeling" of egoism, which springs from a blind instinct, individualism "is based on misguided judgment [and] inadequate understanding."[376] Over time, however, individualism tends to degenerate into pure egoism, because it ignores the public virtues on which society depends. Individualism is a product of the egalitarian democracy that, by destroying aristocracy and other privileged groups, left the individual isolated and defenseless

---

[373] Ibid., 7.
[374] Ibid., 9–10.
[375] Alexis de Tocqueville, *Democracy in America*, ed. J.P. Mayer, trans. George Lawrence (Garden City: Anchor Books, 1969), 2: 507.
[376] Ibid.

against the power of centralized government. And this, Tocqueville warns, is the path to despotism.

Despots abhor any group or organization that promotes loyalty among its members in preference to the state. Despotism cannot take hold unless society has been fragmented into isolated atoms and there no longer exist institutions and organizations that can buffer the individual from the power of Leviathan. And since democracy promotes precisely this kind of social atomism, democracy and despotism "fatally complete and support each other."[377]

II

The reader unfamiliar with the history of political philosophy may become confused at this point, because "individualism" has clearly meant different things to different people. Even critics who agree that individualism leads to "social atomism" sometimes mean different things by this phrase. I will therefore try to clarify matters somewhat by distinguishing between two meanings of "social atomism."

1. The first meaning of social atomism, which emerged from writings of Edmund Burke and other critics of the French Revolution, is perhaps better described as "political atomism." The key point here (which was also expressed by Tocqueville and Lord Acton) is that *intermediate institutions* are essential to the preservation of freedom. Intermediate institutions, such as the Church, guilds, and nobility prior to the French Revolution, are associations that provide their members with various "liberties and immunities" against the power of government. Such institutions, according to their defenders, are indispensable to freedom, because, unlike the isolated individual, they have the power and authority to check the expansion of a centralized state.

According to critics of the French Revolution, when radicals decimated the aristocracy, confiscated church lands, and took other measures that destroyed the power of traditional institutions, they left no effective barriers between the individual and the state. Privileges were abolished in the name of democracy, and everyone was reduced to the equal rank of "citizen." The citizen owed supreme allegiance to the state, and he or she depended on the state alone for security, freedom, and the redress of grievances. No longer were there intermediate institutions with political clout that could serve as a political buffer and protect the individual from the ravages of despotism. No longer was there an effective, real-world check on the abuse of power. The rights of

---

[377] Ibid., 2: 510.

the individual had been stripped of their traditional safeguards and now relied solely on the good intentions of those in power. Democratic reforms, while granting freedom to the people *in theory*, had destroyed those intermediate institutions that had historically preserved freedom *in fact*.

This is what Tocqueville had in mind when he equated the individualism of democracy with the principles of despotism. Democracy, by atomizing society into a collection of separate individuals, had fostered the highly centralized power of the sovereign state, leaving nothing between it and the individual – a solitary atom who stood defenseless against overwhelming power.

There is a good deal to be said for this position. However, it scarcely qualifies as a critique of *liberal* individualism, because its chief proponents (Tocqueville, Acton, and others) were essentially liberal in their political orientation. This objection to social atomism is a critique, not of individualism per se, but of *egalitarian democracy* – and especially that form of democracy that sprang from the French Revolution, which was influenced by Rousseau's theory of the "general will."

Liberals sometimes disagreed over the merits of democracy, but virtually all adhered to the traditional distinction between the "principle" of government and its "form" – a distinction that is found in Jefferson's Declaration of Independence. "Principle" refers to the fundamental purpose of government, whereas "form" refers to its structure (monarchy, democracy, etc.). Liberals agreed the purpose of government is to preserve the rights and freedom of individuals, but they sometimes disagreed about which form of government would best accomplish this goal. There was no question, however, that form should be subordinated to principle, that a democratic form of government is valuable, not for its own sake, but only insofar as it serves the cause of liberty.

2. The second meaning of "social atomism" is usually deployed by critics who reject liberal individualism altogether and who seek to indict this entire school of thought for its allegedly unrealistic prejudices and assumptions about the "abstract individual." The perspective here, which focuses on the relationship between the individual and society, is more philosophical than political. Critics object to liberalism's conception of the autonomous individual who exists in his or her own right, and who controls his or her own destiny, independently of his or her social environment.

Liberalism's notion of the "abstract individual" came under intense fire from Burke, Saint-Simon, Comte, Marx, and other critics of Enlightenment liberalism. The abstract individual, say his or her critics, is an artificial prop of liberal ideology, especially as preached by social contract philosophers and *laissez-faire* economists. A person is organically related to his or her social environment; he or she has no essential nature apart from society. As Marx put it in a famous critique of Adam Smith and other free-market economists, a person can develop into an individual "only in the midst of society":

> Production by an isolated individual outside society – a rare exception which may well occur when a civilized person in whom the social forces are already dynamically present is cast by accident into the wilderness – is as much of an absurdity as is the development of language without individuals living *together* and talking to each another.[378]

Marx's critique has become a catechism for many sociologists, who recite it whenever they hear names such as John Locke and Adam Smith. What is it that critics find so troublesome about the abstract individual? As Marx put it, "*man* is no abstract being squatting outside the world. Man is *the world of man*, state, society."[379]

A person is not an "abstract being," and Marx objects to any theory that treats him or her as such. But compare the wording here to the passage we quoted previously, where Marx refers to "an isolated individual outside society."

Marx uses two words – "abstract" and "isolated" – but he fails to distinguish their meanings. The "abstract individual" of liberalism has nothing in common with the "isolated individual" of Marx. "Abstract" means that particular attributes have been abstracted from real human beings and then integrated to form a single concept. The term "isolated," however, means something quite different: It refers to a person who lives apart from other people, like Crusoe on his island before the arrival of Friday.

The standard objection to the "abstract individual" rests on a crude equivocation. It confuses abstraction (a mental process) with isolation (a physical state). Liberals, contrary to Marxian mythology, did not focus on people apart from their social environment; quite the reverse is true. A person's sociability has been a central concern of individualists at least since the seventeenth century.

In the final analysis, every social theory must employ some abstract concept of human beings. When Marx speaks of "man," he means not this or that particular man, but people in general; he means not a concrete individual, but an abstract individual. Social theorists may disagree with how to construct their theoretical models, but no theorist can dispense with models altogether.

---

[378] Karl Marx, *Grundrisse: Foundations of the Critique of Political Economy*, trans. Martin Nicolaus (London: Penguin Books, 1973), 84.

[379] Karl Marx, *A Contribution to the Critique of Hegel's Philosophy of Right: Introduction*, in *Karl Marx: Early Writings*, trans. Rodney Livingstone and Gregor Benton (New York: Vintage Books, 1975), 244.

The abstract individual – otherwise known as "human nature" – is the foundation of social and political philosophy. We cannot generalize without it; we can only refer to particular human beings. We can say "Bob did this" or "Sue did that," but we cannot generalize without the concept "man." The abstract individual allows us to move from the particulars of history to the generalizations of theory. If a critic believes that a particular concept of the individual has omitted relevant characteristics, then she or he is objecting to a specific abstraction, not to the process of abstraction as such. In this case the critic should offer an alternative model of the abstract individual and argue for its acceptance.

### III

Individualism is commonly described as "social atomism" because it supposedly upholds the view that "society" is nothing more than an aggregate of separate and isolated human atoms. Each atomistic individual – self-contained, rational, and morally autonomous – will interact socially with other individuals only if she or he estimates that a particular association will further her or his own self-interest. Society is thereby reduced to a network of economic calculations whose purpose is to maximize personal utility. There exists no "social bond" other than the egoistic impulse, which means that we always and necessarily treat other people as a means to our ends, rather than as ends in themselves.

There are many variations and permutations of allegations regarding "social atomism," but all of them share the peculiar characteristic of having been formulated by the critics of individualism rather than by its defenders. I can think of no major defender of individualism – from John Locke in the seventeenth century to Adam Smith, Herbert Spencer, and Ludwig von Mises in subsequent centuries – who has advocated the supposed tenets of "social atomism." This is a theory without a theorist, a doctrine without a defender, a villainy without a villain.

Social atomism is a theoretical fiction disguised as *interpretation*. The critic of individualism, unable to cite even a few if any defenses of social atomism, presents this doctrine as an implicit premise or unstated assumption of individualist ideology. Although Adam Smith, Herbert Spencer, and other individualists may not have expressly defended (or even understood) this feature of their own ideology, the critic is blessed with a superior insight that enables him to unmask the hidden premises of individualism. As one such critic, Anthony Arblaster, put it in his history of classical liberalism, "it is more common for ideological assumptions to be concealed and implicit – often so effectively that it is only with the advantage of historical hindsight that they are brought to the surface at all."[380] Social atomism, according to Arblaster, is one such "ideological assumption" of liberal individualism.

Liberalism, according to Arblaster, is based on individualism, both onto-logical and ethical. In the realm of ontology (that branch of metaphysics that investigates the nature of being), liberalism upholds the primacy of the individual human being, who is seen as more "real" than social institutions. Similarly, in the realm of ethics, liberalism attaches a higher moral value to the individual than to any group or collective. "In this way of thinking the individual comes before society in every sense."[381]

After presenting this summary, which is largely unobjectionable, Arblaster protests that "the concept of 'the individual' is both ambiguous and question-begging." Liberalism's stress on the individual puts undue emphasis on "what separates or distinguishes one person from another, rather than on what one person has in common with his or her fellow human beings." The single human being, when viewed in isolation from others and from society, comes to be regarded as complete, self-sufficient, and autonomous. Individualism, according to Arblaster, has emphasized "the inherently anti-social, or at least non-social, character of the human being."

Such sweeping generalizations, however inaccurate, are easier to make than to refute. And they cannot be ruled out of court, because philosophers do indeed work from ideological assumptions that they sometimes fail to iden-tify. Nonetheless it is important to distinguish between two kinds of unstated assumptions, namely those that are *tacit* and those that are *implicit*.

Both tacit and implicit assumptions are ideas that, though relevant to a given argument, are not explicitly identified by proponents of that argument. But there is an important difference between the tacit and the implicit. Tacit ideas are those ideas that a philosopher does not express, but *could* express if questioned or criticized. Every argument contains tacit ideas in this sense, because no argument is completely self-contained. Every argument presup-poses the truth or validity of other propositions that are not expressly identified or included within the argument itself.

Implicit ideas, like tacit ideas, are invisible elements of argument. But whereas tacit ideas constitute a *psychological* link between a philosopher and his or her argument, implicit ideas constitute a *logical* relationship. An idea is tacit if it refers to an unexpressed *belief*, whereas an idea is implicit if it refers to an unexpressed *implication* or abstract *relationship*. Whereas the former is

---

[380] Arblaster, *The Rise and Decline of Western Liberalism*, 9.
[381] Ibid., 14.

psychological, the latter is epistemological. The implicit presuppositions of an argument do not depend on whether they are understood or accepted, but on the inherent logic of ideas.

No informed and fair-minded critic of liberal individualism can claim that its leading proponents believed in "social atomism," whether expressly or tacitly. To claim that Adam Smith and others in his tradition ignored the social nature of people is a crude fiction, as will be readily apparent to anyone who bothers to consult the original sources. In *The Theory of Moral Sentiments*, for example, Adam Smith wrote that "man, who can subsist only in society, was fitted by nature to that situation for which he was made."[382] Similar remarks about the social nature of people appear frequently in the writings of liberal individualists, including those by its modern proponents. Consider this passage by Ludwig von Mises, one of the most radical of modern individualists:

> Modern man is a social being, not only as one whose material needs could not be supplied in isolation, but also as one who has achieved a development of reason and of the perceptive faculty that would have been impossible except within society. Man is inconceivable as an isolated being, for humanity exists only as a social phenomenon and mankind transcended the stage of animality only in so far as cooperation evolved the social relationships between the individuals. Evolution from the human animal to the human being was made possible by and achieved by means of social cooperation and by that alone.[383]

This passage is typical of liberal individualism, as that tradition has developed since the seventeenth century. Thus critics, unable to support the thesis that social atomism is a tacit doctrine of individualism (i.e., one that its proponents accepted but failed to articulate) have no choice but to present social atomism as an implicit feature of individualism. In this view, social atomism is logically implied by individualism, however much its proponents may protest to the contrary.

IV

Standard textbook accounts frequently link nineteenth-century individualism to "Social Darwinism," an unsavory doctrine that supposedly advocated "survival of the fittest" in matters of social policy. Two liberals in particular

---

[382] Smith, *Theory of Moral Sentiments*, 85.
[383] Ludwig von Mises, *Socialism: An Economic and Sociological Analysis*, trans. J. Kahane (Indianapolis: Liberty Fund, 1981), 259.

– Herbert Spencer and William Graham Sumner – are linked by critics to Social Darwinism, so I shall focus on their ideas in an effort to clear up some common misinterpretations.

Neither Spencer nor Sumner held the views that are commonly attributed to them. Social Darwinism, as that doctrine is understood by many critics, is little more than sheer fabrication. For one thing, Spencer's approach to evolution (which he developed independently of Darwin) was essentially Lamarckian. Spencer, unlike Darwin, believed that acquired characteristics are genetically transmitted from one generation to the next, and he placed relatively little emphasis on the process of natural selection. This Lamarckian approach, despite its failures as a *biological* theory, is a far better model of *social* development than is its Darwinian counterpart. Humans do in fact inherit and build upon the "adaptations" of their progenitors – as we see in language, the transmission of knowledge, technology, capital investment, social institutions, and the like.

Both Spencer and Sumner used the phrase "survival of the fittest" – indeed, it was Spencer (not Darwin) who coined the term – and both men lived to regret it, because it made them easy targets for misrepresentation. Spencer complained that his views were being distorted by his critics, and in some cases deliberately so. "I have had much experience in controversy," he wrote in later life, "and my impression is that in three cases out of four the alleged opinions of mine condemned by opponents, are not opinions of mine at all, but are opinions wrongly ascribed by them to me."[384] Sumner became so frustrated by the same problem that he stopped using the phrase "survival of the fittest" altogether, so it never appears in his later writings and speeches.

It is largely owing to the "survival of the fittest" doctrine that Spencer and Sumner have been labeled – or, more precisely, condemned – as Social Darwinists. Social Darwinists, we are told, were infused with a stern and implacable contempt for the poor, disabled, and disadvantaged – those allegedly unfit persons who, by a law of nature, should give way in the struggle for existence to those who are more fit. It is a safe bet that if you consult virtually any standard text on the history of ideas or political philosophy, you will find this view (or a close approximation) attributed to Herbert Spencer and William Graham Sumner.

There are two reasons why this grievous misinterpretation should not be allowed to pass without comment and correction. First, there is a simple matter of historical justice. Both Spencer and Sumner devoted their lives to social betterment – to improving the social and economic conditions of the lower

[384] "Exaggerations and Mis-Statements," in *Facts and Comments* (New York: Appleton, 1902), 151.

and middle classes whom they regarded as the primary victims of government power. And critics, whether they agree or not with liberalism's contention that the lower economic classes are the greatest beneficiaries of a free market, should not be permitted, without protest, to besmirch the reputation of two of liberalism's greatest champions.

Second, there is more involved here than the reputation of two dead liberals. The textbook assaults on Spencer and Sumner are intended, implicitly if not explicitly, to characterize the attitude of *laissez-faire* advocates in general. We have advanced, it is said, from the heartless "dog-eat-dog" attitude of Social Darwinism and *laissez-faire* economics to the compassionate welfare policies of modern governments. We are told that the modern liberal (in contrast to the classical liberal) cares about people more than profits, that she or he values human rights over property rights – and so on, until we drown in a sea of tiresome clichés.

Historical misrepresentations play a major role in political and economic debates, where first impressions often determine whether we will study a given theory in detail. We must be selective, after all; we cannot possibly read what every writer, or even the most important ones, have written about every significant issue. This is where secondary "textbook" accounts play a role in shaping public opinion. The college student who, in his first textbook encounter with Spencer or Sumner, is told that they favored a ruthless Social Darwinism, is unlikely to be enthusiastic about reading these villains for himself in any kind of detail. And should that student ever become a teacher himself, he will teach to his students the selfsame errors that were taught to him.

"Social Darwinism," as that label is commonly understood, is not only an inappropriate label for the ideas of Spencer and Sumner, who never used it themselves; it also represents the opposite of everything they stood for. But what about the phrase, "survival of the fittest" – which they did use? What precisely did they mean by this rather ominous expression?

We should first be clear about what they didn't mean. Spencer repeatedly emphasized that, in using the terms "fit" and "fittest," he was not expressing a value judgment; nor was he referring to a particular characteristic, such as strength or intelligence; nor was he expressing any kind of approval or disapproval; nor was he referring to economic or biological competition. This doctrine "is expressible in purely physical terms, which neither imply competition nor imply better and worse." And, most importantly, *"survival of the fittest is not always the survival of the best."*

> The law [of survival of the fittest] is not the survival of the "better" or the "stronger." ... It is the survival of those which are constitutionally fittest to

thrive under the conditions in which they are placed; and very often that which, humanly speaking is inferiority, causes the survival.[385]

As Spencer pointed out, if a living organism is to survive and prosper, it must adapt to its external environment. This ability to adapt is what Spencer meant by "fitness." If an organism is unfitted to the general conditions of survival – that is, if it fails to adapt – then it will live in a diseased or unhealthy state or, perhaps, ultimately die. To be "fit," therefore, is to be adapted to the requirements of survival, whatever those requirements may be.

In a social context, the "fittest" are those persons who are able to adapt to the survival requirements of their society. If a government decrees that all redheads shall be executed on the spot, then it follows that the persons best fitted for survival in such a society would be non-redheads, or those natural redheads who adapt by changing their hair color or shaving their heads. We can state this "survival of the fittest" principle without condoning the penalty against redheads, and without regarding non-redheads as superior people. It is a simple, inescapable fact: If a government kills redheads, then (other things being equal) you have a better chance to survive – that is, you are more "fit" to survive under the circumstances – if you do not have red hair.

This interpretation, which treats "survival of the fittest" as a value-free description of what in fact *does* occur, rather than as a prescription or approval of what *ought* to occur, was also put forward by Sumner, who tried – in vain, as it turned out – to correct the distorted interpretations of his critics:

> At the meeting of the Liberal Union Club at which I read a paper, it seemed to me that there was some misapprehension in regard to the doctrine of the survival of the fittest. Such misapprehension is very common in spite of many efforts of the leading evolutionists to correct it. It is supposed that the doctrine is that the *best* survive. This is an error, and it forms the basis for all disputes about evolution and ethics. For the word "best" implies moral standards, a moral standpoint, etc.; and if the doctrine were affirmed in that form, it would not be scientific at all, but would be theological, for it would involve the notion that man is the end of creation and that his notions of things are the standard to which things must conform. The doctrine is that those survive who are fittest to survive.[386]

The idea expressed here was central to the sociological methodology of both Spencer and Sumner. Both stressed the fact that human beings adapt to

[385] "Mr. Martineau on Evolution," in *Recent Discussions in Science, Philosophy and Morals* (New York: Appleton, 1878), 339–40.
[386] Sumner, "The Survival of the Fittest," in *On Liberty, Society, and Politics*, 223.

social conditions through the formation of their habits and character. Both believed that character traits play a more important role in society than abstract beliefs and theories. Which character traits emerge in a given society depends largely on the social and political sanctions imposed by that society, on what kinds of behavior are encouraged or discouraged, rewarded or punished. If, for example, a society rewards indolence and penalizes industry, then indolent people will tend to fare better than the industrious. The indolent, having adapted to the conditions of that society, will be rendered more fit than the industrious, who have failed to adapt. This is the meaning of Spencer's oft-quoted remark, "The ultimate result of shielding men from the effects of folly, is to fill the world with fools."

When Spencer and Sumner applied their "survival of the fittest" principle to a free, industrial society, they reached conclusions that differ radically from the position supposedly taken by Social Darwinists. True, the sacrifice of one individual for the benefit of another is the general rule for lower life forms. It is equally true of the lower forms of human society – militaristic, authoritarian societies that Spencer and Sumner (following the legal historian H.S. Maine) called "regimes of status." But as the regime of status gradually gives way to the regime of contract, as voluntary cooperation replaces coercion as the dominant mode of social interaction, we witness a fundamental change in the conditions of social "survival" and its corresponding standard of "fitness."

In a free society, people are able to pursue their own interests as they see fit, provided they respect the equal rights of others. Cooperation in a regime of contract replaces the exploitation in a regime of status – and the "fittest" survive, not by coercing or exploiting others, but by assisting them through the mutual exchange of a market economy. Survival here is achieved by providing others in society with desired goods and services. Here as elsewhere, "survival of the fittest" is an iron law of social existence, but the standard of fitness is far removed from that suggested by the specter of Social Darwinism. Voluntary cooperation, not coercive exploitation, is the standard of fitness in a free society.

Spencer, Sumner, and other liberals clearly understood that market competition differs radically from biological competition, where one organism preys on another to survive. Market competition, unlike biological competition, is able to produce additional wealth through the division of labor, thus making it possible for many people to survive and prosper who otherwise could not. Moreover, the complex division of labor that evolves in a market economy generates specialization, and this specialization generates social interdependence, a condition in which every person must rely on the cooperation and assistance of others for necessary goods and services. The solitary individual cannot produce everything he or she needs or wants in a market economy, so he or she must persuade many others to provide assistance. This condition of survival cultivates the character traits (or virtues) necessary for peaceful interaction – those civilizing *mores*, as Sumner called them, that make social interaction not only productive, but pleasant as well.

Thus, to associate market competition with the biological competition of Darwinism is to misunderstand how liberals viewed the market. Biological competition, where one individual survives at the expense of another, is a zero-sum game; in contrast, market competition is a positive-sum game, where participants gain from their voluntary transactions with others. It is precisely in a free society that Social Darwinism does not apply. In a complex society with an advanced division of labor, where we must give others what they want in order to get what we want, the "fit" are those who can enlist the voluntary cooperation of others. And where success depends upon persuasion rather than coercion, the standard of social "fitness" is measured by one's ability to influence others by offering them something of value, that is, by benefiting them.

But what about the poor, disabled, and disadvantaged? Popular mythology about *laissez-faire* liberals, propagated in one textbook account after another, depicts them as implacable enemies of charity and other measures designed to help those who cannot help themselves. Let us now turn to this controversial issue, again focusing on the writing of Spencer and Sumner.

If we are to understand the views of Herbert Spencer and William Graham Sumner on charity and related issues, we must first understand their roles as pioneers in sociology. Spencer is widely acknowledged as a pioneer in what is known as the "functionalist" school of sociology, while Sumner, during his decades as a Yale professor, did much to establish the reputation of sociology as a legitimate science in American universities.

Spencer and Sumner believed that natural laws (i.e., laws of cause and effect) operate in the social world just as surely as they do in physics, biology, and other natural sciences; the basic purpose of sociology, or a science of society, is to discover and formulate these causal laws. They also believed that causation in society is far more complex and difficult to discern than in the physical world, and that ignorance of this fact has led to many ill-conceived political measures. For example, in his influential book, *The Study of Sociology*, Spencer had this to say about those who offer simplistic political solutions for complex social problems:

> Proximate causes and proximate results are alone contemplated. There is scarcely any consciousness that the original causes are often numerous and widely different from the apparent cause; and that beyond each immediate result there will be multitudinous remote results, most of them quite incalculable.[387]

[387] Herbert Spencer, *The Study of Sociology* (Ann Arbor: University of Michigan, 1961), 2.

Many people are ignorant of physical causation, so it is perhaps no surprise that many more are ignorant of social causation, which is "so much more subtle and complex." Where there is little or no awareness of social causation, "political superstitions" abound, including the belief that government has a special power, transcending that of mere mortals, to solve social problems. In addition,

> The ordinary political schemer is convinced that out of a legislative apparatus, properly devised and worked with due dexterity, may be had beneficial State-action without any detrimental reaction.[388]

William Graham Sumner made a similar point in a number of his essays on sociology. Three facts, he said, are essential to an understanding of social causation. First, social phenomena always present themselves to us in complex combinations. Second, it is by no means easy to interpret these phenomena. Third, we cannot set up social experiments as we do in the physical sciences. Sociology is therefore an extremely difficult discipline, one that requires years of study and observation.

Yet virtually everyone has an opinion about social problems and what is needed to make them better; when some opinions become politically popular, the government attempts to implement them. Sumner put it this way:

> The diagnosis of some asserted social ill and the prescription of the remedy are undertaken offhand by the first comer, and without reflecting that the diagnosis of a social disease is many times harder than that of a disease in an individual, and that to prescribe for a society is to prescribe for an organism which is immortal. To err in prescribing for a man is at worst to kill him; to err in prescribing for a society is to set in operation injurious forces which extend, ramify, and multiply their effects in ever new combinations throughout an indefinite future. It may pay to experiment with an individual, because he cannot wait for medical science to be perfected; it cannot pay to experiment with a society, because the society does not die and can afford to wait.[389]

Sumner, like Spencer, argued that ignorance of, or disregard for, causal laws in social interaction generates the dangerous notion that people, acting through a coercive government, can eradicate any social problems they wish, if only they have good intentions and sufficient determination.

> The assumption which underlies almost all discussion of social topics is that we men need only to make up our minds what kind of society we want, and that then we can devise means for calling that society into existence.[390]

---

[388] Ibid., 5.
[389] William Graham Sumner, "Sociology," in *On Liberty, Society, and Politics*, 186.
[390] Ibid., 187.

This is the basic fallacy in socialism and other utopian schemes to remodel society according to preconceived moral ideals. If, for example, we believe that everyone has a right to the good things in life or to equal wealth, then we need only empower and instruct government to implement these moral ideals. These and similar notions flow from what Sumner called a "sentimental philosophy."

> The sentimental philosophy starts from the first principle that nothing is true which is disagreeable, and that we must not believe anything which is "shocking," no matter what the evidence may be. It touches on one side the intuitional philosophy which proves that certain things must exist by proving that man needs them, and it touches on the other side the vulgar socialism which affirms that the individual has a right to whatever he needs, and that this right is good against his fellow men.[391]

Sumner and Spencer criticized this way of thinking in a manner that was later deployed by F.A. Hayek, Ludwig von Mises, Milton Friedman, and other modern economists. Central to their analysis is the doctrine of unintended consequences, a theory that was especially developed in great detail by Herbert Spencer, who called it the "multiplication of effects."

In social affairs, according to Spencer, "the effect is more complex than the cause."[392] A single cause, such as an economic regulation, will generate a complex network of effects, and each of these effects in turn will cause innumerable other effects, as purposeful human beings adjust and adapt themselves to the new conditions. This is why social legislation, despite the best intentions of legislators, so often leads to unforeseen and detrimental long-term consequences. Spencer, throughout his many books and essays, presented many dozens of examples in which social legislation actually exacerbated the problems they were intended to solve.

Spencer and Sumner emphasized that nature, not people, establishes the conditions of human survival. In our continuous struggle to survive, we must learn to master the forces of nature, and we must learn to cooperate with other people so that they become a help rather than a hindrance in that struggle. In dealing with nature, we have benefited greatly from science and technology. Similarly, in learning to deal with our fellow humans, Spencer and Sumner believed we can learn a great deal from sociology.

Spencer and Sumner, following in the path of Adam Smith and other liberal economists, believed that the greatest discoveries of economic and social science rested on an insight that, though it took many centuries to

---

[391] Ibid., 190.
[392] Herbert Spencer, *First Principles*, 6th ed. (New York: Appleton, 1901), 398.

develop, was relatively simple. If we wish to advance the general welfare, then the best policy is to establish a rule of law that establishes equal rights, and then leave people free to pursue their own desires, interests, and passions as they deem proper.

If a person suffers injustice at the hands of another person, then the government should intervene on behalf of the victim; this is something government has the power to accomplish. But natural evils, such as hunger and disease, do not normally result from human acts of injustice; rather, they are aspects of the human condition that can only be ameliorated, if not eradicated altogether, by human labor and intelligence. These require freedom to operate most effectually.

This theoretical background must be kept in mind when we consider the liberal opposition to welfare legislation. Consider, for example, this passage from Sumner, which again raises the subject of "survival of the fittest":

> We have noticed that the relations involved in the struggle for existence are twofold. There is first the struggle of individuals to win the means of subsistence from nature, and secondly there is the competition of man with man in the effort to win a limited supply. The radical error of the socialists and sentimentalists is that they never distinguish these two relations from each other. They bring forward complaints which are really to be made, if at all, against the author of the universe for the hardships which man has to endure in his struggle with nature. The complaints are addressed, however, to society; that is, to other men under the same hardships. The only *social* element, however, is the competition of life, and when society is blamed for the ills which belong to the human lot, it is only burdening those who have successfully contended with those ills with the further task of conquering the same ills over again for somebody else. Hence liberty perishes in all socialistic schemes, and the tendency of such schemes is to the deterioration of society by burdening the good members and relieving the bad ones. The law of the survival of the fittest was not made by man and cannot be abrogated by man. We can only, by interfering with it, produce the survival of the unfittest. If a man comes forward with any grievance against the order of society so far as this is shaped by human agency, he must have patient hearing and full redress; but if he addresses a man for relief from the hardships of life, he asks simply that somebody else should get his living for him. In that case he ought to be left to find out his error from hard experience.[393]

This is the kind of passage, which we also find in Spencer, that is apt to be viewed in a harsh light by modern readers. But if our goal is understanding

---

[393] Sumner, "Sociology," 190.

rather than political correctness, then we need to keep in mind the earlier background material, especially the remarks about "survival of the fittest." It is unfortunate that Sumner used the terms "good" and "bad" in conjunction with his ideas about survival of the fittest, because these imply a moral judgment that Sumner did not intend. Rather, he meant "good" and "bad" in a functional sense, as when we say that this is a "good" or "bad" knife, depending on how well it cuts. Also, when Sumner said that people ought to learn their errors from "hard experience," this might be interpreted (and has been, by the way) as opposition to voluntary charity and other kinds of assistance to those in need. Again, however, this is not something that Sumner – or Spencer – believed, as they both made clear many times throughout their writings.

Spencer and Sumner opposed state charity – that is, charity that is coercively financed through taxation – but both were in favor of voluntary charity. This, for them, was an all-important distinction, since they believed that coercion changes the essential nature of an act and alters its impact on society in general. Nevertheless, even in their own day the positions of both men were commonly misrepresented. Let us first consider the view of Herbert Spencer.

Spencer opposed coercive, state-enforced charity, but he favored charity that is voluntarily bestowed. As a matter of justice, one should not be forced to help others; but, as a matter of ethics, one may be obligated to help others. Spencer noted with some consternation that his views brought on him "condemnation as an enemy of the poor." In one essay, for example, he pointed out that it was becoming more common for the rich to contribute in time and money to those who were less well off; and this he praised as "a new and better chivalry," "the latest and most hopeful fact in human history" that would eradicate various evils. In addition, the final chapters in Spencer's two-volume work, *The Principles of Ethics*, are devoted to the subject of "positive beneficence," the highest form of society in which people voluntarily help those in need.

This scarcely fits the common picture of a Herbert Spencer devoid of humanitarian sentiments, but one must read Spencer's extensive treatment of this subject to appreciate fully the misrepresentations of his critics. That he was grievously offended by such lies is dramatically illustrated by the fact that he broke off a close friendship of some forty years with Thomas Henry Huxley when Huxley wrote that, according to the Spencerian individualist, a poor man should be left to starve, because charity interferes with the survival of the fittest. In reply to this accusation of "reasoned savagery," Spencer gave this reply: "For nearly fifty years I have contended that the pains attendant on the struggle for existence may fitly be qualified by the aid which private sympathy prompts." Although Huxley later apologized for his error, it still took several years for the friendship to heal.

In Spencer's first book, *Social Statics*, we find a chapter on England's poor laws in which Spencer's views on charity are clearly expressed. This is an especially interesting discussion, because it exemplifies Spencer's "conscience liberalism," a tradition we discussed earlier.

Recall that conscience liberals drew a fundamental distinction between moral duties, which flow from the inner voice of conscience, and legal (or juridical) duties, which pertain to external acts of justice and injustice. This distinction played a crucial role in the centuries-long campaign for freedom of religion.

For conscience liberals, a key question about charity was this: Is it unjust if we refuse to contribute money to a person in need – assuming, of course, that his or her poverty was not caused by a previous act of injustice on our part? To this, Herbert Spencer, and many other conscience liberals, answered "no." It may be considered immoral, depending on our religious and ethical principles, but it is not unjust. One person does not have a right to the honestly acquired wealth of other people, so the rights of a poor person are not violated if others refuse to help him or her.

For Spencer, the principle of conscience applies here as much as it does to our religious beliefs, sexual preferences, and other areas of personal morality. We may, for example, disapprove of our neighbor's religious beliefs and practices, and we have the right, using voluntary methods, to persuade him or her to our point of view. But we do not have the right to force our beliefs upon this neighbor or, what amounts to the same thing, to compel him or her to pay, through taxes, to support an established church. This had long been the guiding principle of dissenters, or Nonconformists, in England – those non-Anglican Protestants who for many decades had suffered under severe legal discrimination. And Spencer chastises some of his fellow dissenters who, while supporting liberty of conscience in religious matters, violated that principle in matters of charity, which is also a question of conscience.

As many Christian thinkers had argued for many centuries, an act that has moral value for the actor when performed voluntarily, from a sense of moral conviction, has no moral worth whatever if it is coercively enforced. This, for Spencer, was an insight with profound implications. The social relationship between benefactor and beneficiary does much to refine and civilize human beings, because it cultivates our sense of sympathy, whereby we identify with the problems and concerns of other people. Spencer's use of the term "sympathy" – a psychological concept that is today better expressed by the word "empathy" – was widely discussed by David Hume, Adam Smith, and other eighteenth-century philosophers, who stressed its role in the civilizing process. According to these philosophers, social interaction becomes more peaceful and harmonious as we learn to identify with other people – as we learn to put ourselves, so to speak, in the shoes of others, and experience the world from their perspective. As we learn to empathize with the beliefs, values, and situations of other people, we become more tolerant of their differences, more respectful of their rights, and more willing to help them voluntarily.

Spencer, like Adam Smith and others before him, believed that a free, "industrial" society, in which there exists a complex division of labor, increases social interdependence, because we must rely on the cooperation of others for goods and services. This society of contract, in contrast to the older society of status, requires that we treat others as equals, not just in a legal sense, but in a personal sense as well. Throughout the eighteenth century, many defenders of the older society of status, such as the writer Samuel Johnson, noted with disgust the tendency of a market economy to break down class barriers and other social distinctions. For example, Johnson noted that his shoe shiner, who in earlier times would have shown great deference to his social betters, because he would have relied entirely on them for his income, had become too independent in England's expanding commercial economy, because there were now plenty of people who could afford to have their shoes shined. Defenders of the society of status constantly complained, therefore, that tradesmen and other workers had become "saucy" and "impertinent."

Adam Smith, in contrast, welcomed this emerging social independence; he was followed in this regard by Spencer and many other liberals, who believed that this sense of equality would, over time, generate more positive acts of beneficence between the haves and the have-nots. But this would be a beneficence that one person extends to his social equals, not the paternalism of the older regime of status, as exemplified by the support given of a feudal lord for his serfs and other dependents.

This fascinating subject deserves far more attention than I can give it here, but the foregoing remarks illustrate the fact that Spencer's views on charity were hardly some kind of knee-jerk reaction or cruel prejudice against the poor. As Spencer saw the matter, the evolving sentiment of social generosity would be seriously curtailed by state-enforced charity. We react negatively to being coerced, so coercive charity, rather than enhancing social sympathy, will serve instead to retard it. State charity corrupts the inner qualities of both benefactors and beneficiaries. Spencer's remarks on this subject deserve to be quoted at length:

> Note again how this act-of-Parliament charity perpetually supersedes men's better sentiments. Here is a respectable citizen with enough and time to spare: a man of some feeling; liberal, if there is need; generous even if his pity is excited. A beggar knocks at his door, or he is accosted in his walk by some wayworn tramp. What does he do? Does he listen, investigate, and, if

proper, assist? No; he commonly cuts short the tale with, "I have nothing for you, my good man; you must go to your parish." And then he shuts the door or walks on, as the case may be, with evident unconcern. Should it strike him the next moment that there was something very woebegone in the petitioner's look, this uncomfortable thought is met by the reflection that so long as there is a Poor Law, he cannot starve and that it will be time enough to consider his claims when he applies for relief. Thus does the consciousness that there exists a legal provision for the indigent act as an opiate for the yearnings of sympathy. Had there been no ready-made excuse, the behavior would probably have been different. Commiseration, pleading for at least an inquiry into the case, would most likely have prevailed; and, in place of an application to the board of guardians, ending in a pittance coldly handed across the pay table to be thanklessly received, might have commenced a relationship good for both parties – a generosity humanizing to the one, and a succor made doubly valuable to the other by a few words of consolation and encouragement, followed, it may be, by a lift into some self-supporting position.

In truth there could hardly be found a more efficient device for estranging men from each other and decreasing their fellow feeling than this system of state almsgiving. Being kind by proxy! Could anything be more blighting to the finer instincts?[394]

Spencer and other liberals were concerned about the dehumanizing effects of bureaucracies, where people are treated as mere ciphers, as interchangeable units to be manipulated and controlled by government employees. By turning what should be matters of personal conscience over to bureaucratic machines, the finer sensibilities of human nature are warped into feelings that generate discord and animosity.

And thus we have the gentle, softening, elevating intercourse that should be habitually taking place between rich and poor superseded by a cold, hard, lifeless mechanism bound together by dry parchment acts and regulations, managed by commissioners, boards, clerks, and collectors, who perform their respective functions as tasks, and kept a-going by money forcibly taken from all classes indiscriminately. In place of the music breathed by feeling attuned to kind deeds, we have the harsh creaking and jarring of a thing that cannot stir without creating discord – a thing whose every act, from the gathering of its funds to their final distribution, is prolific of grumblings, discontent, anger – a thing that breeds squabbles about authority, disputes as to claims, browbeatings, jealousies, litigations, corruption, trickery, lying, ingratitude –

---

[394] Spencer, *Social Statics*, 286.

a thing that supplants, and therefore makes dormant, men's nobler feelings, while it stimulates their baser ones.[395]

Spencer regarded these consequences as more than incidental by-products of state charity – merely negative side effects that are outweighed, in the long run, by its benefits. Rather, governmental programs enmesh themselves into the social fabric, create social conflict between haves and have-nots, and thus frequently exacerbate the problems they are intended to solve. Government, after all, does not create additional wealth but merely redistributes wealth that has been created through social cooperation. It does not therefore eliminate the burdens that come from the struggle to survive, but merely rearranges those burdens, causing untold hardships among working people who are compelled to sacrifice their own welfare for the benefit of others, including a vast administrative machinery.

William Graham Sumner made many of the same points as Herbert Spencer; in his famous essay, "The Forgotten Man," he focused on this perennial victim of governmental programs:

It is plain enough that the Forgotten Man and the Forgotten Woman are the very life and substance of society. They are the ones who ought to be first and always remembered. They are always forgotten by sentimentalists, philanthropists, reformers, enthusiasts, and every description of speculator in sociology, political economy, or political science. If a student of any of these sciences ever comes to . . . appreciate the true value [of the Forgotten Man], you will find such a student an uncompromising advocate of the strictest scientific thinking on all social topics, and a cold and hard-hearted skeptic towards all artificial schemes of social amelioration. If it is desired to bring about social improvements, bring us a scheme for relieving the Forgotten Man of some of his burdens. He is our productive force which we are wasting. Let us stop wasting his force. Then we shall have a clean and simple gain for the whole society.[396]

The appellation of "Forgotten Man," Sumner noted, is somewhat inaccurate, since this person is never thought of at all, at least not by reformers and social speculators. He is a political nonentity who lacks the clout of organized interest groups, who are able to use government to increase their own profits, power, and privileges. Most everybody feels competent to philosophize about social problems and to offer political solutions, but virtually none of these schemes takes into account their impact on the average, hard-working citizen

---

[395] Ibid., 287.
[396] William Graham Sumner, "The Forgotten Man," in *On Liberty, Society, and Politics*, 220–21.

who wishes merely to raise his or her family, provide creature comforts, and be left alone.

These forgotten men and women are the primary producers of wealth in society, and they are also the primary victims of social and economic legislation. They are forced to pay for the so-called rehabilitation of alcoholics and others who have lived improvident lives; they are forced to pay for the inflated profits of merchants and manufacturers who benefit from tariffs and other economic regulations; they are forced to pay for subsidies doled out to rich agricultural interests, who use tax moneys to improve their land; they are forced to pay for the cultural and recreational entertainment of the well-to-do, who demand museums, national parks, and other ways to dispose of leisure time that the forgotten man does not enjoy.

The Forgotten Man, like those with political connections, wishes to better his economic situation, but he must do so by voluntary means, enlisting the cooperation of others. This contrasts with those in government who have at their disposal a powerful coercive mechanism, which permits them to live by expropriating the wealth of others. This leads to what Sumner calls "jobbery," which he defines as follows:

> By jobbery I mean the constantly apparent effort to win wealth, not by honest and independent production, but by some sort of a scheme for extorting other people's product from them.[397]

When government is permitted to extend its activities beyond the equal protection of rights, it becomes a means by which some people exploit others, rather than a means to prevent such exploitation. Or, in Sumner's terms, it becomes a vast system of political jobbery. A free society, in contrast, permits people to do as they like, provided they respect the rights of others, but it also requires that people accept the responsibility and consequences of their own actions, whether good or bad. Freedom and responsibility are two sides of the same coin; one cannot exist without the other.

> The institutions of civil liberty leave each man to run his career in life in his own way, only guaranteeing to him that whatever he does in the way of industry, economy, prudence, sound judgment, etc., shall redound to his own welfare and shall not be diverted to some one else's benefit. Of course it is a necessary corollary that each man shall bear the penalty of his own vices and his own mistakes. If I want to be free from any other man's dictation, I must understand that I can have no other man under my control.[398]

---

[397] Ibid., 217.
[398] Ibid., 207.

# 10

# Methodological Individualism

## I

Liberals have been widely criticized for their view that the individual is the ultimate unit of explanation in the social sciences, and that social institutions can be explained solely in terms of the actions of individuals. This approach – known as "methodological individualism" – was taken for granted by Adam Ferguson, Adam Smith, and other eighteenth-century social theorists; it was not until the nineteenth century that various types of social "holism" challenged this view. The controversy continues to this day; since there is a good deal of misunderstanding about what methodological individualism does and does not entail, let us now examine this theory.

Joseph Schumpeter apparently coined the term "methodological individualism"; he used the term to signify a subset of "sociological individualism."

> By Sociological Individualism we mean the view, widely held in the seventeenth and eighteenth centuries, that the self-governing individual constitutes the ultimate unit of the social sciences, and that all social phenomena resolve themselves into decisions and actions of individuals that need not or cannot be further analyzed in terms of superindividual factors.[399]

Schumpeter regarded sociological individualism as an untenable theory, insofar as it fails to take into account the influence of social factors on individual behavior. This does not mean, however, that we must always consider these formative influences when seeking to explain social phenomena. The economist may analyze a homemaker's economic behavior "without going

---

[399] Joseph Schumpeter, *History of Economic Analysis*, ed. Elizabeth Schumpeter (New York: Oxford University Press, 1954), 888.

into the factors that formed it," and in this case "we speak of Methodological Individualism."[400]

"Methodological individualism" has since acquired a somewhat broader meaning than Schumpeter gave it. Its central tenet is that "all actions are performed by individuals,"[401] or, more specifically, that social phenomena "should always be understood as resulting from the decisions, actions, attitudes, etc., of human individuals, and that we should never be satisfied by an explanation in terms of so-called 'collectives' (states, nations, races, etc.)."[402]

Methodological individualism does not say that only the individual human being is "real" or that social phenomena do not exist. (This issue involves another controversy – that between realism and nominalism – which we shall examine presently.) Methodological individualism says that only the individual is able to think, feel, and act. We can impute actions, purposes, and values only to the singular human being; when we apply such terms to society we enter the domain of metaphor. But this does not mean that "society" cannot be said to "exist" in some fashion. Many things exist that neither think nor act nor feel.


II


Methodological individualism should not be confused with social *nominalism*. The latter is the doctrine that society and social phenomena exist in name only, that they are literally "fictions" (as Jeremy Bentham called them) that cannot be said to exist apart from individuals and their actions.

The difference between social nominalism and methodological individualism may be seen in the writings of Herbert Spencer, who adopted the latter view but not the former. When Spencer posed the question of whether society is "but a collective name for a number of individuals," he answered, "no"; society is an "entity" with identifiable properties. This answer may seem surprising, for was not Spencer a methodological individualist? Yes, but this did not prevent him from maintaining that "society" is a real entity.[403]

---

[400] Prior to Schumpeter, Max Weber (*Economy and Society*, 1: 18) referred to the "individualistic method," and Élie Halévy (*Growth of Philosophic Radicalism*, 504–05) wrote of the "individualistic hypothesis," according to which the individual is "the principle of explanation in the social sciences."

[401] Ludwig von Mises, *Human Action: A Treatise of Economics*, 3rd. ed. (Chicago: Rengery, 1963), 42.

[402] Karl Popper, *The Open Society and Its Enemies*, 5th ed. (London; Routledge & Kegan Paul, 1973), 2: 98.

[403] All quotations from Herbert Spencer in this section are from *The Principles of Sociology*, in *Herbert Spencer: Structure, Function, and Evolution*, ed. Stanislav Andreski (New York: Charles Scribner's Sons, 1971), 107–08.

Spencer dismissed the view "that society is but a collective name for a number of individuals" – in other words, that only individuals exist, while "the existence of the society is but verbal." This nominalist doctrine maintains that the members of a society are essentially identical to a lecturer's audience: an aggregate, a "certain arrangement of persons," that disappears after the lecture is over.

Spencer noted an important difference between an audience and society. The audience is a temporary gathering of individuals who do not exhibit fixed and recurring patterns of interaction. A society, by contrast, exhibits a "permanence of relations among component parts which constitutes the individuality of a whole as distinguished from the individualities of its parts."

The relationship between society and individual human beings is like the relationship between a house and the individual stones that make it up. A house is more than a mere heap of stones randomly arranged; it consists of stones that are "connected in fixed ways." Similarly, a society is more than a heap, or aggregate, of individual human beings; it consists of individuals who exhibit a "general persistence" in their mutual relationships. This permanent element is the "trait which yields our idea of society."

Thus society is more than an aggregate of individuals; it is a *system* of individual relationships. Institutions are recurring and predictable *patterns* of interaction with definite characteristics that can be identified and studied by the sociologist, apart from their concrete manifestations in particular cases. Social institutions are "real" in the sense that they reveal themselves to human consciousness as objective features of the external world. They are discovered rather than invented; we cannot will them out of existence as we can a subjective idea that exists only in the mind. And it is this objectivity that makes an impartial science of society – i.e., sociology – possible.

Spencer, as I said, was a methodological individualist; despite his overuse (and even misuse) of the "social organism" metaphor, he repeatedly emphasized that individual human beings are the ultimate components of every social institution. But we have also seen that Spencer emphatically repudiated social nominalism in favor of realism. He regarded social phenomena as real things, because they exhibit permanent characteristics that can be studied by objective scientific procedures.

The difference between methodological individualism and social nominalism was also noted by Ludwig von Mises.

It is uncontested that in the sphere of human action social entities have real existence. Nobody ventures to deny that nations, states, municipalities, parties, religious communities, are real factors determining the course of human events. Methodological individualism, far from contesting the significance of such collective wholes, considers it as one of its main tasks to describe and to analyze their becoming and their disappearing, their changing structures and their operation. And it chooses the only method fitted to solve this problem satisfactorily.[404]

III

Theories often arise in an atmosphere of intellectual competition, when different theories are put forward to explain the same phenomenon, so we can fully appreciate a given theory only if we know something about its chief rivals. Methodological individualism is typically contrasted with *holism*, according to which (at least some) social entities are unique "wholes" that cannot be reduced to (i.e., explained in terms of) the actions, beliefs, and values of individuals. Holism, according to a popular, if somewhat inadequate, definition, is the doctrine that a social whole (e.g., an institution) is more than the sum of its individual parts – or, alternatively, that the whole is in some way prior to the individuals who comprise it.

Holists have often compared social phenomena to the emergent properties of a chemical reaction. Under certain conditions two parts of hydrogen will combine with one part of oxygen to form water, thereby creating a new substance with emergent properties that are qualitatively different than those of its constituent elements. According to this argument from analogy, individual human beings are "atoms" that, when combined in a particular manner through interaction, produce social "molecules" with new and unique characteristics. John Stuart Mill had this to say about the "chemical method" of reasoning in the social sciences:

> The laws of the phenomena of society are and can be nothing but the laws of the actions and passions of human beings united together in the social state. Men, however, in a state of society are still men; their actions and passions are obedient to the laws of individual human nature. Men are not, when brought together, converted into another kind of substance with different properties, as hydrogen and oxygen are different from water. . . . Human beings in society have no properties but those which are derived from, and may be resolved into, the laws of the nature of individual man.[405]

---

[404] Ludwig von Mises, *Human Action*, 42.
[405] *John Stuart Mill's Philosophy of Scientific Method*, ed. Ernest Nagel (New York: Hafner, 1950), 324–25.

Mill's argument overlooked a major form of holism, which does not claim that individual human beings are qualitatively transformed by social interaction. Holists more often contend that human interaction generates social wholes, or *institutions*, that differ qualitatively from the individuals who comprise them.

Moreover, Mill has been criticized by other methodological individualists for his defense of *psychologism*. This is the label given by Karl Popper to the view that all social phenomena can be explained in terms of the intentions, purposes, and motives of individual human beings. Although psychologism rightly insists that we must reduce the "actions" and "behavior" of collective entities to the actions and behavior of individuals, it erroneously maintains that such explanations must be psychological, that is, that they must ultimately refer to the *conscious* states and dispositions of acting agents. This is a serious error, because many social institutions were not consciously designed but were unintended consequences of human action.

Mill's psychologism, though a species of individualism, should not be confused with methodological individualism per se. Psychologism is inadequate because it fails to take into account the many social institutions, such as money and language, that have developed spontaneously, without conscious planning or foresight. To say that all institutions are the result of individual actions is *not* to say that these institutions are the product of deliberate planning or design. Adam Ferguson put it this way in 1767:

> Mankind, in following the present state of their minds, in striving to remove inconveniences, or to gain apparent and contiguous advantages, arrive at ends which even their imagination could not anticipate, and pass on, like other animals, in the track of their nature, without perceiving its end.... Every step and every movement of the multitude, even in what are termed enlightened ages, are made with equal blindness to the future; and nations stumble upon establishments, which are indeed the result of human action, but not the execution of any human design.[406]

We are largely indebted to Adam Ferguson, David Hume, Adam Smith, John Millar, and other luminaries of the Scottish Enlightenment for our understanding of unintended consequences and their role in the development of spontaneous (i.e., unplanned) social institutions. It is scarcely coincidental that these sociological pioneers were methodological individualists. None would

---

[406] Adam Ferguson, *An Essay on the History of Civil Society* (New Brunswick: Transaction Publishers, 1980), 122.

have seriously entertained the notion that social phenomena are anything more than individuals and their recurring relationships.

Methodological individualism was a dominant theme in Enlightenment social theory, one that was not seriously challenged until after the French Revolution. The Enlightenment stress on reason was inherently individualistic, since reason is a characteristic of the singular human being. The theological mode of explanation (such as the biblical story of the tower of Babel, which had been used to explain the origin of different languages) was in serious disrepair. Although most philosophers acknowledged the influence of divine providence, the deistic God of nature worked from the bottom up, through the voluntary actions of individuals, not from the top down, through the coercive decrees of emperors and kings.

Philosophers sought to explain the harmonious order of nature, and here they were profoundly influenced by the discoveries of Isaac Newton, the patron saint of science. Newton set the stage for a good deal of Enlightenment social theory with these words:

> I wish we could derive the rest of the phenomena of Nature by the same kind of reasoning from mechanical principles, for I am induced by many reasons to suspect that they may all depend upon certain forces by which the particles of bodies, by some causes hitherto unknown, are either mutually impelled towards one another, and cohere in regular figures, or are repelled and recede from one another.[407]

Gravitation was the invisible force of Newton's universe, and philosophers eagerly searched for a moral and social equivalent. Some philosophers, such as Shaftesbury and Voltaire, found the solution in man's natural benevolence ("a delicate and generous sensibility," as Condorcet described it). Other philosophers claimed to have discovered a "moral sense." But self-interest was the undisputed champion of human passions, so here was the leading contender for the moral and social equivalent of gravitation. Here was the force that "impelled" and "repelled" human beings and caused them "to cohere in regular figures" – those social institutions that emerge spontaneously from the pursuit of self-interest.

Social theory was frequently viewed by Enlightenment philosophers as the handmaiden of history. In attempting to explain the origin and development of money, law, language, and other social institutions, philosophers confronted a difficult problem, namely that such institutions were far too complex and

---

[407] Quoted in Basil Willey, *The Eighteenth Century Background* (Boston: Beacon Press, 1961), 138.

intricate to have been consciously planned. They were, as Ferguson put it, "the result of human action, but not the execution of any human design" – so an adequate *historical* account of complex social phenomena was impossible without the assistance of a sophisticated *social* theory.

If theories develop in response to unsolved problems, if they are an attempt to answer difficult questions, then we may say that modern social theory arose with the desire to explain the origin and development of undesigned institutions. In 1882, Carl Menger phrased "the most noteworthy problem of the social sciences" as follows:

> *How can it be that institutions which serve the common welfare and are extremely significant for its development come into being without a common will directed toward establishing them?*[408]

Popper noted that an "action which proceeds precisely according to intention does not create a problem for social science."[409] And in a similar vein, Hayek suggested that modern social theory grew from a desire to explain the origin and development of undesigned institutions:

> The problems which [the social sciences] try to answer arise only insofar as the conscious actions of many men produce undesigned results, insofar as regularities are observed which are not the result of anybody's design. If social phenomena showed no order except insofar as they were consciously designed, there would indeed be no room for theoretical sciences of society and there would be, as is often argued, only problems of psychology. It is only insofar as some sort of order arises as a result of individual action but without being designed by any individual that a problem is raised which demands a theoretical explanation.[410]

The theory of spontaneous order has been taken up by many prominent sociologists (as we see, for example, in Robert Merton's "empirical functionalism" and Anthony Giddens's theory of "structuration"). It has also been developed in great detail by three liberals over the past three centuries: Adam Smith in the eighteenth, Herbert Spencer in the nineteenth, and F.A. Hayek in the twentieth. The significance of spontaneous order theory for methodological individualism is that it offers an attractive third alternative to the extremes of psychologism and holism. The individualist can readily admit that "society"

---

[408] Menger, *Investigations into the Method of the Social Sciences*, 124.
[409] Popper, *Open Society and Its Enemies*, 2: 96.
[410] F.A. Hayek, *The Counter-Revolution of Science: Studies on the Abuse of Reason*, 2nd ed. (Indianapolis: Liberty Press, 1979), 68–69.

(i.e., social institutions in general) results from something more than individual actions – if by this we mean the *intended* outcome of such actions. We may also speak of institutions as possessing emergent properties – if by this we mean properties that emerged *spontaneously*, quite apart from intentions of individual actors.

## IV

It has become fashionable to dismiss methodological individualism as a simplistic and grossly inadequate mode of social explanation. That this is an unfair criticism should be clear from the previous discussion of psychologism and spontaneous order. In recent decades, however, individualism has become associated with "rational choice theory," and other economically oriented schools of thought, and this affiliation has reinforced the view that individualism is based on a simplistic view of human motivation.

This criticism may have merit, to a point (I, for one, have never been impressed by the explanatory power of rational choice theory). But we must understand that individualism, considered as a general method, has been incorporated within different and sometimes conflicting theories of social explanation. Perhaps the best way to reinforce this point is by offering some concrete examples, so I have selected two pioneers of modern sociology: Georg Simmel and Max Weber. Both of these influential men, who continue to occupy a place in the front rank of social theorists, were methodological individualists, but neither can be reasonably accused of adopting a naïve or simplistic approach to sociology.

Society, according to Simmel, "merely is the name for a number of individuals, connected by interaction." It is a concept that "refers to the psychological interaction among individual human beings." Social institutions and organizations "are nothing but immediate interactions that occur among men constantly, every minute, but that have become crystallized as permanent fields, as autonomous phenomena." Society "certainly is not a 'substance,' nothing concrete, but an *event*"; as such, it is something that is constantly being renewed and realized, "something individuals do and suffer." Hence, if we are to remain true to the idea of "society" as an ongoing process rather than as a thing, we "should properly speak, not of society, but of sociation."[411]

---

[411] *The Sociology of Georg Simmel*, trans. Kurt Wolff (New York: Harper and Row, 1959), 9–10. The English "sociation" is translator Kurt Wolff's rendering of the German *Vergesellschaftung*. A more literal, if far more awkward, translation might be "societalization." An early translator, Albion Small, preferred "socialization," but this would now be highly misleading. See Don

Sociation – the ongoing process of interaction – occurs in various forms and in various degrees. With the emergence of new relationships, or with the intensification of old relationships, "the same group becomes 'more society' than it was before." This is why the noun "society" can prove misleading and why "sociation" is a preferable term. There is a natural tendency to reify the concept "society" and thereby treat a dynamic process as if it were a static entity. This reification "is the reason for the peculiar vagueness and uncertainty involved in the concept of society." But "there is no such thing as society 'as such'," because "there is no such thing as interaction 'as such' – there are only specific kinds of interaction." The various forms of sociation do not somehow cause society, nor are they the effects of society. Rather, society is nothing but forms of sociation that have been abstracted from concrete reality and synthesized into a single concept.[412]

These statements by Simmel are epistemological rather than methodological. They reflect his belief that only the individual human being, in contrast to society, is a substantial entity in the ontological sense.[413] Did this ontological individualism commit Simmel to methodological individualism as well? Yes, for if "society" should be characterized as "sociation," if it is an ongoing process rather than an entity, then social phenomena must be understood as the actions of individual human beings.

Simmel's methodology, which is quite sophisticated and complex, illustrates an important point – namely, that, contrary to the misrepresentations of their critics, individualists have not ignored or underestimated the influence of society on the individual.

Simmel's views on this matter may be characterized as a theory of internal relations. In philosophy, the theory of internal relations (which is usually associated with metaphysical idealism) maintains that the identity of a thing (its "essence") depends on its relationship to other things. Perhaps the best way of understanding this complex notion is by offering an example of its metaphysical rival: the theory of external relations. According to this latter doctrine, the identity of a billiard ball – its essential nature – is unaffected by its position on a pool table relative to other billiard balls. The physical characteristics of a given billiard ball (its chemical composition, weight, etc.)

Martindale, *The Nature and Types of Sociological Theory* (London: Routledge & Kegan Paul, 1961), 238, n.1.

[412] Georg Simmel, "The Problem of Sociology," in *Georg Simmel on Individuality and Social Forms: Selected Writings*, ed. Donald N. Levine (Chicago: University of Chicago Press, 1971), 27.

[413] Ontology is that branch of metaphysics that investigates the nature of being as such, i.e., in contrast to particular types of being.

persist and are not affected by its proximity to other physical objects, including other billiard balls.

The defender of internal relations might respond to this example in a number of ways, but such arguments are (fortunately) irrelevant to the present discussion. I am not concerned with the metaphysical merits of this doctrine, but with its application to social theory. In attributing a *social* theory of internal relations to Simmel, I am referring to his argument that *social relationships exist internally, within the consciousness of the individual, and are therefore essential to his or her personal identity.*

Social relationships, according to Simmel, do not exist only in the mind of the sociologist or other observer. Individual human beings are not raw data that, having been observed as discrete "things," are then unified by the observer through a mental act of synthesis. On the contrary, the mental synthesis by which individuals and their actions are unified into social concepts has already occurred within the minds of the individuals themselves. The unity of society is located within the consciousness of the individual. The social bond – that cohesive element that links one person to another – is an *internal* relationship, not an external one. Social connections are internal relationships that exist within the individual's consciousness. The individual is not one thing and his or her social relationships another; rather, the former embodies the latter. Thus, how a person views others does not merely influence (or even "determine") his or her character as an individual, but is itself an essential feature of that selfsame character.[414]

This approach yielded insights that are quite similar to those later developed by the phenomenologist Alfred Schutz (who also embraced methodological individualism). As Simmel pointed out, in everyday life we view others, to some degree, as *general types.* This is necessary because every person is a unique individual, and "we cannot fully represent to ourselves an individuality which deviates from our own."[415] Our knowledge of others is always incomplete, so in deciding how to interact with others we must necessarily rely upon generalizations in some measure that may or may not be accurate in particular cases. These general (or ideal) types are of various kinds, represent different degrees of anonymity, and are usually "unverbalized." We tend, for example, to view members of "my group" (my religion, my country, my occupation, etc.) through the veil of mental categories that will greatly influence our subsequent interactions.

---

[414] See "How is Society Possible?," in *Georg Simmel on Individuality and Social Forms*, 6–22.
[415] Ibid., 9.

This veil does not simply hide the peculiarity of the person; it gives it a new form. Its purely individual, real nature and its group nature fuse into a new, autonomous phenomenon. We see the other not simply as an individual but as a colleague or comrade or fellow party member – in short, as a cohabitant of the same specific world. And this inevitable, quite automatic assumption is one of the means by which one's personality and reality assume, in the imagination of another, the quality and form required by sociability.[416]

As was the case with Herbert Spencer, Simmel's individualism did not lead him into nominalism. From the standpoint of sociology, the individual should not be viewed as more "real" than society. Both are mental categories of interpretation. True, the individual is a "real object," whereas society is an abstraction that "does not exist outside and in addition to the individuals and the processes among them."[417] But this does not mean that "society" is somehow unreal or fictional. Nor does it mean that sociology, which studies the nature of social phenomena, is a bogus science with no authentic subject matter.

Every science, Simmel observed, deals with abstract concepts, and such concepts are a product of the human mind: "human thought always and everywhere synthesizes the given into units that serve as the subject matters of the sciences." The concepts of science "have no counterpart whatever in immediate reality."[418] No science can capture reality in its full richness and variety; it must adopt a one-sided and abstract point of view. Sociology is no exception. Even the individual of methodological individualism is an abstraction (an anonymous type) rather than a specific person. Whether the sociologist refers to the individual or to society will depend on his or her cognitive purpose in a given case. The concepts "individual" and "society" "may be expressed by the symbol of different *distances* between [a given complex of phenomena] and the human mind."

> We obtain different pictures of an object when we see it at a distance of two, or of five, or of ten yards. At each distance, however, the picture is "correct" in its particular way and only in this way. And the different distance also provides different margins for error. For instance, if the minute detail of a painting that we gain at very close range were injected into a perspective gained at a distance of several yards, this perspective would be utterly confused and falsified. And yet on the basis of a superficial conception, one might assert that the detailed view is "truer" than the more distant view. But even this detailed

[416] Ibid., 11.
[417] *The Sociology of Georg Simmel*, 4.
[418] Ibid., 7.

perception involves some distance whose lower limit is, in fact, impossible to determine. All we can say is that a view gained at any distance whatever has its own justification. It cannot be replaced or corrected by any other view emerging at another distance.

In a similar way, when we look at human life from a certain distance, we see each individual in his precise differentiation from all others. But if we increase our distance, the single individual disappears, and there emerges, instead, a picture which has its own possibilities of being recognized or missed. It is certainly no less justified than is the other in which the parts, the individuals, are seen in their differentiation. Nor is it by any means a mere preliminary of it. The difference between the two merely consists in the difference between the purposes of cognition; and this difference, in turn, corresponds to a difference in distance.[419]

V

Near the beginning of his unfinished masterpiece, *Economy and Society*, Max Weber wrote the following paragraph in which we find working definitions of "sociology," "action," and "social action."

> Sociology (in the sense in which this highly ambiguous word is used here) is a science concerning itself with the interpretive understanding of social action and thereby with a causal explanation of its course and consequences. We shall speak of "action" insofar as the acting individual attaches a subjective meaning to his behavior – be it overt or covert, omission or acquiescence. Action is "social" insofar as its subjective meaning takes account of the behavior of others and is thereby oriented in its course.[420]

Line for line, this is probably the most influential paragraph ever written in the history of social theory. The many implications of this passage were unpacked and analyzed by Weber with considerable care in an effort to establish the conceptual foundations of sociology; his labor inspired many others, such as Talcott Parsons and Alfred Schutz, to undertake a similar task. It may be true, as one critic has charged, that *Economy and Society* "is tremendously erudite, but entirely bookish," that "it does not rely on firsthand empirical research, and contains . . . almost no statistical data." It may even be true that most of its definitions are "formally flawed," that it contains "a few hypotheses,

---

[419] Ibid., 7–8.
[420] Weber, *Economy and Society*, 1: 4.

but hardly any explanations," and that its most valuable insights "are buried in long-winded, foggy paragraphs."[421]

\*\*\*

All this may be true – and more. But a criticism can be accurate without being relevant, and relevant without being fair. Most of the preceding remarks fall into one of these two categories. It is not at all clear, for example, what kind of "firsthand empirical research" could possibly be relevant to the methodological task of conceptual clarification, which is essentially a philosophical enterprise. And if Weber's definitions are sometimes ambiguous – as Weber himself would have been the first to acknowledge – then this is an ambiguity with rich potential.

Weber was a major figure in the "interpretive school" of sociology, whose proponents focus on the subjective meaning of social action. This subjective point of view necessarily entails methodological individualism, because "meaning" presupposes a rational being with the capacity to understand, and only the individual human being can possess the requisite state of consciousness. True, some cognitive purposes may require that we treat social collectives (states, associations, business organizations, etc.) as if they were individual persons. In legal theory, as Weber pointed out, we may refer to collective entities "as the subjects of rights and duties or as the performers of legally significant actions."

> But for the subjective interpretation of action in sociological work these collectivities must be treated as *solely* the resultants and modes of organization of the particular acts of individual persons, since these alone can be treated as agents in a course of subjectively understandable action. [F]or sociological purposes there is no such thing as a collective personality which "acts." When reference is made in a sociological context to a state, a nation, a corporation, a family, or an army corps, or to similar collectivities, what is meant is . . . *only* a certain kind of development of actual or possible social actions of individual persons.[422]

Methodological individualism does not mean that the sociologist can (or should) dispense with collective concepts; far from it. In seeking to understand the subjective meaning of action, we must remember that every individual uses collective concepts when interacting with others. They are essential to a person's psychological makeup and so must be taken into account when

---

[421] Mario Bunge, *Finding Philosophy in Social Science* (New Haven: Yale University Press, 1996), 154.
[422] Weber, *Economy and Society*, 1: 13–14.

explaining his or her actions. Collective entities (such as state and society) exist as ideas in the mind of the individual, who often invests them with a moral authority. This subjective belief in the normative authority of collective entities will greatly influence how a person responds to a particular situation.

> Actors thus in part orient their action to [collective entities], and in this role such ideas have a powerful, often a decisive, causal influence on the course of action of real individuals. This is above all true where the ideas involve normative prescription or prohibition.[423]

Suppose we are investigating the role of the "state" in social causation. Whether the state really exists as an ontological entity may interest the philosopher, who may also seek to justify (or criticize) the state's moral claim of sovereignty. But these issues are largely irrelevant for the sociologist, because, whatever the philosopher may decide, many people actually *believe* in the existence of the state and act *as if* this entity has legitimate authority over their lives and the lives of other citizens. Although it would be theoretically possible for the sociologist to replace all references to the "state" and other collective entities with newly coined words that refer instead to the subjective beliefs of individuals, this procedure would be "extremely pedantic and cumbersome."

Collective concepts can also serve as an explanatory tool for the sociologist, who may wish to analyze the functional relationship between social "wholes" and their individual "parts." However, this kind of analysis, which depends on a tenuous comparison of societies to living organisms, is of limited value. At best, functionalism can serve as a "practical illustration" of interdependent social processes. At worst, the organic implications of functionalism can lead to the dangerous reification of social wholes, causing us to treat abstract ideas like concrete things.

Functionalism, which encourages us to view individuals and institutions as functional "parts" of the social whole, can do no more than point the way to an adequate sociological explanation. A functional analysis can open, but should never close, an explanation of social action. This is because we can know far more about the individual members of a society than we can ever know about the individual parts of an organism. The social scientist, unlike the natural scientist, is not limited to describing the functional relationships, uniformities, and other *external* characteristics of the individual elements that constitute her or his subject matter. We can *understand* the *actions* of individual human beings, whereas we can only *explain* the *behavior* of cells. Sociology can *interpret* the meaning of individual actions from the inside out,

[423] Ibid., 1: 14.

so to speak, whereas natural science can only *describe* the external behavior of entities.

Weber tried to rescue methodological individualism from a number of common misconceptions. For example, it "is a tremendous misunderstanding to think that an 'individualistic' *method* should involve what is in any conceivable sense an individualistic system of *values*."[424] The methodological individualist need not be a moral or political individualist. Nor need she or he adopt a rationalistic approach to human behavior, such as we find in rational choice theory and other modern schools of economic thought. To investigate the motives of action and the subjective framework in which they arise does not mean that all actions result from the "rational" calculation of economic costs and benefits. Even socialistic communities, which display a good deal of economic irrationalism, can be explained by methodological individualism.

> The real empirical sociological investigation begins with the question: What motives determine and lead the individual members and participants in this socialistic community to behave in such a way that the community came into being in the first place and that it continues to exist?[425]

One commentator has noted that "no one is more insistent than Weber that the fundamental unit of investigation must always be the individual."[426] Weber, wrote Alfred Schutz, "reduces all kinds of relationships and structures, all cultural objectifications, all realms of objective mind, to the most elementary forms of individual behavior." Never before had the project of reducing social phenomena "to the behavior of individuals been so radically carried out as it was in Max Weber's initial statement of the goal of interpretive sociology."[427] Weber's interpretive method, while highly suggestive, tends to raise more questions than it answers. Nonetheless, his basic insights are sound, and we can survey these without enmeshing ourselves in the complex controversies that have surrounded his work.

Perhaps the best way to understand Weber's overall approach is to examine his treatment of social institutions. (Here as elsewhere I use the term "institution" in a broad sense to signify any form of patterned interaction.) If all institutions must be understood in terms of individuals and their subjectively meaningful actions, then where exactly are these institutions located? Where is their spatial position, so to speak, relative to the individual?

---

[424] Ibid., 1: 18.
[425] Ibid.
[426] Frank Parkin, *Max Weber* (New York: Tavistock Publications, 1986), 17.
[427] Alfred Schutz, *The Phenomenology of the Social World*, trans. George Walsh and Frederick Lehnert (Chicago: Northwestern University Press, 1967), 6.

Weber regarded institutions as existing in the human mind in the form of beliefs, expectations, and dispositions. "The social relationship . . . consists entirely and exclusively in the existence of a probability that there will be a meaningful course of social action. . . . " An institution (a state, church, association, marriage, etc.) is said to exist when individuals orient their actions toward others with the expectation that those others will probably respond in a certain way. "Let it be repeated," wrote Weber, "that it is *only* the existence of the probability that, corresponding to a given subjective meaning, a certain type of action will take place which constitutes the 'existence' of the social relationship."[428]

Consider what would happen if people no longer granted any moral or legal legitimacy to a "state," and if they no longer displayed the appropriate attitude and behavior toward this institution. In such a case, according to Weber, the "state" would cease to exist. Some people might continue to represent themselves as governmental agents, the physical corridors of power might remain standing – but all such facts would be sociologically irrelevant, since "there is no longer a probability that certain kinds of meaningfully oriented action will take place."[429] If self-proclaimed rulers had to enforce every decree at the point of a gun, the victims might obey, but the subjective meaning of this obedience would be the same as if they had complied with the demands of a criminal gang. If the decrees of an institution are not *subjectively* perceived as legally binding, if an institution lacks the moral authority to elicit certain types of actions, then that institution is not a "state."

Thus an institution, sociologically considered, is precisely what people *believe* it to be, nothing more and nothing less. This is what it means to say that the "state" and other institutions can exist nowhere but in the minds of individuals.

---

[428] Weber, *Economy and Society*, 1: 27–28.
[429] Ibid., 27.

# Epilogue

By the end of the nineteenth century, classical liberalism had been eclipsed by a "new" liberalism that justified state interference in social relationships to a far greater extent than most old liberals, such as Herbert Spencer, were willing to sanction. Various explanations have been offered for the decline and fall of classical liberalism, including one by Spencer himself, who suggested that the public at large did not understand the true nature of the beneficial reforms for which old liberalism was responsible.

According to Spencer, the old liberals abolished or mitigated grievances suffered by large segments of the population, and these reforms had been brought about by relaxing the scope of governmental interference and thereby expanding the range of individual liberty. But most people, seeing that these beneficial results had *something* to do with government, failed to differentiate between the repeal of onerous laws and the passing of new laws:

> For what, in the popular apprehension and in the apprehension of those who effected them, were the changes made by Liberals in the past? They were abolitions of grievances suffered by the people, or by portions of them: this was the common trait they had which most impressed itself on men's minds. They were mitigations of evils which had directly or indirectly been felt by large classes of citizens, as causes to misery or as hindrances to happiness. And since, in the minds of most, a rectified evil is equivalent to an achieved good, these measures came to be thought of as so many positive benefits; and the welfare of the many came to be conceived alike by Liberal statesmen and Liberal voters as the aim of Liberalism. Hence the confusion. The gaining of a popular good, being the external conspicuous trait common to Liberal measures in earlier days (then in each case gained by a relaxation of restraints), it has happened that popular good has come to be sought by Liberals, not as an end to be indirectly gained by relaxations of restraints, but as the end to

be directly gained. And seeking to gain it directly, they have used methods intrinsically opposed to those originally used.[430]

Explanations for the decline of classical liberalism were also offered by Ludwig von Mises and Friedrich Hayek, who were largely responsible for carrying the torch of liberalism during its dark years in the first half of the twentieth century. Mises wrote that Enlightenment liberals "blithely assumed that what is reasonable will carry on merely on account of its reasonableness. They never gave a thought to the possibility that public opinion could favor spurious ideologies whose realization would harm welfare and well-being and disintegrate social cooperation."[431]

Hayek, in contrast, focused on a deficiency in liberal principles themselves as a major factor in the decline of liberalism:

> It is thus a misunderstanding to blame classical liberalism for having been too doctrinaire. Its defect was not that it adhered too stubbornly to principles, but rather that it lacked principles sufficiently definite to provide clear guidance.... Consistency is possible only if definite principles are accepted. But the concept of liberty with which the liberals of the nineteenth century operated was in many respects so vague that it did not provide clear guidance.[432]

Although all of the preceding explanations have merit, I have focused in this book on the one offered by Hayek. In particular, I have discussed how the presumption of liberty, when not accompanied with clear criteria of defeasibility, sometimes became so diluted as to be rendered ineffectual as even a theoretical barrier to the growth of state power. This was especially true for those liberals who placed more stress on the "public good" or "social utility" than they did on natural rights; and when the Benthamites later excluded natural rights altogether from the liberal lexicon, the game was essentially over. Without this moral foundation, liberals were reduced to quibbling over what governmental measures did and did not promote the public good, when there were no longer definite standards to decide such matters from a liberal perspective. It is scarcely coincidental that those nineteenth-century liberals, such as Thomas Hodgskin and Herbert Spencer, who protested most vigorously against the incursion of state power were also strong advocates of natural rights.

[430] Herbert Spencer, "The New Toryism," in *The Man Versus the State*, 14–15.
[431] Ludwig von Mises, *Human Action*, 864.
[432] F.A. Hayek, *Law Legislation, and Liberty*, vol. 1, 61.

I also discussed another aspect of this problem, one for which the natural-rights liberals were themselves responsible. This was the failure of most Lockean liberals – Thomas Hodgskin, Auberon Herbert, Lsyander Spooner, and the early Spencer of *Social Statics* were among the exceptions – to confront the radical implications of their own theory of consent. The critics of Locke and his followers were substantially correct when they pointed out that the appeal to "tacit consent" was little more than a ruse to escape the uncomfortable implications that a consistent theory of consent would have for the legitimacy of all governments, past and present. Moreover, many governmental measures that clearly violated the presumption of liberty could readily be justified by an appeal to tacit consent.

This brings us to a related point, namely the rather uneasy alliance between classical liberalism and democracy. Although liberals often led the movements for democratic reforms in various countries, they were also concerned that these reforms might end up substituting one form of absolute sovereignty (that of "people") for another. The distinction between the "form" of government and its animating "principle" had long been a mainstay of the liberal tradition, and many liberals feared that a democratic form of government would eventually swamp the liberal principle that the power of government should be limited to the protection of individual rights. Many liberals looked for a solution in a constitutional form of government that would prohibit a majority from violating the rights of individuals and minorities, but this ideal proved easier to advocate in theory than to implement in practice.

In the final analysis, some problems faced by classical liberals were beyond their control. Unlike some competing political movements, such as nationalism and socialism, which could appeal directly to human emotions, liberalism always had an ethereal quality to it. This was the nature of the beast, because freedom, when viewed as the absence of coercion, cannot be directly perceived by the senses but must instead be understood by the mind. And for this, abstract concepts and theories are essential.

Although liberals developed sophisticated theories in economics, sociology, and other disciplines as a means of tracking the effects of freedom in social relationships, there was little hope that these theories would be known, much less understood, by the average person. (This problem has become even more acute in the modern age of television sound bites where an advocate of classical liberalism might have only 30 seconds to explain the concept of spontaneous order. It is much easier to say that the government ought to do something.)

Lastly, I will mention another problem to which I made only indirect references in this book, one that is related to the interdisciplinary approach to freedom that became a hallmark of classic liberalism during the eighteenth

century. This call for an interdisciplinary defense of freedom is largely a thing
of the past, owing to the modern age of academic specialization. (Perhaps the
last liberal to attempt an ambitious undertaking of this sort was Ludwig von
Mises, especially in *Human Action*.)

In 1867, J.S. Mill warned of the enervating effects of hyperspecialization:

> In every generation, and now more rapidly than ever, the things which it
> is necessary that somebody should know are more and more multiplied.
> Every department of knowledge becomes so loaded with details, that one
> who endeavors to know it with minute accuracy, must confine himself to a
> smaller and smaller portion of the whole extent: every science and art must
> be cut up into subdivisions, until each man's portion, the district which he
> thoroughly knows, bears about the same ratio to the whole range of useful
> knowledge that the art of putting on a pin's head does to the field of human
> industry. Now, if, in order to know that little completely, it is necessary to
> remain wholly ignorant of the rest, what will soon be the worth of a man, for
> any human purpose except his own infinitesimal fraction of human wants
> and requirements? His state will be even worse than that of simple ignorance.
> Experience proves that there is no one study or pursuit, which, practiced to
> the exclusion of all others, does not narrow and pervert the mind; breeding
> in it a class of prejudices special to that pursuit, besides a general prejudice,
> common to all narrow specialties, against large views, from an incapacity
> to take in and appreciate the grounds of them. We should have to expect
> that human nature would be more and more dwarfed, and unfitted for great
> things, by its very proficiency in small ones.[433]

Mill understood, of course, that no one person can become an expert in a
variety of specialized fields, which is why he distinguished between a general
knowledge and a superficial knowledge of a given discipline. He believed that
a general knowledge – that is, a knowledge of fundamental principles – is
possible and desirable in a number of disciplines, and that such knowledge is
essential to education.

It is interesting to note that Mill and Spencer were both products of home
schooling, that neither earned university degrees, that both did interdisciplinary work, and that Spencer (who once observed that most defenders of
freedom worked outside of universities) joined Mill in expressing concern
about the unintended consequences of academic specialization.

The widespread appeal of liberal ideas during the eighteenth century was
indebted to its stress on developing a comprehensive "science of man," as

---

433 John Stuart Mill, "Inaugural Address at Saint Andrews," *The Six Great Humanistic Essays*, ed.
    Albert William Levi (New York: Washington Square Press, 1963), 318–19.

David Hume, Adam Smith, and their contemporaries called it. This was conceived as an interdisciplinary discipline in its own right, one that included moral and political philosophy, psychology, and the social sciences. This project, however it might be evaluated today, attracted the best intellectuals of the time and thereby contributed greatly to the development of liberal ideology. There was a general agreement among Enlightenment liberals, including those who stressed the moral foundations of liberalism, that freedom could not be defended adequately from a single, narrow point of view and that an interdisciplinary approach was essential to the survival of liberalism.

Despite the many problems and challenges that confronted classical liberalism, it experienced a remarkable revival during the latter decades of the twentieth century, as young intellectuals flocked to it in search of an alternative to a range of competing ideologies, from conservatism to socialism, that looked to the coercive measures of government as a solution for social problems. The idea of freedom had once again become popular and exhilarating, but what if anything this new generation of old liberals will learn from the struggles, successes, failures, and errors of their predecessors remains to be seen.

# Index

*Note to index*: An *n* following a page number indicates a note on that page.